Buddhism and Christianity in Dialogue

The Gerald Weisfeld Lectures 2004

Edited by
Perry Schmidt-Leukel

scm press

British Library Cataloguing in Publication data

A catalogue record for this book is available
from the British Library

Bible quotations are from the New Revised Standard
Version, published by HarperCollins Publishers,
copyright © 1989 by the Division of Christian
Education of the National Council of Churches of
Christ in the USA, and are used by permission.
All rights reserved.

0 334 04008 6/9780 334 04008 8

First published in 2005 by SCM Press
St Mary's Works, St Mary's Plain,
Norwich, Norfolk, NR3 3BH

www.scm-canterburypress.co.uk

SCM Press is a division of
SCM-Canterbury Press Ltd

Printed and bound in Great Britain by
William Clowes Ltd, Beccles, Suffolk

Contents

Foreword

After forty years of being an entrepreneur, why the Gerald Weisfeld Lectures?

In 1991, after I sold my main business, I thought I might find in universities a way of aiding the good and great thinkers in the world in their search for world harmony and peace.

So it followed that, as a start, I initiated a 'Chair for Economics of Peace' at Tel Aviv University. In 1993 the Chair became a reality. Later I asked myself is it really economics or money that is to blame for all the current unrest in the world or is it more likely to be divisions of race, religion and ethnicity?

I contacted Glasgow University and was met with an enthusiastic response from the then principal, Sir Graeme Davis. As a result the 'Chair of World Religions for Peace' at Glasgow University came into being. I think it is fortunate that Professor Perry Schmidt-Leukel who is a specialist in Buddhist-Christian dialogue and in inter-faith relations in general became its incumbent. Since my own background is Jewish and later Christian, my interest in inter-faith relations is a very personal one.

My initial idea was that religions have more in common than is usually perceived. I am convinced that there are still a number of commonalities to be discovered and that differences should not be misused for sowing division and disruption. For it was, I thought, in the distillation of the faiths that the ultimate truths could lie. Simplistic one might think, but my instinct, on which I have learned to rely, told me that since we, humanity, share one shape and form physically, we may find that the different faiths may also share deep and significant commonalities. Do they not point to the same ultimate divine ground? If we contemplate the vastness of this galaxy with its billions of stars and then the billions of galaxies how have we the temerity really to believe we can pontificate on the realities contained within it?

From the perspective of the Abrahamic religions there are only two real possibilities, either there is a divine creator of everything or everything is there just by an absurd accident. Enlightened self-interest would inevitably favour the former since it is naturally attracted to the idea of a higher power/creator, one who would have to love us very much not to destroy his creation. This seems to be exactly the huge danger of our age that we might be in the midst of devastating the part of the world in which we live. How is this seen by the great religions of the East, by Hinduism, Buddhism and Chinese religions? And what is their role? It came to me that if there was indeed a higher power, who had our best interest at heart, then surely any belief system that had the aim of improving our behaviour towards each other and our care for the world would be ripe for adoption and use. Would this not satisfy the God from whom all good things come?

I participated in a series of inter-faith gatherings, and recently in a conference in Brussels attended by over one hundred Muslim imams and Jewish rabbis. To me the experience of religions meeting in open-mindedness, friendship and serious mutual interest seems to confirm my instinct, for there is already a large measure of agreement. It is my hope that the Gerald Weisfeld Lectures make – in the best possible scholarly form – their own contribution to a further exploration of this exciting and crucial field, and I am extremely pleased that through SCM Press they are now presented to a wider public.

Gerald Weisfeld
Easter 2005

Notes on Contributors

Karl Baier studied cultural anthropology, philosophy and theology at the University of Vienna where he is now Assistant Professor at the Institute for Christian Philosophy, Catholic Faculty. His main research interests are in the fields of phenomenology and hermeneutical philosophy, philosophical anthropology, philosophy of religion, spirituality, intercultural philosophy and Buddhist-Christian dialogue. Since 2002 he has been head of the postgraduate university programme on spirituality and inter-religious dialogue at the University of Salzburg. He is also a member of the Executive Board of the Austrian Institute for Existential Analysis (Österreichisches Daseinsanalytisches Institut) and of the editorial staff of *Polylog: Zeitschrift für interkulturelles Philosophieren*. Among his numerous publications on European and intercultural philosophy, yoga and Buddhist-Christian dialogue is a book on the history of yoga in the West: *Yoga auf dem Weg nach Westen* (Königshausen & Neumann, 1998). More recently he has published 'Open Art Work versus Art of Openness: Umberto Eco's occidental Work-Aesthetics and John Cage's Buddhist Alternative' (*Satya Nilayam. Chennai Journal of Intercultural Philosophy* 3 (2003), pp. 28–47).

Kenneth Fernando is a classics honours graduate of the University of Peradeniya in Sri Lanka. He received his theological training at Cuddesdon College in Oxford, England. He holds a Diploma in Pāli and Buddhist studies from the University of Kelaniya, Sri Lanka. He was Director of the Ecumenical Institute for Study and Dialogue in Colombo from 1983 to 1992 and Bishop of

Colombo from 1992 to 2003. He has been active in various social concerns and inter-faith activities and has participated in peacemaking efforts in his own country. He was a co-president of the Christian Conference of Asia from 1995 to 2000 and served as a co-president of the Network of Inter-Faith Concerns of the Anglican Communion from 1998 to 2003. He has several articles in journals mainly in his own language to his credit and has recently brought out a new book in English, *Rediscovering Christ in Asia* (ISPCK, 2005).

Elizabeth J. Harris is Honorary Lecturer in Buddhist and Interfaith Studies at the University of Birmingham and Secretary for Inter Faith Relations for the Methodist Church in Britain. She gained her doctorate in Buddhist studies in Sri Lanka and before taking up her present position, she was a Research Fellow at Westminster College, Oxford. She is a member of the executive committees of the Inter Faith Network for the United Kingdom and the Churches' Commission on Inter Faith Relations, and of the Advisory Committee of the European Network for Buddhist-Christian Studies. Her publications include: *What Buddhists Believe* (Oneworld, 1998); *Ananda Metteyya: The First British Emissary of Buddhism* (Buddhist Publication Society, 1998); *Meeting Buddhists* (Christians Aware, 2004); and *Theravāda Buddhism and the British Encounter: Religious, Missionary and Colonial Experience in Nineteenth Century Sri Lanka* (RoutledgeCurzon, forthcoming).

John Makransky is Associate Professor of Buddhism and Comparative Theology at Boston College and Senior Faculty Advisor to Kathmandu University's Centre for Buddhist Studies in Nepal. He received his PhD in Buddhist studies at the University of Wisconsin-Madison based on Fulbright research with Tibetan and Indian scholars in Asia. His research focuses on ways that practices of Indian Mahāyāna and Tibetan Buddhism have informed developing doctrines of Buddhahood. He is the author of *Buddhahood Embodied: Sources of Controversy in India and Tibet* (SUNY, 1997) and co-edited *Buddhist Theology:*

Critical Reflections by Contemporary Buddhist Scholars (RoutledgeCurzon, 2000). His article 'Buddhist Perspectives on Truth in Other Religions: Past and Present' appeared in *Theological Studies* 64 (2003), pp. 334–61. Professor Makransky has practised and studied Buddhism since 1978 under the guidance of Nyingma, Kagyu and Gelug teachers of Tibetan tradition. In 2000 he was installed as a Tibetan Buddhist Lama in the lineage of Nyoshul Khen Rinpoche, and teaches at meditation retreats for the Dzogchen Center throughout the United States.

Minoru Nambara is Professor Emeritus of Comparative Cultural Studies, University of Tokyo. His main area of research is in the exploration of the mystical traditions. He studied comparative religion at the University of Marburg, Germany, and wrote his doctoral thesis on the concept of 'nothingness' in Eastern and Western mysticism. Among his publications are: 'Die Idee des absoluten Nichts in der deutschen Mystik und seine Entsprechungen im Buddhismus' (*Archiv für Begriffsgeschichte* 4 (1960), pp. 143–277); *Das Christentum und die nichtchristlichen Hochreligionen, eine internationale Bibliographie* (compiled together with Ernst Benz, Brill, 1961); *The Philosophy of Jacob Boehme* (Bokushin, 1976); *Padurea de la inceputul lumii* (Cluji, 1995); *Philosophische Pilgerfahrt zwischen Ost und West: Marburger Vorlesungen* (Dietrich Reimer, 2000).

Perry Schmidt-Leukel is Professor of Systematic Theology and Religious Studies, University of Glasgow, and Founding-Director of the Centre for Inter-Faith Studies. He has published widely in the areas of philosophy/theology of religions and Buddhist-Christian dialogue, including *'Den Löwen brüllen hören': Zur Hermeneutik eines christlichen Verständnisses der buddhistischen Heilsbotschaft* (Schöningh, 1992); *Theologie der Religionen: Probleme, Optionen, Argumente* (Ars Una, 1997) and *Gott ohne Grenzen: Eine christliche und pluralistische Theologie der Religionen* (Gütersloher Verlagshaus, 2005). Among his edited books are *Wer ist Buddha? Eine Gestalt und ihre Bedeutung für die Menschheit* (Diederichs, 1998); *Buddhist Perceptions of*

Jesus (EOS-Verlag, 2001); *War and Peace in World Religions* (SCM Press, 2004); and *Buddhism, Christianity and the Question of Creation: Karmic or Divine?* (Ashgate, 2006).

Hozan Alan Senauke is a Soto Zen priest and teacher in the tradition of Shunryu Suzuki Roshi. He was ordained by Sojun Mel Weitsman in 1989. Alan serves as *tanto* or head of practice at Berkeley Zen Center in California, where he lives with his wife, Laurie, and their two children, Silvie and Alexander. From 1991 through the end of 2001, Alan was Executive Director of the Buddhist Peace Fellowship (BPF). Alan is one of the founders of Think Sangha, a group of Buddhist-activist intellectuals and writers. As BPF's Senior Advisor, he continues to work as a social activist around national and international issues of peace, human rights, structural violence and the development of a socially engaged Buddhism. In another realm, Alan has been a student and performer of American traditional music for more than forty years.

Kiyoshi Tsuchiya is Lecturer in Eastern/Comparative Religions and Literature and Theology at the University of Glasgow, where he gained his doctorate with a thesis on Coleridge's poetics and theology. He worked for the Centre for the Study of Literature, Theology and the Arts till 2003, and currently is Co-Director of the Centre for Inter-Faith Studies. His recent publications include *Coleridge's Mystical Heritage: The Mirror Metaphor and the Formation of the Pentad* (Edwin Mellen, 2000); 'Noh and Purification: The Art of Ritual and Vocational Performance', in *Studies of Literary Imagination* (Georgia State University Press, 2001, pp. 93–114); and 'Buddhism', in L. Ridgeon (ed.), *Major World Religions* (RoutledgeCurzon, 2003, pp. 59–115). His major research interest is in exploring a way to recover transcendentalism in practice and examining the philosophical nature of Japanese aestheticism.

1. Intimate Strangers:

An Introduction

PERRY SCHMIDT-LEUKEL

Oh, East is East, and West is West,
and never the twain shall meet

Rudyard Kipling[1]

deep within each of us
there is a Buddhist and a Christian engaged in a profound encounter

Aloysius Pieris[2]

Strange Resemblances and First Encounters

As the first Buddhist scriptures reached the West in the course of the nineteenth century, scholars were puzzled by the large number of parallels or similarities between Buddhist and New Testament narratives and sayings. As a result of this unexpected discovery, a number of biblical scholars became convinced that the New Testament was heavily influenced by Buddhist sources. Intensive research was undertaken to verify the supposed dependency, but despite enormous efforts, the findings proved to be rather slim. Richard Garbe concluded in 1914 that some sort of Buddhist influence – and probably indirect influence at that – could be assumed for no more than a few narratives[3] and

---

1 'The Ballad of East and West', verse 1.

2 Aloysius Pieris, 1988, *Love Meets Wisdom: A Christian Experience of Buddhism*, Maryknoll: Orbis, p. 113.

3 (1) Simeon's prophecy, (2) Jesus' temptation, (3) Peter's walk on the water, (4) bread multiplication.

for the phrase 'wheel of births' in James 3.6.[4] The hypothesis of
a far more substantial Buddhist influence on the New Testament
is still put forth from time to time[5] but more sober studies have
basically confirmed Garbe's modest assessment.[6] Similarly, no
suspicion of a significant influence of Christian ideas on later
developments in Mahāyāna Buddhism or even on Mahāyāna
scriptures has ever been substantiated.

So we must conclude that, for all practical purposes, Buddhism and Christianity developed without taking any notice
of each other. At least for Western Christianity Buddhism was
a largely unknown religion and remained a stranger for about
1500 years. The earliest explicit remark on Buddhism within
Christianity is a brief statement by Clement of Alexandria from
about 202 CE. In his *Stromata* 1:15 he wrote: 'Some . . . of the
Indians obey the precepts of the Boutta, whom on account of
his extraordinary sanctity they have raised to divine honours.'[7]
A very small number of scattered remarks on the Buddha can
be found in a few other early Christian writings but have little
more to add. Nevertheless, there is one interesting field where we
may indeed reckon with the possibility of a significant indirect
Eastern influence, and that is the mystical philosophy of Neo-
Platonism as one of the roots of Christian, Muslim and Jewish
mysticism. The hypothesis of a dependency of Neo-Platonism on

---

4 R. Garbe, 1914, *Indien und das Christentum: Eine Untersuchung
religionsgeschichtlicher Zusammenhänge*, Tübingen: J.C.B. Mohr.

5 See, for example, E.J. Bruns, 1971, *The Christian Buddhism of St.
John: New Insights into the Fourth Gospel*, New York: Paulist; R.C. Amore,
1978, *Two Masters, One Message*, Nashville: Abingdon; C. Lindtner, 2001,
'Review Article: The Bible and the Buddhists', in *Buddhist Studies Review*
18, no. 2, pp. 229–42; D.M. Derret, 2004, 'The Buddhist Dimension of
John', in *Numen* 51, pp. 182–210.

6 Cf. N. Klatt, 1982, *Literarkritische Beiträge zum Problem christlich-
buddhistischer Parallelen*, Köln: Indica et Tibetica.

7 Quoted from David Scott, 1985, 'Christian Responses to Buddhism
in Pre-Medieval Times', in *Numen* 32, pp. 88–100 (89). For an overview
on the relations between India and the Mediterranean world in classical
antiquity see W. Halbfass, 1988, *India and Europe*, Albany: SUNY,
pp. 2–23. For an overview on Buddhist-Christian encounter in pre-modern
and modern times see: Henri de Lubac, 1952, *La Rencontre du Bouddhisme
et de L'Occident*, Paris: Aubier.

Indian thought is based on several grounds: first, on structural similarities between the metaphysics of Plotinus (205–70 CE) and Vedāntic ideas; secondly, on speculations about the possibly Indian origin of Plotinus' teacher Ammonius Sakkas; and thirdly on the remark in Porphyrius' *Vita Plotinii* (3:15–17) that Plotinus, after the death of Ammonius, tried to get to Asia in order to study the philosophy of the Persians and Indians. The attempt failed and Plotinus never reached India. But we may assume that he knew at least so much about Eastern ideas as to be seriously attracted to them. In the end, however, all these considerations remain speculative. Even if there were some Indian influence on Christian mysticism as mediated by Neo-Platonism, Christianity has not been aware of it. Moreover, any supposed Eastern influence on Neo-Platonism does not in itself explain how Neo-Platonism could have become such a strong feature of the mystical strands in all three of the Abrahamic religions. Rather, there must be some natural affinity between these religions and Neo-Platonism that allowed the latter to develop into such a powerful factor within them.

The situation was of course very different for the Nestorian Christians who began spreading eastwards quite early, settling in South India, along the Silk Road and in China.[8] Their encounters and exchanges with Buddhists and Taoists in Central Asia and in China did not remain without consequences for their theology. Far from merely instrumentalizing Buddhist or Taoist terminology as a means to a more effective evangelization, they sought 'a way to reconcile the teaching and insights of East and West' and 'created a synthesis of Tao, Christ, and Buddha', as Martin Palmer rightly points out.[9] A Nestorian scripture

---

8 Cf. A.C. Moule, 1930, *Christians in China Before the Year 1550*, London: SPCK; R.C. Foltz, 1999, *Religions of the Silk Road*, New York: St. Martin's Griffin; H.-J. Klimkeit, 1993, *Gnosis on the Silk Road*, San Francisco: Harper.

9 Martin Palmer, 2001, *The Jesus Sutras: Rediscovering the Lost Religion of Taoist Christianity*, London: Piatkus, p. 3. Palmer presents a new translation of the early Nestorian documents which have been translated by P.Y. Saeki, 1937, *The Nestorian Documents and Relics in China*, Tokyo: The Academy of Oriental Culture.

ascribed to the seventh-century Nestorian missionary Alopen, for example, draws an analogy between Christian negative theology and the Mahāyāna teachings on 'perfection of wisdom' (*prajñā-pāramitā*) and 'emptiness' (*śūnyatā*) – an analogy so far-reaching as to equate 'emptiness' with God: 'The holy One of great wisdom [*prajñā-pāramitā*] is equal to pure emptiness [*śūnyatā*] itself and cannot be taken (a view thereof).'[10] Accordingly the relation between God and the world is defined in Taoist-Buddhist terms as a dynamic non-dualism, such that God is the beingless ground of the world's being:

> The One Sacred Spirit simply is, existing in wu wei ['non-action'], being in beinglessness and beyond touch. Existing in non-existence never extinguished into nonbeing. All that exists does so as the manifestation of the beingness of the One Sacred Spirit.[11]

Nothing, however, of the Nestorian knowledge and understanding of Buddhism was transmitted to the Christian countries in the West. Western Christianity remained cut off from any direct contact with the East by the Muslim empire, which formed a tight barrier between East and West and was almost entirely impenetrable. Only very few missionaries – as for example the friar William of Rubruck (1215–70?) – or adventurers like Marco Polo (1254?–1324) managed to find their way to Asia and back. Their reports, distorted and fantastic as, in part, they were, created the scanty image of Buddhism that prevailed in Western Christianity for centuries. This image was based upon three hardly compatible components: (1) Buddhist doctrine was viewed as atheism in so far as a personal creator God seems to be rejected or as pantheism in so far as everything seemed to be seen

---

10 *Discourse on Monotheism* 58; transl. from Saeki as quoted in Scott, 'Christian Responses to Buddhism', p. 94.

11 *Discourse on Monotheism*. Here quoted from Palmer, *The Jesus Sutras*, p. 149. Palmer calls this text 'The Sutra of Origins' and renders its Chinese title as 'Second Part of the Preaching' (cf. *The Jesus Sutras*, p. 55). Insertion in brackets: P. S-L.

as divine,[12] (2) Buddhist practice was viewed as idolatry in so far as it seemed to focus on the veneration of idols, namely sacred images of Buddhas and Bodhisattvas or statues of ancestors,[13] and (3) the Buddhist founder was viewed as a saintly figure who unfortunately was no real saint because he had been a pagan.[14] Ironically, throughout the Middle Ages the Buddha had been anonymously venerated as a Christian saint under the names of Barlaam and Josaphat which presumably go back to *bhagavān* ('the venerable one') and *bodhisattva* ('enlightenment-being', a Buddha-to-be). Nineteenth-century research had been able to demonstrate that the legend of Barlaam and Josaphat – among the most popular devotional narratives in the Middle Ages – was a Christianized version of the Buddha legend, which had reached the West through some Persian and probably Syrian or Arabic travesties.[15]

As far as early Buddhist knowledge of Christianity is concerned our information is even scantier. The name of Jesus is mentioned in the *Kālacakra Tantra* 1:154 (tenth century?). There is, however, no doubt that Jesus is perceived there as one of the prophets of Islam and not as the central figure of Christianity.[16] Accordingly, the negative association with 'powerful, merciless *mlecchas* (barbarians)' refers not to Christianity but to Islam, experienced by Buddhists at that time as a genuine threat. This would seem

---

12 P. Jackson (trans.), 1990, *The Mission of Friar William of Rubruck: His Journey to the Court of the Great Khan Möngke 1253–1255*, London: The Hakluyt Society, p. 231.

13 Cf. Jackson, *The Mission of Friar William of Rubruck*, pp. 150–56; *Il Milione* III, Sir Henry Yule (trans.), 1871, *The Book of Ser Marco Polo, The Venetian, Concerning the Kingdoms and Marvels of the East*, 2 vols, London: John Murray, vol. 2, pp. 256–60.

14 Cf. Marco Polo's frequently quoted statement on the Buddha: 'if he had been a Christian . . . he would have been a great saint of Our Lord Jesus Christ, so good and pure was the life he led.' *Il Milione* III, Sir Henry Yule, *The Book of Ser Marco Polo*, vol. 2, p. 258.

15 P. Almond, 1987, 'The Buddha of Christendom: A Review of the Legend of Barlaam and Josaphat', in *Religious Studies* 23, pp. 391–406.

16 A. Berzin, 2002, 'The Kalachakra Presentation of the Prophets of the Non-Indic Invaders', in *The Berzin Archives*: www.berzinarchives.com/kalachakra/kc_pres_prophets_islam_full.html.

to apply also to the negative statements about 'the Messiah' in the Central Asian *Insādi Sūtra.*[17]

In China Christianity was known as the 'luminous religion' (*ching chia*o). The fact that the Nestorians presented Christianity in a positive relation to Buddhism and Taoism had obviously been helpful in achieving official recognition. The famous inscription on the Nestorian stele of Xi'an (erected in 781) quotes the imperial proclamation which in 638 had authorized the propagation of Christianity with the argument that religious truth and saintly life are not confined to any specific region or system:

> The way has no unchanging name,
> Sages have no unchanging method;
> Teaching is established to suit the land,
> That all living may be saved.[18]

Here we see strong evidence that Christianity was perceived – at least at some stages – as an acceptable variation of genuine religious insight. The further fact that the Nestorians proudly quoted such a view might indicate that they possibly subscribed to it.[19] Be that as it may, by the ninth century both Christians

---

17 H.-J. Klimkeit, 1985, 'Christian-Buddhist Encounter in Medieval Central Asia', in G.W. Houston (ed.), *The Cross and the Lotus: Christianity and Buddhism in Dialogue*, Delhi: Motilal Banarsidass, pp. 9–24 (14f.).

18 Quoted from Moule, *Christians in China*, p. 39.

19 Adam Ching-ching, the author of the Xi'an inscription, is known for his close co-operation with a Buddhist monk on the translation of Buddhist scriptures. For this he was officially rebuked by the court with the argument that the Buddhist and the Christian monks 'differ in customs and are wholly opposed to one another in their religious practices, Ching-ching must preach the teaching of messiah (*Mi-shih-hê*) and the Buddhist monk (*Sha-mên*) make known the *sūtra* of Buddha. We wish to have religious teachings well defined that men may have no uncertainty. Truth and error are not the same . . .' (quoted from Moule, *Christians in China*, p. 69; see also: C. Cary-Elwes, 1957, *China and the Cross: Studies in Missionary History*, London: Longmans, pp. 33–5). In such a hostile climate it is theologically significant that Adam quoted the former imperial view of a legitimate religious diversity.

and Buddhists became victims of the persecution of 'foreign', non-Chinese religions.

What is surprising is that – at least to date – we know of no Buddhist comments upon or responses to Nestorian Christianity. Were Christians too strange for the Buddhists to deal with? Or too familiar? Or are the hints of possible Christian echoes within Buddhism too subtle to be clearly identifiable?[20]

Strangers Become Enemies

The situation changed dramatically in modern times. By then, Nestorian Christianity had almost entirely disappeared from Central Asia and China.[21] But now the technological progress in ship-building enabled the Western nations to sail around the Muslim barrier and proceed to Asia. In the sixteenth century the Portuguese, accompanied by missionaries, arrived in Sri Lanka, China and Japan. The result was by and large a catastrophe. At first, Buddhists welcomed the Europeans as representatives of a new and possibly interesting version of religious truth. But rather soon the aggressive, polemical attitude of the Christian missionaries and their obvious alliance with Portuguese economic and military interests led to the firm conviction that Christianity was the imperialistic religion of an imperialistic people. From now on we do indeed find various Buddhist texts responding to Christianity – but all of them extremely critical and adversarial.[22] Moreover, the disputes did not remain theoretical. When a Portuguese colony was established in Sri Lanka, Buddhists

---

20 This is obviously the suspicion of Yves Raguin, 1998, *Le Christ Chinois: Héritages et espérance*, Paris: Desclée de Brouwer, Bellarmin.

21 Primarily, it may be presumed, as a result of the extremely intolerant politics carried out in the fourteenth century by Tamberlaine (Timur-i-Leng) in Central Asia and by the early Ming Dynasty in China. See Cary-Elwes, *China and the Cross*, p. 37.

22 Iso Kern, 1992, *Buddhistische Kritik am Christentum im China des 17. Jahrhunderts*, Bern: Peter Lang; George Elison, 1973, *Deus Destroyed: The Image of Christianity in Early Modern Japan*, Cambridge, MA: Harvard University Press.

became victims of expulsion and cruel persecution.[23] Triumphantly the Portuguese claimed that they had captured the holy tooth relic – the ancient symbol for Sri Lanka's dedication to Buddhism – and had taken it to Goa where they destroyed it (a claim the Buddhist guardians of the relic denied).[24] In China the anti-Christian tracts of Buddhist authors led to some minor forms of anti-Christian measures.[25] In Japan, however, the suspicion of the rulers that the Christian missionaries were only preparing the way for a colonialist invasion not only brought about the seclusion of the country for more than 200 years, but also triggered one of the fiercest and most sanguinary persecutions that Christians had ever had to endure.[26]

While Japan was thus spared from colonial conquest, almost all the other Buddhist countries of Asia became subject to the rule of Western Christian nations at one stage or another during the subsequent centuries. Sri Lanka came, first, under Portuguese dominion (1505–1658), then Dutch (1658–1795), and finally British (1795–1948). This meant the subjugation of Sri Lanka by Catholic, Reformed, Anglican and Methodist Christians – a rather impressive spectrum of Christian denominational diversity but all of them with the same three goals: power, profit, proselytism. During the nineteenth century Britain also conquered Buddhist

---

23 Cf. the judgement of the sober historian K.M. De Silva: 'In Sri Lanka the Portuguese record of religious persecution, coercion and mindless destruction of places of worship sacred to other faiths was unsurpassed in its scale and virulence.' K.M. De Silva, 1981, *A History of Sri Lanka*, London: C. Hurst; Berkeley: University of California Press, p. 128. See also: Tennakoon Vimalananda, 1963, *Buddhism in Ceylon under the Christian Powers*, Colombo: M.D. Gunasena & Co., pp. xxiv–xxxiv.

24 R. Gombrich, 1991, *Precept and Practice*, 2nd edn, Delhi: Motilal Banarsidass, p. 122.

25 Kern, *Buddhistische Kritik am Christentum im China des 17. Jahrhunderts*, pp. 1–49.

26 Cf. G. Voss, H. Cieslik (trans.), 1940, *Kirishito-Ki und Sayo-Yoroku: Japanische Dokumente zur christlichen Missionsgeschichte des 17. Jahrhunderts*, Tokyo: Sophia University; C.R. Boxer, 1974, *The Christian Century in Japan. 1549–1650*, Berkeley: University of California Press; Ikubo Higashibaba, 2001, *Christianity in Early Modern Japan: Kirishitan Belief and Practice*, Leiden: Brill, pp. 126–60.

Burma and extended its influence to Buddhist Thailand. At the same time France set up its rule over 'Indochine': Vietnam, Laos and Cambodia. China became the object of greed for Britain, Portugal, France, Germany and Russia. Japan followed the example of the Christian nations, extending its rule over parts of China and Korea and justifying its military adventures (as for example in the Russo-Japanese war at the beginning of the twentieth century) as a battle between 'the army of God' and 'the army of the Buddha', among other things. For 'Russia is not only the enemy of our country but of the Buddha as well.'[27] By now, Buddhism and Christianity had turned from strangers into bitter enemies.[28]

From Controversy to Dialogue

The hostile situation is also reflected in the sort of judgements that followers of both religions tended to pass on each other at the turn of the nineteenth to the twentieth century. While, for example, the great reformer and modernist of Theravāda Buddhism, Anagarika Dharmapāla (1864–1933), classified Christianity as one of the most primitive and destructive cults,[29] Archibald Scott wrote in his widely read comparison of Buddhism and Christianity: 'Christianity seems to be superior to it, not in the sense that the infant is superior to the embryo, but as man is superior to the animal . . .'[30] The mood expressed

---

27 B. Victoria, 1997, *Zen at War*, New York: Weatherhill, p. 30.

28 What Notto Thelle has stated for Japan can well be considered as a generally valid characterization of the situation at the end of the nineteenth century: 'In the 1890s Buddhists and Christians confronted each other as equal adversaries.' N. Thelle, 1987, *Buddhism and Christianity in Japan: From Conflict to Dialogue, 1854–1899*, Honolulu: University of Hawaii Press, p. 247.

29 See, for example, his 'Buddhagama and the Religions of the World', in A. Dharmapala, 1989, *The Arya Dharma of Sakyamuni Gautama the Buddha*, repr. of the 1st edn, 1917, Calcutta: Maha Bodhi Book Agency, pp. 1–13.

30 A. Scott, 1971, *Buddhism and Christianity: A Parallel and a Contrast*, repr. of the 1st edn, 1890, Port Washington: Kennikat Press, p. 41.

in such statements was characteristic of the various controversies in South and East Asia between Christian missionaries and Buddhist representatives.[31] But Buddhist-Christian controversies were now no longer confined to the East.

In the wake of Western colonialist expansion Western knowledge about Buddhism increased considerably. Missionary letters and tracts containing reports on Buddhism were augmented by the lengthy records of travellers and official delegates detailing the customs of the newly discovered Asian countries and frequently addressing religious issues as well. But it was not until the nineteenth century that Buddhist scriptures were brought to the West where they were published, translated and eagerly studied. The negative flavour of Buddhist terms like *nirvāṇa* ('fading out, extinction'), *nirodha* ('cessation'), or *śūnyatā* ('emptiness') threw up the question as to whether the ultimate position of Buddhism was akin to mysticism and negative theology or whether it amounted to a kind of atheist and nihilist world-view.[32] By no means was this a purely academic issue. For the first time in the history of the Occident, the influence of anti-Christian atheism and materialism, as formulated in the eighteenth century, came to extend beyond intellectual circles, becoming the world-view of common people as well. Was Buddhism to be regarded as an ally of those atheistically minded Westerners who saw themselves as the progressive, enlightened vanguard of humanity? Or was it just another version of the medieval mystical religiosity, which did not at all accord with the enlightened mentality of the nineteenth century, and which put both religion's critics and religion's defenders in a rather awkward position? Additional weight to this debate was the generally accepted, but erroneous

31 See K. Malalgoda, 1976, *Buddhism in Sinhalese Society 1750–1900*, Berkeley: University of California Press; Thelle, *Buddhism and Christianity in Japan* (see fn. 28).

32 Cf. G.R. Welbon, 1968, *The Buddhist Nirvāna and Its Western Interpreters*, Chicago: University of Chicago Press. For a detailed account of the Western academic exploration of Buddhism see J.W. de Jong, 1974, 'A Brief History of Buddhist Studies in Europe and America', in *The Eastern Buddhist* 7, no. 1, pp. 55–106, no. 2, pp. 49–82.

opinion that Buddhism would constitute the religion of the majority of humankind.[33]

For many decades the interpretation of Buddhism as atheism and nihilism dominated in the West, even influencing Buddhist self-understanding in the East to some extent, particularly among those Asian Buddhist intellectuals who had studied Buddhism in contemporary English books. Seen as an atheist philosophy Buddhism met with fierce criticism from Christian apologetics; for the same reason it was welcomed by Western intellectuals like Schopenhauer and Nietzsche. Finally, towards the end of the nineteenth and the beginning of the twentieth century, a Western form of Buddhism emerged, born out of the interaction between inner-Western debates and Buddhist texts, but having almost no direct contact with Asian Buddhists.

In the latter regard the situation was different in the United States, where a certain ongoing presence of Asian Buddhists – primarily channelled through Hawaii – had been an ingredient in the modern encounter quite early on. However, it was not until the middle of the twentieth century that polemical, apologetic controversy gradually gave way to the more open and constructive communication that can be called Buddhist-Christian dialogue[34] – though even today this process is by no means complete.

---

33 The error was based on the false assumption that more or less all Chinese were Buddhists.

34 There are several excellent overviews available, for example: H. Dumoulin, 1974, *Christianity Meets Buddhism*, LaSalle: Open Court Publishing; J. Spae, 1980, *Buddhist-Christian Empathy*, Chicago: The Chicago Institute of Theology and Culture; P. Ingram, 1988, *The Modern Buddhist-Christian Dialogue: Two Universalistic Religions in Transformation*, Lewiston: Edwin Mellen Press; W. Lai and M. von Brück, 2001, *Christianity and Buddhism: A Multicultural History of Their Dialogue*, Maryknoll: Orbis. My own work (P. Schmidt-Leukel, 1992, *'Den Löwen brüllen hören': Zur Hermeneutik eines christlichen Verständnisses der buddhistischen Heilsbotschaft*, Paderborn: Schöningh) focuses on the hermeneutical aspects of Buddhist-Christian dialogue. Two international journals are dedicated to Buddhist-Christian dialogue: *Buddhist Christian Studies*, published by the University of Hawaii Press, and *Dialogue*, published by the Ecumenical Institute, Colombo, Sri Lanka.

The fact that dialogue has been gaining the upper hand over polemical confrontation can be traced to a number of factors. On the Christian side a major motive is surely the regrettable way, highly criticized by several theologians, in which Christianity had introduced itself – and thereby Jesus Christ – to the Asian Buddhist world during the centuries of Western colonialism.[35] Lynn de Silva (1919–82), one of the great pioneers of Buddhist-Christian dialogue, has expressed this most clearly at the Fifth Assembly of the World Council of Churches in Nairobi in 1975:

> Dialogue is urgent and essential for us in Asia in order to repudiate the arrogance, aggression, and negativism of our evangelistic crusades which have obscured the gospel and caricatured Christianity as an aggressive and militant religion. As a result of this Jesus Christ appears in the eyes of people of other faiths as a religious Julius Caesar . . .
>   . . . Dialogue therefore is essential in order to dispel the misunderstandings and prejudices of the past created by our negative attitude to other faiths and thereby create a healthy atmosphere where we can receive as well as give, listen as well as proclaim.[36]

---

35 In this context it is worth mentioning that the situation in Korea is markedly different. Korea is the only traditionally Buddhist country in Asia where Christianity has experienced significant growth during the twentieth century so that it is now almost on a par with Buddhism. One of the reasons for this exceptional situation may very well be that Korea has not been colonized by a Christian nation but rather by a Buddhist one, so that Christianity enjoys here a far higher credibility than elsewhere in Asia. For this insight I am indebted to the research work currently carried out by Jeeeun Choi, one of my postgraduate students. For the religious situation in Korea see J. H. Grayson, 2002, *Korea: A Religious History*, rev. edn, London: RoutledgeCurzon; J.H. Grayson, 1985, *Early Buddhism and Christianity in Korea: A Study in the Emplantation of Religion*, Leiden: Brill.

36 D.M. Paton (ed.), 1976, *Breaking Barriers: Nairobi 1975. The Official Report of the Fifth Assembly of the World Council of Churches*, London: SPCK, p. 72.

Another major factor compelling Christians towards a serious dialogue with Buddhists has been the acknowledgement of the high moral standards and contemplative wealth of Buddhist religious practice. Must there not be a great deal of truth in a religion which brings about such splendid fruits? The experiences of Christians such as Thomas Merton (1915–68) and Hugo M. Enomiya-Lassalle (1898–1990) who dared to immerse themselves in Buddhist spirituality and meditational training prepared the ground for a growing theological interest in exploring the corresponding Buddhist wisdom.

On the Buddhist side the interest in dialogue with Christianity has been, generally speaking, more reserved. The suspicion is still rife that the new Christian enthusiasm for open dialogue and exchange might simply be yet another strategy in the unaltered goal of religious conquest. Nevertheless, there are now many Buddhists seriously dedicated to dialogue with Christianity and among their motivations two are outstanding.

One motive, inextricably linked to the philosophical work of the so-called Kyoto School,[37] is a Buddhist interest in better comprehending the role that Christianity had and perhaps continues to have in the formation and development of the modern world. This interest is part of the overall Japanese project, in the wake of the Meiji reform, to discover the secrets of Western success in modernity in order that Japan might benefit from them. The Kyoto philosophers, coming primarily out of a Zen or Amida Buddhist background, acquired an excellent knowledge of the Western history of ideas and the role of Christianity within it. It is illuminating that their own discussion of Christianity mirrors, in a certain sense, the Western debates over Buddhism in the nineteenth century, for repeatedly their reflections have turned to the question of Buddhism's relationship to the two great thought-forms in which the West has had to confront the idea of nothingness, namely: in the mysticism of Meister Eckhart and the nihilism of Friedrich Nietzsche. Kyoto philosophers

---

37 Cf. F. Franck (ed.), 1982, *The Buddha Eye: An Anthology of the Kyoto School*, New York: Crossroad.

like Kitarō Nishida (1870–1945), a lifelong friend of Daisetsu
Suzuki (1870–1966), Keiji Nishitani (1900–90), Hajime Tanabe
(1885–1962), Shin'ichi Hisamatsu (1889–1981), Yoshinori
Takeuchi (1913–2002), Shizuteru Ueda (b.1926) and Masao Abe
(b.1915), hugely contributed to the development of Buddhist-
Christian dialogue. While much of the thinking within the Kyoto
School has been marked by the idea that Buddhism would be
better equipped than Christianity to deal with the challenges of
modernity in the long run, there seems to be indications of a current trend towards recognizing that both traditions have been
similarly hit by a mushrooming secularization which but under-
scores the necessity to work together in the search for adequate
responses.[38]

The Buddhists' philosophical interest in the West was comple-
mented by a Western philosophical interest in the East, the latter
arising out of the wish to overcome a static concept of being.
This can be seen in Martin Heidegger's (1889–1976) existential-
ism[39] as well as – though in a quite different form – in Alfred
North Whitehead's (1861–1947) process philosophy.[40] Hence
a number of theologians involved in dialogue with the Kyoto
School display a certain nearness either to existentialist thinking[41] or to process philosophy/theology.[42]

---

38 See, for example, H.-M. Barth, K. Kadowaki, E. Minoura and M. Pye
(eds), 2004, *Buddhismus und Christentum vor der Herausforderung der
Säkularisierung*, Schenefeld: EB-Verlag (contributions partly in English).

39 Heidegger's interest in the East and contacts with Japanese scholars
is well documented in Hartmut Buchner (ed.), 1989, *Japan und Heidegger:
Gedenkschrift der Stadt Meßkirch zum hundertsten Geburtstag Martin
Heideggers*, Sigmaringen: Jan Thorbecke Verlag.

40 Cf. A.N. Whitehead, 1996, *Religion in the Making: Lowell Lectures,
1926*, New York: Fordham University Press; C. Hartshorne, 1984, 'Toward
a Buddhisto-Christian Religion', in K.K. Inada and N.P. Jacobson (eds),
Buddhism and American Thinkers, Albany: SUNY, pp. 1–13.

41 See, e.g., H. Waldenfels, 1980, *Absolute Nothingness*, New York:
Paulist; F. Buri, 1997, *The Buddha-Christ as the Lord of the True Self*,
Macon: Mercer University Press.

42 See, e.g., J. Cobb, 1982, *Beyond Dialogue: Toward a Mutual
Transformation of Christianity and Buddhism*, Philadelphia: Fortress;
Ingram, *The Modern Buddhist-Christian Dialogue* (see fn. 34).

A second motive of Buddhist interest in Christianity is nothing less than what Notto Thelle called the 'admiration for the person of Jesus'.[43] This holds true for almost all branches of Buddhism, and even the worst anti-Christian Buddhist polemicists at the height of reciprocal intellectual mud-slinging usually found some words of praise for the founder of this much-blamed religion. Buddhist spiritual masters and reformers like Bhikkhu Buddhadāsa (1906–93) in Thailand and Thich Nhat Hanh (b.1926) from Vietnam entered into dialogue with Christianity primarily out of their undisguised appreciation of Jesus as an enlightened teacher, a 'new Dharma door',[44] whose 'Sermon on the Mount . . . is far more than enough and complete for practice to attain emancipation'.[45] Quite obviously, this is also a key motive in the fourteenth Dalai Lama's involvement in Buddhist-Christian dialogue.[46]

Another motive needs to be mentioned – one common to both Christians and Buddhists: their jointly felt responsibility to alleviate the suffering of fellow beings, to hear and respond to the 'cries of the world' and contribute to the world's inner and outer peace. One of the major manifestations of this is the Buddhist-Christian co-operation in global organizations such as the World Conference of Religions for Peace[47] (in whose establishment Buddhists have made a crucial contribution) or in the International Network of Engaged Buddhism.[48]

No doubt in historical terms the Buddhist-Christian dialogue is still a very recent, young and possibly fragile phenomenon. But neither can there be a doubt that thanks to dialogue no

---

43 Thelle, *Buddhism and Christianity in Japan* (see fn. 28), p. 249.

44 Thich Nhat Hanh, 1996, *Living Buddha, Living Christ*, London: Rider, p. 39.

45 Bhikkhu Buddhadāsa, 1967, *Christianity and Buddhism*, Bangkok: Sublime Life Mission, p. 29.

46 See Dalai Lama, 1998, *The Good Heart: A Buddhist Perspective on the Teachings of Jesus*, Boston: Wisdom Publications.

47 H.A. Jack, 1993, *WCRP: A History of the World Conference on Religion and Peace*, New York: World Conference on Religion and Peace.

48 See S.B. King and C.S. Queen (eds), 1996, *Engaged Buddhism*, Albany: SUNY.

small number of Buddhists and Christians have ceased to be enemies and have become friends. But have they also ceased to be strangers?

The Nature of Dialogue

Whatever the specific motives for dialogue might be, to a large extent it continues to be about mutual understanding. Do we understand the other as the other understands him- or herself? That such an understanding must be the regulative ideal that we need to pursue in genuine dialogue has hardly been disputed. But what does this require? Some pioneers of dialogue such as Raimundo Panikkar have gone so far as to proclaim that we understand the beliefs and faith of other men only if we share them.[49] This might be an exaggeration.[50] But at its core is something quite true, namely, that understanding entails a shift of perspective, a kind of 'passing over' to where the other is.[51] A full consent to what the other believes or a sharing of the other's faith as a prerequisite for true understanding may indeed be too much to ask; nevertheless we ought to become able to see and understand the *why* of the other's belief, the motives of the other's faith. As Wilfred Cantwell Smith has phrased it:

> To understand any human behaviour, any human feeling, any human hope or vision, is to recognize that if you had been in that situation, you would have had that particular act or quality or value-judgement as one of your options.[52]

---

49 'I can never understand his position as he does – and this is the only real understanding between people – unless I share his view; in a word, unless I judge it to be somewhat true.' See R. Panikkar, 1978, *The Intrareligious Dialogue*, New York: Paulist, p. 9. See also R. Panikkar, 1975, 'Verstehen als Überzeugtsein', in H.G. Gadamer and P. Vogler (eds), *Neue Anthropologie*, Band 7, Stuttgart: Georg Thieme Verlag, pp. 132–67.

50 For a critique of Panikkar's thesis see Schmidt-Leukel, *'Den Löwen brüllen hören'*, pp. 379–97.

51 See J. Dunne, 1972, *the Way of All the World*, Houndmills: Macmillan.

52 W.C. Smith, 1997, *Modern Culture from a Comparative Perspective*, ed. John W. Burbidge, Albany: SUNY, p. 134.

Dialogue can and should be a means of striving for such an understanding. The shift of perspective involved has often been described as seeing through the other's eyes. So says Smith:

> . . . to understand the faith of Buddhists, one must not look at something called 'Buddhism'. Rather, one must look at the world – so far as possible, through Buddhist eyes.[53]

If we come somewhere near to accomplishing that, one of the things that we will see through the eyes of the other is ourselves. Do I understand how the other sees me and do I understand *why* the other sees me like that? When in the course of dialogue we begin to ask these questions our hermeneutical efforts reach a *second*, highly significant *phase*. Not only may we now learn more about the other but we may learn more about ourselves – through the eyes of the other and with the help of the other. As is the case in other inter-faith dialogues, the Buddhist-Christian dialogue too has started to enter that phase.[54] In order to make these efforts explicit and allow them to become a topic of our dialogue we must start to speak comparatively: We must start to speak about *both* traditions, sharing our mutual perceptions and reflections born in reciprocal comparisons, exchanging our insights into the other for their insights into us. This does not mean a fall back into the distanced, ostensibly 'neutral' operations of comparative religion. It means rather to enter a new field – the field of comparative theology,[55] which can only be done dialogically.

---

53 Smith, Modern Culture from a Comparative Perspective, p. 132.

54 See, for example, R.M. Gross and T.C. Muck (eds), 2000, *Buddhists Talk About Jesus: Christians Talk About the Buddha*, New York and London: Continuum; P. Schmidt-Leukel (ed.), 2001, *Buddhist Perceptions of Jesus: Papers of the Third Conference of the European Network of Buddhist-Christian Studies (St Ottilien 1999)*, St Ottilien: EOS-Verlag; P. Schmidt-Leukel, 2002, 'Christian Perceptions of Buddha: Proceedings of the European Network of Buddhist-Christian Studies' Conference Held in Lund, May 2001', in *Swedish Missiological Themes* 90, no. 1.

55 See F.X. Clooney, 1995, 'Comparative Religion: A Review of Recent Books (1989–1995)', in *Theological Studies* 55, pp. 521–50. Pioneering work has been done by Clooney himself in relation to Hinduism and Buddhism and by Keith Ward in a multi-religious perspective. For

But there is a *third phase* of dialogical understanding, one that is marked by the challenge of mutual transformation. If we learn to understand the other as the other understands him- or herself, and if we further learn to see ourselves through the eyes of the other, the next question will inevitably arise: Can we integrate the truth that we might have discovered in the other's tradition – which is to say, can we incorporate what we have learned about the other into our own religious self-understanding? And can we incorporate into our own self-understanding the truth that we learn about ourselves when we perceive ourselves through the other's eyes?

To a large extent mutual transformation will take place through mutual inspiration with 'catalyst effects'. The encounter with Buddhist meditational practice, for example, inspires a revitalization of Christian contemplative practice; listening to the Buddhist philosophy of 'emptiness' creates a renewed interest in the Christian tradition of 'negative theology'; the encounter with Christian social ethics and charity reminds Buddhists of the social implications of their own bodhisattva ideal – and so on. But mutual transformation can go further. It can touch the innermost core of a religious tradition's self-understanding.[56]

---

an overview and discussion of Ward's work see T.W. Bartel (ed.), 2003, *Comparative Theology: Essays for Keith Ward*, London: SPCK.

56 In particular, James Fredericks (and sometimes Francis Clooney as well) has suggested that we approach comparative theology as an alternative to the kind of questions treated within the so-called 'theology of religion'. However, to avoid questioning the self-understanding of religions in their encounter with other traditions would mean losing the theological dimension of comparative theology, and then we would either have to go back to comparative religion or to choose the 'retreat to commitment'. Cf. J. Fredericks, 1999, *Faith Among Faiths: Christian Theology and Non-Christian Religions*, New York: Paulist; J. Fredericks, 2004, *Buddhists and Christians: Through Comparative Study to Solidarity*, Maryknoll: Orbis. For a critique of Fredericks and Clooney, see P. Schmidt-Leukel, 2005, 'Limits and Prospects of Comparative Theology', in N. Hintersteiner (ed.), *Naming and Thinking God in Europe Today: Theology in Global Dialogue*, Amsterdam and New York: Rodopi, pp. 447–58.

Traditionally both Buddhists and Christians have related to one another and to other religions in general either by claiming that they alone teach the path to salvation or at least that they teach it in a uniquely superior form. Hence whatever truth there might be in the other religious traditions (if any at all), it is either not sufficient to attain salvation[57] or it provides only a fragmentary basis with a diminished chance of salvation. In any case, one's own tradition is incomparably superior and hence it would be ideal and desirable that everyone should become a member of it. The value of the other religions – or of the other denominations/forms within one's own tradition – is at best a provisional one: They constitute the lower steps which may lead up to the solemn heights of one's own sect/school/church. A transformation of these *exclusivistic* or *inclusivistic* forms of religious self-understanding would bring us to the *pluralistic* position, whereby another religion is seen neither as totally wrong, nor as an inferior path, but rather as teaching a different and nevertheless equally valid path to salvation.[58] This is the challenge that an in-depth encounter of Buddhism and Christianity holds ready for the members of both traditions.

This challenge does not arise in the abstract. It appears precisely when Buddhists and Christians turn, seriously and dialogically, towards a comparative understanding of their visions of human existence: the human predicament and its prospect of liberation; the relation of human existence to ultimate reality; the role played

---

57 This is the tenor of the frequently misunderstood Buddhist parable of the elephant and the blind men (see *Udāna* 6:4). While the enlightened Buddha is in the situation of the king who sees the elephant in full, the rival teachers are compared to blind men who have only a limited perception of a few aspects of the truth. According to the concluding verses of *Udāna* 6:5 and 6:6, their partial insight is insufficient in order to achieve liberation. See on this also A. Grünschloß, 1999, *Der eigene und der fremde Glaube: Studien zur interreligiösen Fremdwahrnehmung in Islam, Hinduismus, Buddhismus und Christentum*, Tübingen: Mohr Siebeck, pp. 202ff.

58 Cf. P. Schmidt-Leukel, 2005, 'Exclusivism, Inclusivism, Pluralism. The Tripolar Scheme: Clarified and Reaffirmed', in P. Knitter (ed.), *The Myth of Religious Superiority*, Maryknoll: Orbis.

by their founding figures, Jesus Christ and Gautama Buddha, in mediating ultimate reality to human beings. The way Christians and Buddhists judge one another in these areas is not without its impact on their assessment of the chances for a fruitful mutual co-operation and joint contribution towards the inner and outer peace of the world. And, by the same token, the practical experience gained in their mutual co-operation is not without consequences for their mutual understanding and assessment.

The Dialogue at the 'Weisfeld Lectures'

The chapters of this book document the second series of 'Gerald Weisfeld Lectures',[59] organized by the Centre for Inter-Faith Studies[60] (University of Glasgow), which took place in Glasgow during May 2004 as part of the events leading up to the Dalai Lama's visit to Scotland. Two lectures were given each week, one by a Christian and one by a Buddhist, both of them speaking on the same topic and both of them speaking comparatively, though from the perspective of each one's own tradition. At the end of both lectures the discussion was opened with each speaker's response to the other. This structure has been preserved in the subsequent chapters. For purposes of publication the lectures have been rewritten after the actual experience of the dialogue itself.[61]

The first theme, 'Human Existence in Buddhism and Christianity', is taken up from a Christian perspective by *Elizabeth Harris* who teaches at the University of Birmingham and has a long-standing involvement in inter-faith dialogue, particularly with Theravāda Buddhism. Her Buddhist dialogue-partner is *Kiyoshi Tsuchiya* who teaches hermeneutics and Eastern religions in the Department of Theology and Religious Studies at Glasgow

---

59 The first series was held in 2003 and is published as *War and Peace in World Religions*, ed. Perry Schmidt-Leukel, London: SCM Press, 2004.

60 See http://www.religions.divinity.gla.ac.uk/Centre-Interfaith/index. htm.

61 I am grateful to Carolina Weening for her editorial assistance with the chapters by K. Baier, M. Nambara and P. Schmidt-Leukel.

University. Harris points out what she understands as a basic commonality in the Buddhist and Christian analysis of the human condition. For both traditions human existence is ambivalent: on the one hand, it is deeply pervaded by the roots of evil – craving and ignorance, according to Buddhism, sin, according to Christianity; on the other hand, it offers a way out, a genuine possibility of salvation or liberation. However, says Harris, Buddhism and Christianity both 'converge and diverge'. Both traditions see human self-centredness at the root of the problem, and in their respective paths of salvation we find convergences too. The differences, however, become apparent, so Harris, in the active function of God for the salvific process within Christianity as well as in the role of reincarnation within the Buddhist analysis of human existence, which is without any parallel in Christianity.

Tsuchiya agrees that both traditions understand the self as the major source of the human predicament, but holds that they interpret this in quite different senses. While the self is seen as sinful but nevertheless real in Christianity, Buddhism sees the self as an unwholesome illusion. Hence there are two different, even contradictory forms of self-understanding: a 'relational', individualistic *ego* dominant in Christianity, and a sort of cosmological *ego*, characteristic for Buddhism, particularly within the Zen-Taoist tradition from which Tsuchiya speaks. He illustrates this point challengingly with a comparative analysis of Kafka's story of Gregor Samsa's metamorphosis into a beetle and Chuang-tzu's famous butterfly dream. This difference of self-concepts is, so Tsuchiya, crucial for the respective Christian and Buddhist understandings of transcendence and cosmos: personal transcendence versus cosmological transcendence, anti-naturalism versus naturalism.

In her response Harris raises the question whether Tsuchiya's representation of Christianity is sufficiently comprehensive. Are there not dimensions in Christianity supportive of a non-dualist approach to nature and human existence? Tsuchiya, in his reply, admits that the ultimate religious goals might converge, but insists on an at least 'possibly contradictory' religious orientation with specific dangers on both sides, so that there is room for mutual constructive challenge.

This debate continues in the dialogue on the second topic: 'Ultimate Reality in Buddhism and Christianity'. *Karl Baier*, who teaches intercultural philosophy at the University of Vienna, presents a Christian perspective heavily informed by its mystical tradition. *Minoru Nambara*, who taught comparative cultural studies at the University of Tokyo, is well known as a Buddhist expert in Western and Eastern mysticism. Baier offers a comparative analysis of the deconstructive efforts of Nāgārjuna and Nicholas Cusanus, both of whom employed the so-called 'fourfold negation' in order to introduce their non-dual and non-conceptual views of the relation between ultimate and non-ultimate reality. For Baier the obvious affinities between these two (sub-)traditions are even increased in the current situation. For 'by means of transformative encounter Buddhism and Christianity cease to be independent bodies of thought'.

Sketching the transformation of Buddhism as it passed from India into China[62] and Japan, Nambara holds that for Chinese Buddhism 'this very world is, in and of itself, the ultimate subject, the ultimate reality'. Zen practice, accordingly, is 'a way' where 'no metaphysical flowers blossom'. To live by the bottomless ground of everything, which is in itself no-thing, is to live with nature as 'neither its master nor its slave'. The biblical God, understood as one who can create nature and destroy nature, is profoundly at variance with the Buddhist view. Nambara agrees, however, that through the possibly Indian-inspired Neo-Platonic tradition a Christian understanding of the Ultimate could more closely approximate Buddhism's. This may be said also of

---

62 Malcolm David Eckel pointedly characterized the 'transformation that took place when the wine of the Indian Buddhist tradition was poured into its Chinese bottles' with the phrase: '"Nature" in the Indian tradition was a world to be transcended, while in East Asia it took on the capacity to symbolize transcendence itself.' M.D. Eckel, 1997, 'Is There a Buddhist Philosophy of Nature?', in M.E. Tucker and D.R. Williams (eds), *Buddhism and Ecology: The Interconnection of Dharma and Deeds*, Cambridge, MA: Harvard University Press, p. 339.

Meister Eckhart's intellectual mysticism, and perhaps even more appropriately (though somewhat differently) of Jacob Boehme's Christocentric mysticism, marked as the latter is by a simple lifestyle celebrating the resurrection of nature in its true form before the 'fall' – that is, before its disturbance through man's self-centred desire. 'Neither science nor civilization quenches its thirst nor heals its ills.' But true religion can. It is, says Nambara, living the truth, and this in turn is the fruit of 'the pure and simple soul', found in those who often live in poverty, without the comforts of civilization. If we care for religion, it is their reality that we need to experience first.

Of course, Baier grants in his response, there are indeed dualistic tendencies at work in the definition of the relation between God and the world in the biblical and post-biblical Christian tradition. But does Nambara not underestimate the non-dualistic strands which are equally present? On what grounds would it be justified to single them out as 'un-Christian'? Is this not merely serving the agenda of immunizing the traditional superiority claim of Buddhism – or of a particular Zen-Taoist version of it? Does dialogue not call us beyond such conventional strongholds? But, asks Nambara in his reply, are not these differences undeniably obvious in the approach to nature as manifested in the Western Christian tradition on the one hand and in the Eastern Buddhist tradition on the other? And how far would Christians be prepared to go when it comes to the insight into the interplay between language and dualism? From a Buddhist perspective, says Nambara, it is not enough to affirm that God or the Other is ineffable. 'Rather, negative propositions disclose a dimension . . . beyond all opposites, appearing and yet always escaping all souls, whether Buddhist or Christian.'

With the third topic the dialogue focuses on 'Buddha and Christ as Mediators of the Transcendent'. In *my own* contribution, I suggest a reconstruction of how the idea of incarnation developed in Buddhist and Christian thinking, triggered by the experience that the Buddha embodied the Dharma he taught and Christ the kingdom he proclaimed. Two structural similarities are set forth: first, Buddha and Christ both mediate the transcendent by pointing away from themselves towards something different, thereby making the transcendent symbolically and yet really present; second, the force behind this process of embodiment is regarded as stemming from the Ultimate itself. This analysis inevitably throws up the question of the uniqueness of incarnation: Can Christians accept Buddhist claims of the Buddha as an embodiment of the Ultimate, and can Buddhists accept the respective claims made by Christians for Christ?

In his Buddhist presentation of the topic *John Makransky*, an ordained Tibetan lama and expert in the Indo-Tibetan tradition of Buddhism who teaches at Boston College, acknowledges the basic similarity of Buddhist and Christian incarnation beliefs but raises the question as to whether Buddha and Christ do not differ significantly in their salvific role, the former being seen as the one who teaches the way to liberation, the latter seen as the redeemer from sin through his atoning sacrifice. Despite this difference Makransky appreciates Christ as someone who 'indeed functions somehow as a mediation of ultimate reality as I, a Buddhist, understand that reality'. But what sense is to be made of this from a Mahāyāna perspective? In response to this question Makransky suggests a Buddhist version of Mark Heim's 'multiple ends'-version of inclusivism. Through their mediators Christianity and Buddhism are indeed related to the ultimate reality with a significant overlap in their liberating features. But this relationship is differently conceptualized and, from a Buddhist perspective, does not achieve in Christianity the same depth of insight into the empty, non-dual nature of the Ultimate. Consequently Christian and Buddhist salvific ends are neither simply the same nor fully equivalent. There is room for further friendly debate over which of the two traditions provides the more adequate insight and practice with regard to the Ultimate.

In my response to Makransky I challenge Heim's model, asking whether it really fulfils what many believe it promises, namely: to do full justice to religious diversity. According to my understanding it does not combine diversity with equal validity, which is – as I see it – what we would need in order to develop an appropriate understanding of Buddhism and Christianity.

Makransky, however, in his own reply holds that both religions can learn from each other so long as they accept an authentic salvific value of the other without necessarily admitting a full soteriological equivalence.

At least one aspect of Buddhist and Christian practice is addressed with the last topic, 'Buddhism, Christianity and their Potential for Peace'. *Kenneth Fernando*, retired Anglican Bishop of Colombo, Sri Lanka, writes out of his long experience of dialogue with Sri Lankan Theravāda Buddhism and his intimate involvement, alongside leading Buddhist monks, in the peace efforts related to the country's ethnic conflict. Confessing a rather deplorable record of Christianity's frequently violent behaviour in the past, and acknowledging a much more laudable Buddhist record in this regard, Fernando presents an interpretation of biblical motives that can effectively nourish a Christian contribution to peace work; work that has to be multi-religious, both in his country and globally.

As someone who has participated for many years in precisely that type of work, the ordained Zen Buddhist Hozan Alan Senauke from the Buddhist Peace Fellowship emphasizes that the crucial task, from a Buddhist point of view, is to take the insight into the roots of evil within one's own self-entanglement and translate it to the level of social and political activity; and to do so without creating new unwholesome sentiments of aversion or hatred.

While there is much agreement on these basic points, the responses echo an exciting exchange on the spiritual significance of, on the one hand, hope and optimism and, on the other hand, non-attachment with regard to the outcome of our actions. What if our peace efforts fail? Do we then need that sort of hope against all hope, the kind of optimism that flows from the eschatological dimension of the Christian faith in the Kingdom of God? Or do we need the Buddhist equanimity that faces unshaken the reality of aggression as part of the all-pervasive reality of suffering (*duḥkha*)? Does this mark a juncture where Buddhist and Christian spiritualities diverge, or are both in need of particularly that sort of inspiration which is such a prominent feature in the spirituality of the other?

When it comes to Buddhism and Christianity, the relationship between how they differ and what they have in common is a quite peculiar one. Their encounter has been stamped from the very outset with the mixed and puzzling impression of their utter strangeness on the one hand together with their deep familiarity on the other. This ambivalent impression can also be sensed in the various contributions to the dialogue here documented. The goal of dialogue and the reflection which accompanies it is neither to ignore or remove the differences between Buddhism and Christianity, nor to neglect or negate their familiarity. A sense of strangeness will always be in the air perhaps when Buddhists and Christians meet. But befriended through dialogue and matured in mutual understanding they may become quite intimate strangers – and they may even share Aloysius Pieris' judgement, that that there is a Buddhist and a Christian deep within each of us.[63]

---

63 See again Pieris, *Love Meets Wisdom*, pp. 110–35.

Part I

Life and Death

2. Human Existence in Buddhism and Christianity:
A Christian Perspective

ELIZABETH HARRIS

Introduction

I started to write this chapter in Sri Lanka, on the balcony of a hotel, looking directly over the sea. Palm trees framed the view. Waves broke with a continuous rhythmic beat. The sun was dipping from the vertical, threading the water with silver. A more relaxing and beautiful sight would be difficult to find. It breathed tranquillity. But I could have picked up my pen overlooking a very different scene. A few months before that I had been to Jaffna, in the north of Sri Lanka. I was taken through an area that had been home to a thriving Muslim community before the Liberation Tigers of Tamil Eelam (LTTE) evicted all Muslims from Jaffna in October 1990.[1] Every house was in ruins, exquisite stone tracery work cracked and broken. The mosque, open to the skies, had been deliberately desecrated. It was a symbol

---

1 Much has been written about Sri Lanka's ethnic conflict. Among the most useful are: K.M. De Silva, 1998, *Reaping the Whirlwind: Ethnic Conflict, Ethnic Politics in Sri Lanka*, Delhi: Penguin; Rohan Gunaratne, 1998, *Sri Lanka's Ethnic Crisis and National Security*, Colombo: South Asian Network on Conflict Research; Kumar Rupasinghe (ed.), 1998, *Negotiating Peace in Sri Lanka: Efforts, Failures and Lessons*, London: International Alert; S.J. Tambiah, 1992, *Buddhism Betrayed? Religion, Politics, and Violence in Sri Lanka*, Chicago: University of Chicago Press. A remarkable novel that charts Sri Lanka's twentieth-century history through the eyes of the Tamil people is: A. Sivanandan, 1997, *When Memory Dies*, London: Arcadia Books.

of the destruction Sri Lanka has suffered in over two decades of war, destruction that has touched all communities and faiths, but most particularly those in the north and east of the country.

Beauty and pain, loveliness and ugliness, are interwoven in most countries of the world and in most human experience. How do we give meaning to this? How is sense to be made of the fact that we are born, grow old and die; that in life we not only hope, love and enjoy but suffer, despair and sicken? What are we here, in this world, as humans, to be or to do? These are questions that all religions attempt to answer. My task here is to look through Christian lenses at the narratives and doctrinal frameworks that Buddhism and Christianity offer.

I am glad, though, that my task is to give 'a' Christian perspective and not 'the' Christian perspective. To give 'the' Christian perspective would have been impossible. For how we make sense of human existence is contextually situated. It is conditioned not only by the religion we belong to but also by our life journeys. It is conditioned by whether we are male or female, rich or poor, young or old, part of a majority community or a minority community, an activist or a mystic or both. Most particularly it is affected by how much suffering we have experienced or witnessed. This paper will therefore be rooted in my own journey, as a middle-class, white Christian woman, who, in her mid-thirties, in 1986, travelled to Sri Lanka to immerse herself in Buddhism. The following factors are particularly important.

My appreciation of Buddhism initially arose through relating to the Pāli Canon of Theravāda Buddhism and the Theravāda Buddhist practice of the people of Sri Lanka, although, since returning to Britain in 1993, I have encountered other forms of Buddhism: Zen, Pure Land, Japanese lay movements such as Risshō Kōsei Kai, Vajrayāna or Tibetan Buddhism, and new Western movements such as the Friends of the Western Buddhist Order. Nevertheless, it is the texts and practices of Theravāda Buddhists that I will draw on most in what follows, and the language I will use for technical Buddhist terms is Pāli.

As for my Christian formation, I was born into a Methodist family and still identify myself as a Methodist. But my religious interests have never run on 'Methodist' lines alone. By the time I began to study Buddhism, I had two overriding interests. The first was the use of silence in prayer, contemplation and intro-spection. The second was a commitment to social justice, rooted in awareness of the inequalities within the global economy, the hegemony of the West, and the scandalous gap between rich and poor. When, in my teenage years, I rejected the Christian faith I had been nurtured in, it was Jesus' Nazareth Manifesto and the message of prophets such as Amos that brought me back.[2] If Christianity was about social justice I was interested!

Significant also is that I was thrown into one of the most turbulent periods of Sri Lanka's history between 1986 and 1993. In the late 1980s two wars were tearing the country apart, one between the Indian Peacekeeping Force and the LTTE in the north, and the other between the government forces and a mili-tant Sinhala group in the south, the Janatha Vimukti Peramuna (JVP). Thousands were killed. People of all communities and all religions suffered. Questions concerning the meaning of human existence, and indeed the message of Buddhism, were refracted through the life and death issues of these conflicts.

I will divide this chapter into three parts. First, I will look at some of the narratives through which Buddhism and Christian-ity define the human condition. Then I will turn to Buddhist and Christian responses to that condition. Lastly, I will consider Buddhist and Christian responses to death. I hope to show that Buddhist and Christian perspectives both converge and diverge. At certain points, they touch each other and even interlock. At other points they move apart: not, I believe, into exclusive and antagonistic camps, but into a space where mutually transforma-tive dialogue can take place.

---

2 See Luke 4.16–19 when Jesus is recorded as applying verses from the prophet Isaiah that refer to bringing good news to the poor, to his own role; and Amos 5.21–24, which ends with these words: 'But let justice roll down like the waters and righteousness like an ever-flowing stream.'

The Human Condition

Let me start with Buddhism and a myth of beginnings that is found in the *Aggañña Sutta* of the Pāli Canon. The Buddha is presented as telling the myth in response to the complaint of one follower that the Brahmins consider themselves to be superior to all other castes. The myth concerns the dissolution and re-evolving of worlds. One world, the Buddha narrates, passes away. Some beings who had been within it are reborn in one of the radiant heavens. When the world begins to re-evolve, these beings are reborn into the world as humans. They are at first made of mind, self-luminous, undifferentiated, glorious, long-lived. The *sutta* narrates how these beings gradually become gross and solid, losing their luminosity and their longevity, dividing into comely and ugly, male and female, and eventually into different trades and occupations. The key to this development, which is also pictured as a descent into immorality, is craving and the growth of individualism. The luminous beings see a tasty sweet crust on the earth and begin to devour it with craving, tearing away lumps at a time. The tasty crust disappears and a mushroom arises for their food. The craving of the beings develops further. They divide into comely and unlovely, pride in beauty entering. Creepers and then rice appear. The beings divide into male and female, and lust arises. A pivotal moment is when one being begins to hoard rice rather than take only what is needed for the day. This leads to stealing and jealousy, and eventually to the election of a king to control immorality through state power.

The key to an understanding of the human condition in this *sutta*, and throughout the Theravāda Canon, is the presence of the divisive force of egotistical craving (*taṇhā*), and its relationship to three factors: greed, hatred and delusion (*lobha, dosa, moha*). The suffering, pain and existential anguish in human experience, arising because we are born, grow old and face numerous pains such as being separated from those we love, are attributed to the presence of craving. Numerous metaphors are used as illustration. There is the famous 'fire' sermon in which the Buddha claims that all our senses are on fire with craving:

Bhikkhus, all is burning. And what, bhikkhus, is the all that is burning? The eye is burning, forms are burning, eye-consciousness is burning, eye-contact is burning, and whatever feeling arises with eye-contact as condition – whether pleasant or painful or neither-pleasant-nor-painful – that too is burning. Burning with what? Burning with the fire of lust, with the fire of hatred, with the fire of delusion; burning with birth, aging, and death; with sorrow, lamentation, pain displeasure, and despair, I say.[3]

The same is said of the other senses, including the mind, which Buddhists see as a sense. This passage indicates that craving comes into being, in the Buddhist world-view, through a process of cause and effect, as our senses interact with sense objects, causing feelings to arise that in turn condition attraction and aversion, greed and hatred. As the interaction takes place, the conditioned reactions that we have built up from birth (and in previous lives) also kick in. Another graphic description comes from the *Aṅguttara Nikāya* of the *Sutta Piṭaka* of the Pāli Canon:

Monks, I will teach you the craving that ensnares, that floats along, that is far flung, that clings to one, by which this world is smothered, enveloped, tangled like a ball of thread, covered as with blight, twisted up like a grass rope, so that it does not pass beyond the Constant Round, the Downfall, the Way of Woe, the Ruin . . .[4]

This is the human condition, according to Buddhism. Humans are locked in a self-made prison through their greed, hatred and delusion. And part of delusion, *moha*, is placing the 'I' or the ego

---

3 From the *Salāyatanasamyutta, Samyutta Nikāya*, iv 19. See Bhikkhu Bodhi (trans.), 2000, *The Connected Discourses of the Buddha*, Boston: Wisdom, p. 1143.

4 *Aṅguttara Nikāya* ii 211; translation taken from: F.L. Woodward (trans.), 1992, *The Book of the Gradual Sayings (Aṅguttara Nikāya)*, vol. 2, Oxford: Pali Text Society, p. 225.

in the centre, not realizing that all our constructions of an 'I' are impermanent and empty. The *sutta* I've just quoted continues:

> Monks, when there is the thought: I am – there come the thoughts: I am in this world; I am thus; I am otherwise; I am not eternal; I am eternal; Should I be; Should I be in this world; Should I be thus; Should I be otherwise. May I become; May I become in this world; May I become thus; May I become otherwise. I shall become; I shall become in this world; I shall become thus; I shall become otherwise. These are the eighteen thoughts which are haunted by craving concerning the inner self.[5]

In Buddhist narratives, craving, expressed through greed and hatred, is seen operating not only at the individual level but also at the institutional and corporate levels, for instance in the state that denies economic justice to its inhabitants by refusing them means of livelihood. As a handful of texts in the Theravāda Canon show, such institutional greed can push a society towards lawlessness and even bestiality.[6] The net result is a world smothered in craving resulting in war, violence, injustice and pain.

When Christian missionaries in Asia first encountered this analysis of the human condition, their initial reaction was that it was nihilistic and pessimistic. 'Buddhism is one vast system of negations – of hope destroying negations', claimed the Baptist missionary, H.A. Lapham in the 1890s.[7] Thomas Moscrop, Methodist, writing in the same period, says something similar:

> Buddhism – a religion without God and without hope in the world – is too pessimistic, too cold, too antagonistic to

---

5 *Aṅguttara Nikāya* ii 212.

6 Two notable *suttas*, both of which carry narrative parables, are: *Kūṭadanta Sutta* (*Dīgha Nikāya* i 127–49), in which a monarch is advised to foster economic justice in order to curb the lawlessness of his realm, and the *Cakkavatti Sīhanāda Sutta* (*Dīgha Nikāya* iii 58–79), which shows a monarch's failure to give wealth to the poor leading to societal breakdown.

7 Quoted in John Brown Myers (ed.), 1893, *Centenary Celebration of the Baptist Missionary Society 1892–93*, London: Baptist Missionary Society, p. 192.

the constitution of human nature to take the world captive. Buddhism cannot succeed for it says, 'There is no good, but all is evil in human existence'.[8]

I will not make the mistake these missionaries made. Buddhists would say that the analysis of the human condition that I've just outlined is realistic rather than pessimistic.[9] It is how things are. Moscrop is grossly at fault to say that, for the Buddhist, 'all is evil in human existence'. Buddhism does not deny that human life contains joy and happiness. Indeed, the ultimate bliss of *nibbāna* (= *nirvāṇa*), the goal of spiritual practice, is possible in this very life. But, at a worldly level, if it is not the fruit of the religious path, it is as impermanent as all other phenomena and prone to corruption through self-seeking. Most important is that the cosmos is not seen as hostile, indifferent or antagonistic to human life. Humans are not victims of chance, fate or a capricious external power. The cosmos is seen as functioning according to a just, impartial law of cause and effect, through which wholesome action produces wholesome fruits and unwholesome action, unwholesome fruits: the law of *kamma* ('action' = *karma*). It is a cosmos in which trust can be placed, one in which liberation from greed is possible. Furthermore, all Buddhist traditions stress the preciousness of human birth. Of all the *gatis* or realms of existence – five in the Theravāda tradition, six in some Mahāyāna traditions – human birth is one of the hardest to obtain.[10] It is a privilege and an opportunity. For it is only as a human that the work for liberation can begin. For

---

8 T. Moscrop, 'Present Day Buddhism in Ceylon', in *Ceylon Friend* (Colombo: Wesleyan Mission Press) 16 Oct. 1889, pp. 92–5 (95).

9 For instance see Walpola Rahula, 1959, *What the Buddha Taught*, London and Bedford: Gordon Fraser (now republished by Oneworld), p. 17: 'First of all, Buddhism is neither pessimistic nor optimistic. If anything at all, it is realistic, for it takes a realistic view of life and of the world.'

10 In one passage of the Pāli Canon, the difficulty of gaining a human birth from one of the hells is likened to the possibility of a blind turtle, who came to the surface of the ocean once in every hundred years, pushing his neck through a yoke with a single hole, thrust into the ocean by a man (*Saṃyutta Nikāya* v 455–7).

craving is not an inherent property of existence. It can be uprooted and replaced by the compassion and wisdom that is *nibbāna*.

I find many touching points between this and Christian perspectives, informed by the Jewish thought from which it grew. Here too there are narratives of a fall from purity into dis-ease and dislocation. In the third chapter of Genesis, primordial inno-cence and wholeness is destroyed when Eve succumbs to the temptation to taste the fruits of the tree of knowledge. The result is not the wisdom that the serpent promises and Eve craves, but self-consciousness and individuation. 'I was afraid because I was naked and I hid myself', Adam says to God when he is drawn into the discourse.[11] Alternatively, there is the story of the tower of Babel, also in the book of Genesis. It begins, 'Now the whole earth had one language and the same words': a picture of harmony.[12] The people then come together and aspire to improve themselves by building towards heaven: 'Come, let us build ourselves a city, and a tower with its top in the heavens, and let us make a name for ourselves', they exclaim.[13] But this striving leads to confusion. The universal language breaks down. There is individuation and dissolution as the people of the earth split and spread, divided by language and identity.

The Buddhist and Christian myths, on the surface, seem to dif-fer. In the *Aggañña Sutta*, craving is already present within the minds of the luminous beings that come to a re-forming earth. There is no intermediary between the object of craving and the mind. In the first Christian myth, there is an intermediary: the temptation comes from without in the form of a serpent. In the second, it is God who is seen to sow the confusion that splits a once united human community. At a deeper level, this difference breaks down. For at the heart of both of the Christian myths I have mentioned, as in the *Aggañña Sutta*, is greed or the wish for the promotion of self, corporately or individually. I can see this more clearly because of my knowledge of Buddhism. The world into which humans are born, according to the Christian myths I have referred to, becomes one in which 'Mammon' reigns, an

---

11 Genesis 3.10.   12 Genesis 11.1.   13 Genesis 11.4.

Aramaic word denoting wealth, power and riches.[14] It is one where ignorance or the blatant flouting of the will of God causes the poor to be oppressed and unrighteousness to flourish. But human existence within the Christian world-view, as in Buddhism, is precious, this time because it is a gift from God. God is the one who 'forms' humans in the womb, knows them and gives them life – for a purpose.[15] Again, the cosmos is not hostile to human life. It is potentially nurturing. And, as in Buddhism, there is the possibility of release from Mammon. Mammon, and the alienation from God this represents, is not inherent. A renewed relationship with God is possible.

Responses to the Human Condition

John Hick has suggested that the great world religions are different forms of 'cosmic optimism'.[16] He presents this as a generalization from the distinctive affirmations of each religion 'about the ultimate character of reality as this affects human beings'.[17] Do Buddhism and Christianity fall into this? I believe that they do, but in different ways. This section concerns the affirmations in Buddhism and Christianity that respond to the human condition I have outlined and the path that is embedded in them. Narrative can again be used to probe this, narrative connected with two people, Siddhattha Gotama (Sanskrit = Siddhārtha Gautama), the Buddha, and Jesus of Nazareth, the Christ. Both are presented as embodying a response to the human condition. The Buddha is the embodiment of the Dhamma, the truth and wisdom that upholds the cosmos. One who cannot grasp the Dhamma, cannot 'see' the

---

14 See Matthew 6.24, Luke 16.9–13 in which Jesus warns his disciples that they cannot serve God and 'Mammon', translated in contemporary versions as 'wealth'.

15 See, for example, Isaiah 44.2, 24.

16 John Hick, 2000, 'The Religious Meaning of Life' in Joseph Runzo and Nancy M. Martin (eds), *The Meaning of Life in the World's Religions*, Oxford: Oneworld, p. 274.

17 Hick, 'The Religious Meaning of Life', p. 274.

Buddha.[18] Jesus is the embodiment of the 'Word'.[19] Both figures communicated and developed their message in debate with the religious ideas of their time. As Richard Gombrich has repeatedly illustrated, the early Buddhist texts of the Theravāda Canon are best understood if they are seen in the context of debate with Brahmanism and the Hindu Sanskrit tradition.[20] And Christian biblical scholars have learnt that the New Testament cannot be studied in isolation from the Jewish tradition of the first century CE.

It is important, therefore, to look at the Buddha and Jesus in action, spreading a view of human existence in two particular contexts. I will argue that both offered a counter-cultural message rooted in a call which went something like this: 'The way you view the world is wrong! Change your way of looking and acting.' I begin with a parable from the Theravāda Canon that lies at the heart of the Buddhist tradition. Mālunkyāputta, a disciple of the Buddha who has left home and family to become a celibate renunciant, decides that the Buddha has not answered some of the most important questions about life: Is the world eternal? Is the soul the same as the body? Does the Buddha exist after death? He is shown saying to himself that he will abandon his discipleship if the Buddha can't answer these central metaphysical questions. When he shares this with the Buddha, the Buddha asks, 'Did I promise to answer these questions when you renounced?' Mālunkyāputta has to say 'No'.

After this, the Buddha gives an illustration well known throughout the Buddhist world. A man is fatally wounded by

---

18 See the *Itivuttaka* 90–1, in which the Buddha claims that even a monk who seizes the corner of the Buddha's robe and follows close on his heels will be aloof from him if he has a mind that is full of greed and hatred. The Buddha adds, 'For this monk, monks, beholds not Dhamma, and, in failing to behold Dhamma, beholds not me.' Peter Masefield (trans.), 2000, *The Itivuttaka*, Oxford: Pali Text Society, p. 79.

19 See John 1.14.

20 See, for example, Richard F. Gombrich, 1996, *How Buddhism Began: The Conditioned Genesis of the Early Teachings*, London and Atlantic Highlands, NJ: Athlone Press.

an arrow tipped with poison. Relatives call a doctor. Before
the wounded man will allow the doctor to remove the arrow,
however, he insists on having certain questions answered. These
include: Was the man who wounded me a noble, a Brahmin, a
merchant or a worker? Was he dark or brown or golden-skinned?
Does he live in such a village or town or city? Was the bow that
wounded me a longbow or a crossbow? And so on. If that man
had waited for the answer to all his questions, the Buddha points
out, he would have died. The message for Mālunkyāputta is that
if he waits for the answers to his speculative questions before
starting on the path, he also will die of the poison within him.
Then come the well-known words:

> And what have I declared? 'This is suffering' – I have declared.
> 'This is the origin of suffering' – I have declared. 'This is the
> cessation of suffering' – I have declared. 'This is the Way
> leading to the cessation of suffering' – I have declared.[21]

These are the Four Noble Truths, the house within which the
whole of Buddhism lies.

The Theravāda texts suggest that the society in which the
Buddha taught was one in which vigorous, sometimes violent,
debate about metaphysical questions was common. The Pāli
Canon refers to those who go about breaking into pieces the
speculations of their adversaries.[22] The Buddha's message in
this situation was that speculation about questions not linked
to removing the causes of human suffering was pointless. What
was important was action to pull out the poison that gives rise
to pain and suffering.

The Buddha was drawn into wide-ranging debates as a result
of this message. One focal debate was with those the texts call

---

21 Bhikkhu Nanamoli (trans.), 1995, '*Cūla-Mālunkya Sutta*: The
Shorter Discourse to Mālunkyāputta', in *The Middle Discourses of the
Buddha*, Boston: Wisdom, p. 536 (*Majjhima Nikāya* i 431).

22 See, for example, *Kassapa Sīhanāda Sutta*, *Dīgha Nikāya* i 162–3.

'Eternalists' (*sassatavāda*), who believed in the existence of
an eternal soul separate from the body, and 'Annihilationists'
(*ucchedavāda*), materialists who believed that all life returned to
the elements at death. The Buddha rejected both. In fact he said
that both could be traced to the craving within the mind: craving for eternal existence in the eternalists; craving for sensual
pleasures in the annhilationists, a 'live now, tomorrow we may
die' philosophy. In their place he suggested a Middle Path rooted
in cause and effect or dependent origination, *paṭiccasamuppāda*.
There is nothing that is unchanging within the human person, he
declared. The human person is a verb not a noun. It is continually
changing as five factors interlock with each other in a continuum
of cause and effect: *rūpa* (physical body), *vedanā* (feelings), *saññā*
(perception), *sankhāra* (mental formations), *viññāna* (consciousness). None of these is the soul, according to this structure. The
person is the sum total of the relationship between the five. Each
of us is a process, an ever-changing process of cause and effect
that continues after death into new births. Put in another way,
the message was: 'Change the way you construct your idea of
self. Release yourself from promoting, protecting and pamper-
ing an "I" that in reality doesn't exist.'

Another counter-cultural message concerned ritual. One
brahmanical view was to see harmony in society as the result of
correct ritual and the fate of a person after death as dependent
on the prayers said. The Buddha offered another model. The
head of a village, for instance, in one *sutta*, is shown asking the
Buddha to comment on those who claim that they can send a
person heavenward through prayers and ritual. The Buddha
gives an example. Suppose there is a person who has destroyed
life, taken what is not given, engaged in sexual misconduct,
spoken falsely and been full of ill will. Imagine then a group
of people, after his death, attempting to send him to heaven by
prayers. This would, the Buddha continues, be like a person
hurling a huge rock into a pool of water and then a group of
people gathering to pray for the rock to rise up from the water.
The rock could not rise. Likewise, a person who had broken
moral norms could not be saved from the consequences of his

deeds.[23] Suffering could not be eradicated by ritual, only by a threefold discipline of morality, mind culture and wisdom (*sīla, samādhi, paññā*), for the causes of suffering were not external but located within the human mind.

The critique took a different form with non-brahmanical groups. The *Cūḷadukkhakandhasutta*, for instance, shows the Buddha in dialogue with some Jains, who were standing upright on a rock, believing that such intense austerity would lead to liberation by burning up the effects of evil deeds done in the past. They are shown declaring to the Buddha that happiness is to be achieved through pain.[24] The Buddha challenges them with questions such as: 'Do you know what you did in the past that has to be worn away?' 'Do you know that so much evil is worn away, that so much more is to be worn away or that when so much evil is worn away, all ill will be worn away?' The Jains can answer none of these questions, nor can they describe how skilled and unskilled states of mind that lead to unwholesome deeds arise. Their view is false, the Buddha implies. Know your mind and heart. Learn how greed and hatred appear and what triggers their arising. Realize that volition is also action and can have negative and positive results. And change your way of relating to the world so that you can change your future. That was the Buddha's message.

These are just a handful of examples of the Buddha honing a response to the human condition on debate. More could be selected: his challenge, for instance, to the caste structure[25] or to an epistemology that reified tradition above experience.[26] And behind it was an ethic that placed the arising of compassion at

---

23 *Gāmaṇisaṃyutta, Saṃyutta Nikāya* iv 312–13.

24 *Majjhima Nikāya* i 91–95, here 93–94.

25 See, for example, *Aggañña Sutta* (*Dīgha Nikāya* iii 80–98); *Madhura Sutta, Majjhima Nikāya* ii 83–90; *Kaṇṇakatthala Sutta, Majjhima Nikāya* ii 125–33; *Assalāyana Sutta, Majjhima Nikāya* ii 147–57. In all of these the Buddha is seen challenging the fourfold brahmanical caste system.

26 See, for example, *Caṅkī Sutta, Majjhima Nikāya* ii 164–77 in which the Buddha contrasts the preservation of truth with awakening to truth.

the centre. For when greed is defeated, the Buddha taught, compassion arises.

There was urgency in this message. As one canonical passage puts it:

> What others speak of as happiness
> That the noble ones say is suffering
> What others speak of as suffering,
> That the noble ones know as bliss[27]

What parallels can be seen in Christianity? Jesus was also in debate with religious leaders of his time. Contemporary scholarship suggests the teaching of Jesus was close to that of the Pharisees, one of three Jewish sects that flourished at the time of Jesus, rather than in opposition to it as populist readings of New Testament material have suggested.[28] The Christian doctrine of the resurrection of the dead came from them. But although close to them, he debated with them, vigorously. And I find it significant that his debate with them, as recorded in the gospels, focuses on the need for consistency between teaching, and action, thought, mind and behaviour.[29]

As the Buddha, Jesus is seen questioning the benefits of ritual and what was considered to be religious Law. Matthew 12

---

27 *Saḷāyatanasaṃyutta, Saṃyutta Nikāya* iv 127. Translation taken from Bodhi, *The Connected Discourses of the Buddha*, p. 1209.

28 A good reference text is: Helen P. Fry, 1996, *Christian-Jewish Dialogue: A Reader*, Exeter: University of Exeter Press; see, for example, pp. 141–2, a quote from Marvin Wilson, 1989, *Our Father Abraham*, Grand Rapids: Eerdmans; or pp. 150–1, a quote from an official Roman Catholic Statement of 1974 affirming that the teachings of Jesus were 'closer to those of the Pharisees than to those of any other group of his period'.

29 See Matthew 23.1–36 in which the teaching of the Pharisees is not condemned but their actions are, for example v. 25: 'Woe to you, scribes and Pharisees, hypocrites! For you clean the outside of the cup and of the plate, but inside they are full of greed and self-indulgence. You blind Pharisee! First clean the inside of the cup, so that the outside also may become clean.' (Translation from the New Revised Standard Version.)

shows Jesus plucking heads of grain from growing corn on the Sabbath and healing a man with a deformed hand, in defiance of the Jewish prohibition of work on the Sabbath. On being challenged, he is recorded as answering:

> Suppose one of you has only one sheep and it falls into a pit on the Sabbath; will you not lay hold of it and lift it out? How much more valuable is a human being than a sheep! So it is lawful to do good on the Sabbath.[30]

In a way similar to the Buddha's rejection of the brahmanical caste structure, he challenged judgements that stigmatized groups of people – those the gospels call 'sinners and tax-gatherers', who had either made themselves ritually impure by their actions or had collaborated with Rome's imperial power.[31]

Jesus is also recorded as saying this:

> He said to them, 'Then do you also fail to understand? Do you not see that whatever goes into a person from outside cannot defile, since it enters, not the heart but the stomach, and goes out into the sewer?' . . . And he said, 'It is what comes out of a person that defiles. For it is from within, from the human heart, that evil intentions come: fornication, theft, murder, adultery, avarice, wickedness, deceit, licentiousness, envy, slander, pride, folly. All these evil things come from within and they defile a person.'[32]

These could be the words of a Buddhist in their message that the categories of pure and impure are not connected with external acts or diet but with what is going on in the mind and heart of an individual. One of the Pāli words used for 'mind' in the Theravā-da Canon is *citta*, a word that embraces both mind and what is referred to here as heart.

---

30 Matthew 12.11–12 (translation from the New Revised Standard Version).

31 See, for instance, Mark 2.16–17.

32 Mark 7.18–23.

Then there is the passage in the Sermon on the Mount in which Jesus overturns a series of maxims taken from popular religious culture:

> You have heard that it was said to those of ancient times, 'You shall not murder'; and, 'whoever murders shall be liable to judgement'. But I say to you if you are angry with your brother or sister you will be liable to judgement; and if you insult your brother or sister, you will be liable to the council . . .[33]

And again:

> You have heard that it was said, 'You shall love your neighbour and hate your enemy.' But I say to you, Love your enemies and pray for those who persecute you, so that you may be children of your Father in Heaven . . .[34]

There is a counter-cultural tenor in these teachings similar to that found in the Theravāda Buddhist texts.

A central theme within the first three gospels of the New Testament, Matthew, Mark and Luke, was that the Kingdom of Heaven, or the Reign of God, had broken into human existence through the teachings and actions of Jesus. It is an elusive, paradoxical concept: an eschatological future reality and yet already present; about the mighty acts of a transcendent God yet rooted in metaphors and stories that are drawn from the day-to-day experience of the people of Galilee. So the Kingdom is likened to a mustard seed, the smallest of all seeds when sown, the greatest of shrubs when mature.[35] It is like yeast that slowly permeates the whole of the dough.[36] It is a space that the rich will find it difficult to enter because of their love of wealth.[37] It will not

---

33 Matthew 5.21–22.
34 Matthew 5.43–45.
35 Mark 4.30–32; Matthew 13.31–32; Luke 13.18–19.
36 Matthew 13.33.
37 See Matthew 19.16–26; Mark 10.17–27 where a rich person is told to sell his possessions and give all he has to the poor.

come with fanfares but is already present in human communities.[38] It involves a rebirth within this life[39] and is demonstrated though acts of healing and restoration such as those carried out by Jesus himself. Methodologically, these images remind me of the Buddha's use of the empirical to draw people towards the transcendent with a 'come-seeish' invitation.

The reign of God in these gospel pictures is a society renewed through the breaking in and proliferation of compassion, the empowerment of the poor and the victimized, the defeat of egotistical greed and the renewal of relationships. That this is possible, that this is part of the potential of human existence, is implicit throughout.

If these points alone were taken from the New Testament, a case could be made that the Buddha and Christ communicated, and indeed embodied, a similar view of existence, defined by a realistic appraisal of the human condition and the conviction that the transformative – the Dhamma or the Kingdom of God – could break in. Differences between the two, however, should also be faced. Buddhism and Christianity touch but also diverge. And the divergences can be seen most clearly in the concepts of God and grace in Christianity, and rebirth in Buddhism.

Part of the Buddhist view of existence is that it is because of our undefeated craving and ignorance that we are bound to repeated rebirths across the five or six realms of being which make up *saṃsāra*, the realm of birth and rebirth. 'What do you think, bhikkhus?' the Buddha asks. 'Which is more: the mother's milk that you have drunk as you roamed and wandered on through this long course – this or the water in the four great oceans?' The answer is, mother's milk.[40] Ubbirī, an early Buddhist nun, is recorded as gaining enlightenment when the Buddha asks her, when she is still a queen, which daughter she is mourning for,

---

38 See Luke 17.20–21 where Jesus affirms that the Kingdom is 'among you'.

39 See John 3.1–8.

40 *Saṃyutta Nikāya* ii 180–1. Translation taken from Bodhi, *The Connected Discourses of the Buddha*, p. 653.

adding that 84,000 of her daughters had been buried in the same cemetery.[41]

A human existence for the Buddhist is a precious opportunity to gain liberation precisely because it lies within the meta-narrative of births and rebirths too many to record, of being born, sickening, growing old and dying, time and time again, simply because our craving for existence has not been overridden. Nothing corresponds to this in Christianity, however many hints there might be in the Bible that the Jews believed a prophet could come back to the world again.[42]

To pass to the concept of God, within all the schools of Buddhism, the Buddha is seen as more than merely a man. In the Theravāda tradition he is born a human but becomes an *acchariya manussa*, a wonderful man, a being who, at his enlightenment, enters a category far beyond the human. He becomes teacher of gods and humans, and, in at least one commentarial text, the one who brings others into *nibbāna*.[43] In Mahāyāna Buddhism, the historical Buddha is merely one face of cosmic Buddhahood, eternally present. In both schools, a Buddha, in his infinite compassion, can help people towards liberation by entering the world for their deliverance, but cannot walk the path for them, even within Pure Land Buddhism where the concept of 'other power' is strongest. Deliverance is offered through teaching, inspiration and example. This resonates with Christianity

---

41 From the narrative connected with *Therīgāthā* 51–3.

42 See Matthew 11.13, when Jesus links John the Baptist with the coming of Elijah, or Matthew 16.13–14 and Luke 9.19 where the disciples report to Jesus that some think he is Elijah, Jeremiah or another prophet returned.

43 In a note to Chapter VII of the great fifth-century CE commentarial work by Bhadantācariya Buddhaghosa, the author explores the twin characteristics of wisdom and compassion in the Buddha and links the two in a number of assertions, several of which link the Buddha with delivering others, for example, 'It was through understanding that he himself crossed over, and through compassion that he brought others across.' Bhadantācariya Buddhaghosa (trans. Bhikkhu Nanamoli), 1991, *The Path of Purification (Visuddhimagga)*, Kandy: Buddhist Publication Society, 5th edn, Note 9, pp. 773–4.

but does not equate with the Christian concept of Godhead. In Christianity, God as creator, sustainer, saviour, pain-bearer and grace-giver cannot be written out of the picture. Imagine the Psalms without a God who intervenes on the side of the oppressed. They could not exist. Written by those familiar with suffering, they affirm the power of a God who saves, as these verses suggest: 'Deliver me from my enemies, O my God; protect me from those who rise up against me.'[44] 'For God alone my soul waits in silence; from him comes my salvation. He alone is my rock and my salvation, my fortress.'[45]

To pass to Jesus, the experience and conviction of the early church was that Jesus could not simply fit into the Jewish category of Messiah, an anointed one sent by God to usher in a new era on earth. Although it is doubtful that Jesus himself made any comprehensive claim about his own identity, other than through the phrase, 'Son of Man', the early Christians developed the doctrine of the Trinity to make sense of what they believed God had done through Jesus. A contested doctrine throughout the Church's history, the definition that gained most support was that Father, Son and Holy Spirit were three substantive realities within One reality, God. Jesus, therefore, was God, of one substance with God. Mary was 'Mother of God'. And in the cross and resurrection of Jesus, God took into God's self the pain, violence, suffering and sin of humanity in order to defeat them. To quote a contemporary theologian, trinitarian theology presents God as the 'one life that occurs between Jesus and his Father by their Spirit'.[46]

Many Christians place this – God's action through the cross and resurrection – at the centre of their view of human existence. It is a meta-narrative which says that all the weaknesses, failures and imperfections that humans are prone to are met and transformed through the proactive grace and love of God as it reaches

---

44 Psalm 59.1.
45 Psalm 62.1.
46 Robert W. Jenson, 2000, 'Trinity', in *The Oxford Companion to Christian Thought*, Oxford: Oxford University Press, p. 716.

down towards humanity to draw it up into the divine life. It is both similar to and different from that of Buddhism, which is inseparably bound to narratives of the Buddha as teacher and compassionate deliverer.

Perspectives on Death

How then do these similarities and differences express themselves in relation to views of death? Both Buddhism and Christianity affirm continuity after death and reject materialism. The cry of the early Christian church was that death had been defeated, swallowed up in victory, in the action of God through Jesus. Humans who had been sentenced to death because of their sin were now in receipt of the gift of eternal life. Death was now the gate through which heaven could enter and so it could be greeted without fear, in faith. And acts such as Jesus raising Lazarus from the dead were taken as a sign of what was to come.[47]

Buddhism says something similar. Death is to be greeted as part of life, not to be feared. It encourages engagement with the reality and process of death, doing this perhaps more effectively than Christianity. For instance the narrative of the raising of Lazarus can be can be contrasted with the Buddhist story of Kisāgotamī. Kisāgotamī comes to the Buddha carrying the dead body of her young son. She pleads for help and the Buddha offers it. He tells her to bring some mustard seed from one of the houses nearby, adding that it must come from a house in which no one had died. She leaves him expectantly but, of course, fails to find a household that had not known a death. She, therefore, comes to accept the death of her son and gains enlightenment, becoming a nun.[48]

Let me give two examples that have been part of my recent experience. Both concern Western Buddhist nuns living in Sri Lanka. The first is Ven. Miao Kwang Sudharma. She is

---

47 John 11.1–44 in which Jesus is seen to raise his friend Lazarus from the dead although he had been dead four days.

48 From the narrative connected with *Therīgāthā* 212–23.

seventy-six years old and lives in a small kutie near Anurad-hapura in the north-west of the country, dependent on villagers for her food. In her kutie is a coffin. It lies at the foot of her bed. She bought it so that the villagers who support her will not have to bear the cost of a coffin when she dies. But it also serves as a meditation object for her. Each day she does *maraṇa bhāvanā*, meditation on death, using the coffin. 'I want to be ready for death. I want to be prepared,' she said to me.

The second nun is Sr Nyanasiri. When I visited her in 2003, she had survived a heart attack and had rejected medication, pre-ferring to experience the ageing process naturally. On her wall was an artist's representation of death – a shadowy yet dynamic personified force. 'It may come to me at any time', she told me. 'If you hear of my death before you come again, do not grieve. I am ready. I am not attached to life. I want nothing.'

When I arrived in Kandy, in Sri Lanka, in April 2004, it was happening. She was dying in a nursing home. She had refused food and drink, and could only communicate with difficulty. I spent two whole nights with her, as her organs stopped func-tioning. At some points she did not know how to handle the pain within her body and was crying out for help. But, at the moment of death, I believe she was where she had trained herself to be. She had been unconscious for about eighteen hours, but regained consciousness. At the moment of death, she was fully mindful of what was happening and tranquil, not clinging to life or to anything material. That is the death Buddhists hope for. Many believe that the state of one's consciousness at death is important in determining the next rebirth. If at death one is clinging to life, battling against death, then one will surely be reborn in *saṃsāra*. If one is free of attachment, then liberation from rebirth will be closer.

Buddhism and Christianity here touch and diverge. In both religions there is an awareness that birth and death are ongoing processes within life. Passing from death to life is a reality in the present for many Christians, echoing the following verse: 'We know that we have passed from death to life because we love one another. Whoever does not love abides in death', the writer of the first letter of John exclaims (1 John 3.14). Buddhists might speak of attaining *nibbāna*, the 'deathless', in this life or of living and dying every moment, as thoughts, feelings and mental states arise and pass.[49]

Concluding Thoughts

I prefer to speak of touching points between religions rather than identical insights. The religions of the world are not the same but neither are they different. They touch, and even embrace each other, in many ways. When Buddhism and Christianity are taken together, the similarities in their view of human existence leap out. Both see it as dislocated, out of joint. Both pinpoint greed and selfishness, *taṇhā* or Mammon, as a root cause of this. Both point to the dangers of a wrong concept of self. For the Christian mystic, the antidote is self-naughting in the presence of God. For Buddhists, it is similar – a realization that liberation arises when the concept of an unchanging 'I' is got rid of altogether. For both, non-attachment and compassion, or altruistic love, are two sides of one reality: non-attachment to the self and its greeds leading to compassion for the pain and suffering of others. Both emphasize action rather than simply belief or ritual, as a response to the human condition. It is important to remember that one message of the Christian gospels is that it is those who do the will of God who are closest to God[50] and those who

---

49 For instance, 'One should not regard the relation of living-dying objectively *from outside*. This relation needs to be awakened *from within*. In this manner, the living-dying relation is not seen as a sequential change from the former to the latter. Rather, we are living and dying at each and every moment . . . The understanding of human existence as something constantly undergoing "living-dying" is the fundamental standpoint of Buddhism.' Masao Abe, 2000, 'The Meaning of Life in Buddhism', in J. Runzo and N. Martin (eds), *The Meaning of Life in the World Religions*, Oxford: Oneworld, pp. 153–61 (155).

50 Matthew 7.21: 'Not everyone who says to me, "Lord, Lord", will enter the kingdom of heaven, but only one who does the will of my Father in heaven.'

take up their cross in discipleship of Jesus who will find that they are where God is.[51]

However, as I have shown, there are divergences too. I would like to suggest that these should be allowed to interrogate each other rather than competitively vie with each other. Let us picture the differences as two iconic postures that stretch across time, embodying the Christian and Buddhist views of human existence.

The first is Jesus hanging on a cross, Jesus as God, the second person of the Trinity, dying an excruciatingly painful death as a common criminal. By this act, he takes into himself the world's darkness and pain, the incarnation of a God who suffers with those who suffer, pours grace and love into the world, and calls humans into a relationship with God's self and a path of self-sacrificial love.

The second is the Buddha seated in meditation. To evoke this image let me quote from words I coined for a radio broadcast in 1993, describing the massive images of the Buddha, carved into the rock, at the Gal Vihāra in Polonnaruwa in Sri Lanka:

> Peace seems to radiate from them and has done for over 800 years. Yet it is not the peace of indifference or apathy. It is the peace of wisdom and compassion, which arises when the heart-rending nature of human violence and human greed is fully realized. It is not an anguished, twisted scream of torture at the nature of the world's inhumanity, but a silent, gentle embodiment in stone of empathy, compassion and strength.[52]

This icon calls people not so much into a relationship but on to a way that leads to the realization of wisdom and compassion, through a discipline of morality and mind culture.

For me, as a Christian, I need both of these iconic images or

---

51 See, for example, Luke 9.23: 'If any want to become my followers, let them deny themselves and take up their cross daily and follow me.'

52 Elizabeth J. Harris, 1994, *A Journey into Buddhism*, Bodhi Leaves No. 134, Kandy: Buddhist Publication Society, p. 22.

postures, as I seek to make sense of human existence. I cannot speak for the Buddhist, who might find the idea of a crucified God strange to say the least. But I am content that the two figures, embodying two views that touch and diverge, should face one another, as long as by doing so, they encourage us all to embark on or continue in a religious path that challenges the greed, or the Mammon, that is wreaking havoc within our world.

3. Human Existence in Buddhism and Christianity:

A Buddhist Perspective

KIYOSHI TSUCHIYA

Life and Death in Chinese Buddhism and Christianity

The topic I was given, 'Human Existence in Buddhism and Christianity', is challenging in a twofold way. It points directly to what Henri Bergson called the only valid question for philosophy, 'Where do we come from? What are we? Where are we going to?' There are different ways to respond, and equally different ways to come to the question. 'Buddhism and Christianity' denotes one such difference. My task here is to make sense of this difference. It inevitably begins with my personal response to the question. Therefore, the task would examine not only my academic competence but also my personal strength as to how well or badly I face up to the question.

Moreover, my presentation is not going to be even-handed, because I already have my preferences. Let me here summarize them as the Buddhist teaching of rising above life and death and the Christian faith in eternal life. One of the benefits of a comparative study like this is that it reminds us of how ludicrous these doctrines are. Our life has its beginning and end, and at the same time we are living and dying at every moment. 'Life and death' is our biggest paradox, and this is our indubitable starting point. Placed next to each other, the two doctrines immediately reveal each other's extraordinariness. Buddhism teaches us to rise above life and death even when we are never indifferent to what happens to us and others. Similarly, the Christian faith; our strong, venerable attachment to life is not likely to warrant our hope of eternal life. The Buddhist way to deal with the paradox is to leave it as it is. The Christian way, in contrast, is to sort it out, to separate life from death, and in its process to bring in the strongest dichotomy we have ever had, 'good and evil'. Christianity and Buddhism do not need each other to point out the extremity of their doctrines. Both Christianity and Buddhism have defended their doctrines from the very beginning by revising, reinterpreting, and reinforcing them. It is unlikely, therefore, that the Christian doctrine merges with the Buddhist teaching even in this day of constant exchange. Therefore the difference demands interpretation.

I suspect that in his or her eternal life a Christian will retain his or her personality. The eternal life itself is the result of the relational approval (God's love or God's acceptance). I do not doubt that the promise of eternal life could genuinely be transcendental. The point is that this transcendentalism is a personal and relational one. My question here is whether this transcendentalism 'can' end up strengthening the grip of ego, and if it does, whether there is or should be a way out of it.

I ask this because my upbringing has taught me quite a different form of transcendentalism. What I expect for myself at the end of my life is a release from myself. I see myself as naturally decomposable. Not only my body but also my soul will dissipate when I die. The world is indifferent to my existence or non-existence, and at the end of my time I would like to endorse, gracefully if possible, this indifference. My life is a brief series of rather insignificant accidents, in which, however, there are certain experiences of joy and happiness, sadness and suffering. When it comes to its end, I would feel simultaneously sad and relieved. The origin of this sentiment is undoubtedly the Taoist and Buddhist heritage. Here is a quotation from Chuang-tzu.

Man's life between heaven and earth is like a white colt passing a crack in the wall – suddenly it's finished. Rapidly surging, all things come forth; smoothly subsiding, all things reenter.

Having evolved they are born, then they evolve again and are dead. Living things are sorrowed by it, mankind is saddened by it. But it's only the untying of a heavenly bow-case, the emptying of a heavenly book-bag. With a flurry and a flourish, the soul departs, and then the body follows. This is the great returning!

From formlessness to form, from form to formlessness.[1]

For life is the disciple of death and death is the beginning of life. Who knows their regulator? Human life is the coalescence of vital breath. When it coalesces there is life; when it dissipates there is death. Since life and death are disciples of each other, how should I be troubled by them? Thus the myriad things are a unity.[2]

Let me explain briefly why the use of Taoist materials is not a deviation from the given title. Chinese Buddhism began when the Chinese took genuine interest in this 'foreign', by this they meant barbarian, philosophy and practice. In accepting Buddhism, the Chinese thinkers made an extensive use of Taoist philosophy. They never abandoned their traditional learning because Buddhism did not demand that and the Chinese did not see the need of giving it up. Conversion did not take place if it meant a radical change in the participant's world-view and lifestyle. While Taoism was not so successful in becoming an organized religion, it left its distinct elements in Chinese and Japanese Buddhism. In this sense the Chinese acceptance of Buddhism was the earliest example of our comparative study. The passages quoted above were written at least a few hundred years prior to the arrival of Buddhism in China. Here we can see how the basic Buddhist teachings of transition (impermanence), non-self and reincarnation (transmigration) were made compatible with this

1 Victor H. Mair, 1994, *Wandering on the Way: Early Taoist Tales and Parables of Chuang Tzu*, Honolulu: University of Hawaii Press, pp. 216–17.

2 Mair, *Wandering on the Way*, p. 212.

Taoist view of life. The teaching of transition (impermanence) turned out to be readily translatable as the incessant movement of the Yin and Yang spirits. Nothing is to remain as it is. And if we are a part of this cosmic movement, there is no such thing as our 'selves'. Karma is the only notion absent in Chuang-tzu. Chuang-tzu only declares, 'life and death are disciples of each other'. But even the teaching of karma was interpreted as everyone being in charge of one's smooth transition and made compatible with the Taoist effort of regaining the Tao. For most Chinese Taoist indifference was identical with the Buddhist wisdom. Most Chinese, including Chinese Buddhists, followed this serene optimism and left little room for karma and suffering, with the most notable exception of Pure Land Buddhism. Their preference of Mahāyāna Buddhism over pre-Mahāyāna Buddhism is indicative of this optimism. The diminishing importance of the historical Buddha, together with the development of Mahāyāna Buddhology that presented the notion of dharmakā-ya as the cosmic body, suited well the Chinese transcendentalism that was essentially non-personal. It was further strengthened by the fact that bodhisattvas' practice always listed wisdom as the last stage of practice. Chinese Buddhism always found a place for compassion, but it was usually regarded as a by-product of enlightenment practice. Chuang-tzu declares that when one rises above life and death, 'the myriad things are a unity'. This vision is what the Taoist means by union with the Tao, as much as what the Chinese Buddhist means by enlightenment.

The union is simultaneously visionary and transformative. The best description of it is found in Lao-tzu.

There is a thing, formless yet complete. Before Heaven and Earth it existed. Without sound, without substance, it stands alone without changing. It is all pervading and unfailing. One may think of it as the mother of all beneath Heaven. We do not know its name, but we term it Tao. Forced to give an appellation to it, I should say it was Great.[3]

---

3 Tao te ching, 25.

This 'thing' is the origin or the root of everything, and simultaneously the principle that runs through everything. Its manifestation is different at every moment, hence it is also said to be the constant change. It is nameless, that is, it comes across as nothing when we try to grasp it. Its action is called non-action because it exercises no contrivance or effort.

This is a record of an ecstatic experience comparable to that known in the West as the mystical union with the absolute. This experience is self-transformative and generative of various kinds of practices from meditation to devotion. One notable difference is that while Taoist philosophy leaves it entirely open as to what to do to reach one's union with the Tao and what to expect from it, the mystical union in the West has always been placed within the context of Christian or other religious doctrine. It is rarely seen as the universal source of religion and art, the source of religious life and artistic creation that is prior to any contextualization. It is sometimes presented as one side of the coin representing the individualistic and a-historical side as against the communal and historical side, the unitive as against the dividing, non-ethical and inclusive as against ethical and exclusive side. It is sometimes seen as the elementary stage of religion that is on its way to becoming a properly organized religion or as a trigger of the revival movement in which the participants attempt to revisit the source of their tradition. Often it is seen as degenerate sentimentality, fanciful delusion in which one imagines to rise beyond one's finiteness into the infinite, a symptom in which one dreams of mixing those that are never to be mixed. Mysticism always existed within European Christianity, though not at the centre but on the periphery, often as an unwelcome or insignificant element.

In China, the openness of the Taoist union resulted in its being the central point of all the subsequent philosophical schools in China, and the source of inspiration of all the subsequent Chinese arts. This, and not the lineage from Bodhidharma, is the true origin of Zen Buddhism. Recent studies have suggested that Shinran's spontaneity (*jinen-hōni*), which is seen by some as the last stage of Shinran's practice, is spiritually comparable with Taoist spontaneity, although Shinran's way, as he himself saw it, is through his thorough pessimism and equally thorough dependency upon Amida's grace. Can we not see in these different treatments of mystical experience the fundamental distinction that we tend to think lies between Christian Europe and Taoist/Buddhist East but could in reality be the basic distinction that lies within most religious traditions? The difference, I think, is this. In Taoism, the Tao is 'a thing', that is, it is not a person. Hence our approach to it is meditative, therefore adaptable to a broad spectrum of mystical speculation. In the West, the absolute is never a thing. It is almost always a person, a person with will and judgement. Therefore our approach is inevitably relational. This difference is crucial. Since the Tao is 'a thing', at the event of our union we are no longer a person. In contrast, if the absolute is a person, even at our union with the absolute we remain personal and relational. What to do with the ego is the basic question concerning all forms of transcendentalism. The two different approaches aim at either resolving the ego or strengthening it. In either way the ego remains paradoxical in the sense that one way is no more promising than the other. What we need to see here is that the Eastern and Western traditions appear divided on this essential orientation. Both Buddhism and Christianity are eclectic traditions, and it is not difficult to find examples that are not in line with their respective orientations. In my view, however, these exceptions do not amount to a denial that an essential difference in their orientations does exist. It is this difference that called us to our comparative study. I would like to present in what follows two extreme examples, one from the East and the other from the West, that epitomize the two opposite orientations.

Release

Chuang-tzu (or: 'Chuang Chou') provides the most vivid depiction of the release from one's personhood.

> Once Chuang Chou dreamt he was a butterfly, a butterfly flitting and fluttering around, happy with himself and doing

as he pleased. He didn't know he was Chuang Chou. Suddenly he woke up and there he was, solid and unmistakable Chuang Chou. But he did not know if he was Chuang Chou who had dreamt he was a butterfly, or a butterfly dreaming he was Chuang Chou. Between Chuang Chou and a butterfly there must be *some* distinction! This is called the Transformation of Things.[4]

This is from the chapter called 'Discussion on Seeing All Things Equal'. The union with the Tao reveals that all things are equal. According to this we are one of those many 'equal things'. When the distinction between Chuang-tzu and the butterfly comes out, it is nothing but an accidental outcome of the autonomous movement of the Tao. His being is cosmological. Taoism thus presents the unquestionable priority of the cosmological ego over the relational ego.

The Taoist union did not give any prescribed context for its doctrine or practice. Chuang-tzu's playfulness is in fact an active rejection of any attempt at appropriation. That is why it has become the source of inspiration of philosophical speculation and artistic creativity throughout Asia. Regaining one's cosmological involvement, by whatever means, became the ideal for Chinese arts, ranging from music, painting, calligraphy, pottery to martial arts. Art is understood as transformative and transcendental since its purpose is to embody a passing phase of the Tao and reproduce a glimpse of the cosmic movement. This is similar to Greek aesthetics, which had a clearly defined cosmological norm for artistic creation. Greek aesthetics was geometrical in vision, mathematical in audition. For the Greeks the clearly defined principle, geometrical or mathematical, was simultaneously cosmological and aesthetic. The Chinese also maintain the cosmic relevance of their art. In the case of the Chinese, however, the word 'cosmic' is not quite appropriate. For the Tao is said to be chaos rather than cosmos. While the

---

4 Chuang-tzu, 1964, *Basic Writings*, New York: Columbia University Press, p. 45.

Greeks found themselves in a world ordered by ratio (ratio is recognizable by their rationality), the Chinese believed that they were a part of the cosmic movement, which was, however, vital and therefore beyond their rational grasp, hence chaotic. The Greek approach was rational while the Chinese approach was distinctly intuitive. The Chinese approach was not stable nor repetitive, and the attempt to reach genuine intuition always involved the practitioner's self-transformation. That is why art in China was thought to be equivalent to religious practice. This is distinctly Chinese practice, and whether the practitioner was Taoist or Buddhist is not a significant question. It should suffice to point to the fact that Zen Buddhists have always been powerful practitioners of these arts. The basis was laid down when Chuang-tzu's playfulness was incorporated into Zen classics such as 'Platform Sutra', 'Transmission of the Lamp' (*Jingde*) and 'Gateless Gate'.

Confinement

We have an account of metamorphosis that is at once surprisingly similar to Chuang-tzu's for the actual event and equally different as to the context in which it happens. Ovid's *Metamorphoses* are similar to Chuang-tzu's in many ways, but they do not give us the contract that we need for a comparative study. There is an account from the modern, Western culture. It is Kafka's *Metamorphosis*, a short experimental story of an ordinary man being transformed into an insect. It is such a hideous, that is, 'good', parody of Chuang-tzu's account that we might seriously wonder if Kafka had actually parodied Chuang-tzu. This is how Kafka's account begins:

> As Gregor Samsa awoke one morning from uneasy dreams he found himself transformed in his bed into a gigantic insect. He was lying on his hard, as it were armour-plated, back and when he lifted his head a little he could see his dome-like brown belly divided into stiff arched segments on top of which the bed-quilt could hardly keep in position and was about to

slide off completely. His numerous legs, which were pitifully thin compared to the rest of his bulk, waved helplessly before his eyes.[5]

This metamorphosis itself is almost identical with Chuang-tzu's. But everything else is in direct contrast. Chuang-tzu's butterfly flies, Kafka's beetle does not. Chuang-tzu's butterfly is in the open air, Kafka's beetle is confined in a small room. Chuang-tzu's butterfly is in joy, Kafka's beetle is in horror. In all these the contrast between the symbolism of freedom and that of bondage cannot be sharper. Chuang-tzu's butterfly is 'flitting and fluttering around, happy with himself and doing as he pleased'. Kafka's beetle is lying on a bed, seeing 'his numerous legs, which were pitifully thin compared to the rest of his bulk, wave[d] helplessly before his eyes'. Moreover, Chuang-tzu's butterfly is likely to be a pretty insect while Kafka's beetle is undoubtedly ugly. All these highlight the difference of the contexts in which their metamorphoses take place. Chuang-tzu's butterfly is alone in the open field. It is in the environment to which it belongs. Chuang-tzu's identity as Chuang-tzu or as a butterfly is equally dreamlike because they are both the result of cosmic evolution. Chuang-tzu's butterfly is cosmological. Kafka's beetle, in contrast, is entirely stripped of his cosmological relevance. Gregor Samsa 'is' the beetle. And 'it was no dream'. Kafka's beetle is alone too, but it is because he is left alone in his room. It is still surrounded by his family and society to which it no longer belongs. Being immersed in relations, Kafka's beetle is forever deprived of his cosmological relevance and remains relational. Kafka gives no explanation as to why his beetle fails to recover its cosmological relevance. Instead he gives a meticulous description of what awaits the unfortunate beetle when it fails to be free.

In the relational context, a metamorphosis is just a grotesque and unacceptable deviation from the norm by which the very context is set. At the event of his metamorphosis, Gregor Samsa

---

5 Franz Kafka, 1961, *Metamorphosis and Other Stories*, trans. Willa and Edwin Muir, Harmondsworth: Penguin, p. 9.

finds himself in solitary confinement. The point is that this
isolation is a relational isolation, caused and maintained within
the relationship he once had. He stays in his room because he fears
that he might upset his relationship with the rest of his family
and others. The first irony is that those who have a relationship
with Gregor Samsa do not accept his withdrawal. He receives
call after call from outside. They demand that their relationships should be maintained and honoured. When their demands
are not met, they are disappointed, angered and insulted. The
menacing calls culminate in a forceful address made by the chief
clerk of his company.

> 'Mr. Samsa', the chief clerk called now in a louder voice, 'what's
> the matter with you? Here you are, barricading yourself in
> your room, giving only "yes" and "no" for answers, causing
> your parents a lot of unnecessary trouble and neglecting – I
> mention this only in passing – neglecting your business duties
> in an incredible fashion. I am speaking here in the name of
> your parents and of your chief, and I beg you quite seriously to
> give me an immediate and precise explanation. You amaze me,
> you amaze me. I thought you were a quiet, dependable person,
> and now all at once you seem bent on making a disgraceful
> exhibition of yourself.'[6]

In this I hear a clear resonance of the biblical passage, 'But
the Lord God called to the man, and said to him, "Where are
you?"' (Gen. 3.9). The beetle eventually comes out in a desper-
ate hope not to offend them any further by his withdrawal. The
second irony is that these callers are those who, when the beetle
does come out, push him back to his confinement in the next
moment. The relationship continues even after that, and the
beetle remains entirely dependent upon it. The only difference is
that the relationship is no longer easy and comfortable but hard
and burdened with unexpected and unexplainable frictions.

---

6 Kafka, *Metamorphosis*, p. 17.

Kafka's beetle tries his best to maintain the relationship even in such an extraordinary circumstance. Because of the twofold irony whatever he attempts ends up increasing the friction in the uncomfortable and unconsoling relationship. For a brief moment, however, even Kafka's beetle ponders on the possibility of freedom. It is pitiably small in scale, but nevertheless genuine freedom. The idea is to remove some furniture from his room so that he should have more space for crawling. But, of course, he decides against it.

> Did he really want his warm room, so comfortably fitted with old family furniture, to be turned into a naked den in which he would certainly be able to crawl unhampered in all directions but at the price of shedding simultaneously all recollection of *his human background*? He had indeed been close to the brink of *forgetfulness* that only the voice of his mother, which he had not heard for so long, had drawn him back from it.[7]

This forgetfulness of 'his human background' is what Chuang-tzu's butterfly achieves in his metamorphosis. And in Chuang-tzu this forgetting is the same as remembering his part in the cosmic evolution. In Kafka, however, one call from his mother is enough for him to decide against his freedom. The beetle declares:

> Nothing should be taken out of his room; everything must stay as it was; he could not dispense with the good influence of the furniture on his state of mind; and even if the furniture did hamper him in his senseless crawling around and around, that was no drawback but a great advantage.[8]

The furniture symbolizes 'his human background', the relationship that was once comfortable. Even when all the comfort is lost and all he finds is friction, Kafka's beetle still chooses to remain in the relationship. For him freedom is nothing but 'senseless

---

7 Kafka, *Metamorphosis*, p. 38. Italics added by K.T.
8 Kafka, *Metamorphosis*, p. 38.

crawling around and around'. He willingly decides against that, for the loss of freedom, according to him, is 'no drawback but a great advantage'. This decision is crucial. With this Kafka's beetle dies a meaningless death. Chuang-tzu's butterfly represented freedom and became a symbol of philosophical and artistic creativity in China (and in Japan). Kafka's beetle, in contrast, embodies 'unfreedom' that marks the end of philosophy and art, because it just does not make sense either philosophically or aesthetically. It is the result of the persistent trend to replace the cosmological context with the relational context. Kafka does not explain why this trend has started or how it operates. For this we need to turn to his spiritual brother, Kierkegaard.

Closure

Kierkegaard presents a clear picture of the mechanism in which internal self-reflection necessarily results in the replacement of the cosmological ego with the relational ego. We find at the beginning of *Sickness Unto Death* the most powerful statement of the ego in its relationality.

> A human being is spirit. But what is spirit? Spirit is the self. But what is the self? The self is a relation that relates itself to itself or is the relation's relating itself to itself in the relation; the self is not the relation but is the relation's relating itself to itself.[9]

Is not this relational ego inevitably a solipsistic, regressive ego? It undoubtedly is, but according to Kierkegaard it is only the preparation for the discovery of a proper relationship with God. From here he develops two dogmatic arguments: that there are good and bad forms of solipsism, and that there are good and bad ways out of it. By good solipsism he means that which

---

9 Søren Kierkegaard, 1980, *The Sickness unto Death: A Christian Psychological Exposition for Upbuilding and Awakening*, Princeton: Princeton University Press, p. 13.

is waiting to be opened, by bad solipsism that which is willing to stay closed. This is how he puts it:

> Such a relation that relates itself to itself, a self, must either have established itself or have been established by another. If the relation that relates itself to itself has been established by another, then the relation is indeed the third, but this relation, the third, is yet again a relation and relates itself to that which established the entire relation.[10]

The first solipsism is the bad one that remains closed and does not reach 'the third'. This is for the pagan. The second solipsism is the good one that reaches 'the third'. This is properly Christian.

We need to remember here that the transcendental ego that addresses itself to what lies beyond it is an inherent paradox of every form of transcendentalism. We need to question, therefore, whether Kierkegaard's judgement on success and failure was made on a purely dogmatic ground.

The distinction he is at pains to make here is whether solipsism just stays on or becomes an entry to the salvific path. Elsewhere he discloses the real intention of introducing the internalized, self-reflective, relational ego. He says:

> The first thing he does is to turn toward himself . . . In turning toward himself, he *eo ipso* turns toward God, and there is a ceremonial rule that says that when the finite spirit would see God, it must begin as guilty. As he turns toward himself, he discovers guilt.[11]

The sole point of his argument is that the distinction between the Christian opening and the pagan closure is more primary, more important, more urgent than any other consideration. Kierkegaard's argument gets into dangerous territory when he deems the pagan closure 'demonic'.

---

10 Kierkegaard, *Sickness unto Death*, p. 13.
11 Kierkegaard, *Sickness unto Death*, p. 107.

The demonic does not close itself up with something, but it closes itself up within itself, and in this lies what is profound about existence [Tilvœrselsen], precisely that unfreedom makes itself a prisoner.[12]

The problem is that this closure is also open exactly the same way as the Christian closure is also open.

The demonic is unfreedom that wants to close itself off. This, however, is and remains an impossibility. The demonic is inclosing reserve [*det Indesluttede*] and the unfreely disclosed. The two definitions indicate, as intended, the same thing, because inclosing reserve is precisely the mute, and when it is to express itself, this must take place contrary to its will, since freedom, which underlies unfreedom from without, revolts and now betrays unfreedom.[13]

This 'unfreedom' is freedom exercised in the demonic, rather than the Christian, context. However, it is apparent that Christian freedom and demonic freedom operate in the same way. Is not Kierkegaard's distinction a dogmatic one? And does it not indicate that in his solipsistic isolation Kierkegaard encounters both the divine grace and the demonic temptation, and that there is nothing to distinguish between the two other than his dogmatic conviction? With his powerful assertion, is he not making a distinction that is impossible to make in reality?

Kierkegaard's line of argument is always the same: the Christian passage from the tree of knowledge to the tree of life, the passage he insists that each individual must take by his or her own choice, is the only legitimate form of transcendentalism. The way he carries out his attack on pagans (by this he means philosophers and aestheticians) is equally dogmatic.

---

12 Søren Kierkegaard, 1980, *The Concept of Anxiety: A Simple Psychologically Orienting Deliberation on the Dogmatic Issue of Hereditary Sin*, Princeton: Princeton University Press, p. 124.

13 Kierkegaard, *Concept of Anxiety*, p. 123.

Transcendentalism is paradoxical from the beginning. As seen before, our ego, a small and ephemeral enclosure of the whole, and its desire for the union with the whole, create an inherent paradox. Whatever form of transcendental practice, philosophical, aesthetical or other, it is a way to live through this paradox. What Kierkegaard does is to pick up this inherent paradox in all forms of transcendentalism and argue that it is damned unless it is 'genuine', by this he means, Christian. One example should suffice. Kierkegaard takes up Socrates' problem of 'the moment of truth'. The paradox is that when one comes to realize that something is true, one must have known it before that moment, otherwise one would not be able to tell whether it is true; but if one already knows that it is true, there could be no 'moment of discovery'. The Platonic solution was the recollection theory in which it was explained that the moment is simultaneously discovery and recollection. In this, every moment is potentially the moment of truth. Kierkegaard snaps at this paradox and says that there are only two moments that are true: the moment of incarnation and the moment of conversion. For Christianity alone allows us to combine the eternal and the moment, hence the Christian truth alone is the genuine truth.[14] In the Platonic paradigm our understanding of the moment is open in the sense that no particular moment is prioritized over other moments. With Kierkegaard this openness is lost. Instead we have a closure that is both historical and dogmatic.

---

14 'It is well known that Christianity is the only historical phenomenon which in spite of the historical, nay precisely by means of the historical, has intended itself to be for the single individual the point of departure for his eternal consciousness, has intended to interest him otherwise than merely historically, has intended to base his eternal happiness on his relationship to something historical.' Søren Kierkegaard, 1962, *Philosophical Fragments* I, Princeton: Princeton University Press, p. 137. The following description of the moment therefore is not about the moment of truth but the moment of conversion. 'In the Moment man becomes conscious that he is born; for his antecedent state, to which he may not cling, was one of non-being. In the Moment man also becomes conscious of the new birth, for his antecedent state was one of non-being.' Kierkegaard, *Philosophical Fragments*, pp. 25–6.

Introspection and Guilt

I have suggested above that Kierkegaard has only one case of solipsistic dead-end but is determined to apply two different descriptions, salvation and damnation, to it. If this is the case, his case is just a dead-end, similar to Kafka's. There is no trace of salvific language in Kafka's *Metamorphosis*. Here closedness and openness which, according to Kierkegaard, correspond to damnation and salvation, are completely relativized. Gregor Samsa's family put him in confinement, but at the same time they never stop approaching him for their love, hate or curiosity. Gregor Samsa's soliloquy represents his intense introspection, and the relationship he nonetheless maintains with his family represents his openness. The point is that both closedness and openness are defined within the relationship. Its absurdity reaches its highest point when he dies from the wound caused by an apple his father threw at him. Is it meant to be understood as divine intervention?

Both Kierkegaard and Kafka give a clear picture of how the cosmological ego dies when the relational ego is born. Kierkegaard's 'new birth' is precisely this. The sole purpose of Kierkegaard's argument is to defend it against 'Christian paganism', the Christian failure to live up to this ideal. In presenting the purely relational ego and its guilt in its purest form, Kierkegaard simply abandons all that to do with the cosmological ego. This is blatantly contrary to our experience. Our first experience is 'the world and I', and this 'I' is the cosmological one. The relational ego comes about only when we begin interacting with others. In order to argue for the primacy of the relational ego, Kierkegaard turns over this precedence and argues that the relational ego is prior to the cosmological ego, that the latter is a sinful deviation from the former. The rest of his argument is an apology, often aggressive, of this overturn, and a persistent attack on all that is to do with the cosmological ego that, according to Kierkegaard, is the breeding ground of Christian paganism. I am meant to have no insight into what happens in this new life. And this is as much Kierkegaard's point as my own acknowledgement.[15] My reply is that this new birth is simply to give up all the possibilities we have in this life. Whatever reward he may or may not allow himself to expect, Kierkegaard in this life is willing to become Kafka's beetle.

Thus far we have identified two basic orientations of religious practice. The orientation we find in the Chinese arts is to keep the priority of the cosmological ego over the relational ego; by contrast, we find in the modern European mind the determination to replace the cosmological ego with the relational ego. What makes European thinkers such as Kierkegaard interesting is that in spite of their determination to the contrary they exhibit a surprisingly accurate insight into what it is like to remain in the cosmological context. In discussing innocence in *The Concept of Anxiety*, Kierkegaard concedes that in innocence there is 'peace and repose', and that it is by definition prior to the experience of anxiety.

> Innocence is ignorance. In innocence, man is not qualified as spirit but is psychically qualified in immediate unity with his natural condition. The spirit in man is dreaming . . . In this state there is peace and repose, but there is simultaneously something else . . . What, then, is it? Nothing.[16]

This is comparable with Lao-tzu's vision of the Tao as vast, as nothing. Kierkegaard also accurately points out the dreamlike

---

15 'The being born, is this fact thinkable? Certainly, why not? But for whom is it thinkable, for one who is born, or who is not born? This latter supposition is an absurdity which would never have entered anyone's head; for one who is born could scarcely have conceived the notion. When one who has experienced birth thinks of himself as born, he conceives this transition from non-being. The same principle must also hold in the case of the new birth. . . But who then may be expected to think the new birth? Surely the man who has himself been born anew, since it would of course be absurd to imagine that one not so born should think it. Would it not be the height of the ridiculous for such an individual to entertain this notion?' Kierkegaard, *Philosophical Fragments*, pp. 24–5.

16 Kierkegaard, *Concept of Anxiety*, p. 41.

quality of this vision. His orientation, however, is not to stay here but to move on to the next stage.

> But what effect does nothing have? It begets anxiety. This is the profound secret of innocence, that it is at the same time anxiety. Dreamily the spirit projects its own actuality, but this actuality is nothing, and innocence always sees this nothing outside itself.[17]

For a Taoist this encounter with 'nothing' is the experience of ecstasy; for Kierkegaard, however, the same is the cause of anxiety. He continues:

> Anxiety is a qualification of dreaming spirit, and as such it has its place in psychology. Awake, the difference between myself and my other is posited; sleeping, it is suspended; dreaming, it is an intimated nothing. The actuality of the spirit constantly shows itself as a form that tempts its possibility but disappears as soon as it seeks to grasp for it, and it is a nothing that can only bring anxiety.[18]

Here again Kierkegaard repeats the same point that our inevitable move from dream to reality necessarily brings about anxiety in us. But the description of the circumstance is clearly comparable with that of Chuang-tzu's metamorphosis. Kierkegaard's 'intimated nothing in dreaming' is essentially the same as Chuang-tzu's playful freedom. The only difference is that for Chuang-tzu dreaming remains prior to reality, for Kierkegaard this priority inevitably turns over. Another example from the same book shows that Kierkegaard was fully versed with descriptions of the mystical union.

> Anxiety may be compared with dizziness. He whose eye happens to look down into the yawning abyss becomes dizzy . . . Hence anxiety is the dizziness of freedom, which emerges when the spirit wants to posit the synthesis and freedom looks down into its own possibility, laying hold of finiteness

---

17 Kierkegaard, *Concept of Anxiety*, p. 41.
18 Kierkegaard, *Concept of Anxiety*, pp. 41–2.

to support itself. Freedom succumbs in this dizziness. Further than this, psychology cannot and will not go. In that very moment everything is changed, and freedom, when it again rises, sees that it is guilty. Between these two moments lies the leap.[19]

For Kierkegaard 'the leap' from dream to reality is inevitable. Consequently, he burdens himself with the impossible task of mediating the infinite and the finite 'not in dream but in reality'. This is what he means by 'the synthesis'. And the very impossibility of this task he calls guilt. Kierkegaard offers no explanation about this leap, why he has to take it, why it is necessary, why he chooses to become Kafka's beetle rather than to remain Chuang-tzu's butterfly. All I can see here is his willingness to do so.[20]

---

19 Kierkegaard, *Concept of Anxiety*, p. 61.

20 There is an example that demonstrates Kierkegaard's sympathetic insight into how 'a pagan' sees his death. It is found in a footnote attached to his statement that death is the punishment of sin. It is interesting that he recorded this insight in a footnote, the insight that he could never find a place for in the body of his text. 'Because the pagan view of sensuousness was more naive, its temporality more carefree, so the pagan view of death was milder and more attractive, but it lacked the ultimate. In reading the beautiful essay of Lessing on the representation of death in classical art, one cannot deny being sadly and pleasurably moved by the picture of this sleeping genius or by seeing the beautiful solemnity with which the genius of death bows his head and extinguishes the torch. There is, if you will, something indescribably persuasive and alluring in trusting oneself to such a guide who is as conciliatory as a recollection in which nothing is recollected. On the other hand, there is something sinister in following this silent guide, because he does not conceal anything. His form is no incognito. Just as his is, so is death, and with that, everything is over. There is an incomprehensible sadness in seeing this genius with his friendly figure bend down over the dying and with the breath of his last kiss extinguish the last spark of life, while all that was experienced has already vanished little by little, and death remains as that which, itself unexplained, explains that the whole of life was a game that came to an end, and in which everyone, the greatest as well as the least, made their departures like school children, extinguished like sparks of burning paper, and last of all the soul itself as the schoolmaster. And so there is also a muteness of annihilation found in the fact that the whole was merely a children's game, and now the game is over.' *Concept of Anxiety*, p. 92.

Introspection and Art

Chinese aesthetics and Christian theology in Europe do not meet very often. There have been, however, some modern Europeans who took a serious interest in Chinese art and left discussions that could potentially be theological. Herbert Read, for example, made a specific reference to an aesthetic norm that was derived directly from Chinese cosmology. Referring to one of the six principles of painting by Hsieh Ho, Read says:

> The first principle is the one that is most difficult to render into a Western language. It expresses a concept of a spiritual energy moving through all things and uniting them in harmony. Cosmic energy might be an adequate phrase, but only on the understanding that it proceeds from a single source and animates all things, inorganic and organic. Spirit resonance is one almost literal translation of the Chinese expression used by Hsieh Ho.[21]

It is yet to be examined how much philosophical and aesthetic influence Read received from this knowledge. It is quite possible that Read's assertion that art is essentially a religious matter is directly related to it.[22] While art in China has always retained its cosmological relevance, modern European aesthetics whose ultimate purpose appears to be to recover art's cosmological origin is probably the least successful branch of European philosophy. Since its revival in the eighteenth century it has struggled with a couple of the basic questions, what beauty is, and where to find it. As for the definition of beauty, aestheticians have had to accept that, whatever the definition, it is either

---

21 Herbert Read, 1967, *Art and Alienation*, London: Thames & Hudson, pp. 40–1.

22 'It [art] is the direct measure of man's spiritual vision. When that vision is communal, it becomes a religion, and the vitality of art throughout the greater part of history is closely bound up with some form of religion.' Herbert Read, 1951, *The Meaning of Art*, London: Faber & Faber, p. 261.

too narrow and specific or too vague and whimsical. Also, they have failed to find the exact locus of beauty. It is either inherent in a beautiful object or lies in the sensitivity of one who perceives it, but their discussion has gone no further. The result of their effort is the constant failure in answering the basic questions with which they began their study. Through this failure, however, European aesthetics has arrived at one assumption and one orientation that would lead us to this assumption. The assumption is that there should be a principle that runs through natural beauty and beauty created artificially, which is also the principle that runs through the act of producing beauty and the act of perceiving it. This assumption is similar to Chinese assumption of the Tao for its sweeping breadth and vagueness. According to it one orientation that would lead to this assumption is disinterestedness, that is, freedom from prejudgement and preconceptions, again similar to Chinese indifference and forgetfulness. Modern aestheticians, Herbert Read for example, came very close to Chinese aesthetics when they realized that this one principle was only an assumption, probably undemonstrable, rather than a premise, and when they recognized that disinterestedness was not a description but a norm that was to be realized in the practice of art. From here Read carried out his examination of the nature of artistic introspection. The result is an argument that looks like a strong counter-argument against Kierkegaard's introspection. His argument, in short, is that what we should discover is not anxiety but playfulness and peace, and it should lead us not to guilt but to artistic creativity. For the first point he just quotes a passage from *A Midsummer Night's Dream*.

> And as imagination bodies forth
> The forms of things unknown, the poet's pen
> Turns them to shapes, and gives to airy nothing
> A local habitation and a name.[23]

---

23 *A Midsummer Night's Dream*, v.i. This quotation appears in Herbert Read, 1960, *The Forms of Things Unknown: Essays towards an Aesthetic Philosophy*, London: Faber & Faber, Epigraph.

This imagination is comparable with dreaming. Its origin is 'nothing'. He makes his second point by quoting from a contemporary artist André Masson.

> I buried myself in the darkness of the earth, a seed eager to burst out towards the light of the day. I desired to be no more than the essence of movement at the birth of things, in order to be more fully exterior. . . I hailed the four elements, I admired the fraternity of the natural kingdom. . . I saw what one sees no more because one sees it too often. . . I am marvelled at the evidence of *correspondence*.[24]

This is a clear example, from a European artist, that introspection does not lead to the Christian penance but to the beginning of artistic creativity. For Read the purpose of art is a release from the grip of the relational ego. He says in *The Meaning of Art*:

> The work of art is in some sense a liberation of the personality; normally our feelings are inhibited and repressed. We contemplate a work of art, and immediately there is a release; and not only a release – sympathy is a release of feelings – but also a heightening, a tautening, a sublimation. Here is the essential difference between art and sentimentality: sentimentality is a release, but also a loosening, a relaxing of the emotions; art is a release, but also bracing. Art is the economy of feeling; it is emotion cultivating good form.[25]

This is an exact reverse of Kierkegaard's project. It is a project to release Kafka's beetle in the open. According to Read this is the only way to recover genuine creativity. Here as well as elsewhere Read carefully guards himself against the dogmatic threat that the denial of guilt means hellish confusion. Art, according to Read, is simultaneously releasing and bracing. In the same book Read says:

---

24 Quoted by Read, *Art and Alienation*, p. 49.
25 Read, *The Meaning of Art*, p. 39.

I would say that the function of art is not to transmit *feeling* so that others may experience the same *feeling*. That is only the function of the crudest forms of art. . . The real function of art is to express *feeling* and transmit *understanding* . . . We come to the work of art already charged with emotional complexes; we find in the genuine work of art, not an excitation of these emotions, but peace, repose, equanimity . . . It is better described as a state of wonder or admiration . . . as a state of recognition. Our homage to an artist is our homage to a man who by his special gifts has solved our emotional problems for us.[26]

Read believes that art is the process of regaining our 'peace, repose, equanimity', in other words, innocence. That is, art can bring us back to the stage where there was no anxiety. This requires a radical reorientation of the Christian legacy in the West. On this ground Read makes this famous statement.

The only sin is ugliness, and if we believed this with all our being, all other activities of the human spirit could be left to take care of themselves.[27]

What is important here is that when we encounter the existential question we should resist a hasty answer. We have seen the two examples of this resistance: the Chinese religion and art with its distinctly fanciful 'answer' and aestheticism of modern Europe with its persistent failure to provide an answer. The Chinese answer is hardly an answer. At least the initial question does not lose its power because of it. And its open-endedness leaves a possibility that the power of the initial question may transform into spirit that initiates artistic creativity. Christianity, in contrast, gives a solid answer. It protects us from the power of the question and allows us eventually to ignore it. By this protection, however, we lose our artistic creativity, and what is left for

---

26 Read, *The Meaning of Art*, pp. 260–1.
27 Read, *The Meaning of Art*, p. 261.

us is to repeat the same answer, and in some bad cases, to get into conflict with others who are equally committed to repeat different answers. A solid answer blocks the power of the initial question and suffocates our creativity. Anxiety as presented by Kierkegaard and Kafka was the expression of their desire for a solid answer, the expression of their despair in which they felt it impossible to live without an answer. The difference in their outcome, Kierkegaard finding the Christian answer and becoming a preacher and Kafka failing to find an answer and ending up describing the absurdity of the quest itself is of less significance.

The purpose of examining the consequence of these two opposite religious orientations is not to decide which is more Eastern or Western. As suggested above, it is more likely that we find the same split in Western Christianity and Far Eastern Buddhism. What amazes me is the clear awareness of the opposite orientation that the European thinkers have while presenting their own orientation. Kierkegaard and Kafka, in presenting the relational ego, are fully aware of the opposite orientation that would lead to the cosmological release. Herbert Read, in reversing their process, is equally aware of their, as well as his own, orientation. They are keenly aware of the whole process, its beginning and the outcome of the orientation that is not theirs. It is because of this awareness that their practice in Europe is inevitably confrontational. In the East there is a long-standing attempt to unite Pure Land Buddhism and Zen Buddhism. Its aim is doctrinal eclecticism, and its approach is more mediatory than confrontational. The participants often exhibit a limited awareness of the opposite, one certainly not as keen as the European ones. These examples, one confrontational and the other mediatory, give us two models that we can adopt for our present dialogue between Buddhism and Christianity. If our dialogue is to reach beyond a predetermined mediatory point, we need to go through the confrontational way. The task is undoubtedly as difficult as persuading Kafka's beetle to fly.

4. Response to Kiyoshi Tsuchiya

ELIZABETH HARRIS

At the heart of Kiyoshi Tsuchiya's paper is confrontation between what he calls two essential orientations: the cosmological ego and the relational ego. The first is linked with the East, particularly the form of Buddhism in China that is fused with Taoism. It is light, playful and marked by self-forgetting. The second is linked with the Christian West. It is heavy, ugly and marked by clinging to the egocentric hope of eternal life for the self. Tsuchiya admits that both the East and West offer other models: the Pure Land Buddhist tradition stresses the relational; the aesthetic vision of Herbert Read touches cosmic self-forgetting. This does not change his view that the contrast between the two orientations lies at the heart of the difference between Buddhism and Christianity.

I appreciate much in this argument. Buddhism and Christianity are not the same, and can appear to speak of different goals and different models of the 'self'. What Tsuchiya calls the relational is as central to the Christian as non-dual, cosmic interconnectedness is to the Taoist Buddhist. I have no difficulty in recognizing that, from a Buddhist perspective, Christianity's seeming fixation with personal salvation and eternal life for the soul is suspect. In fact Buddhists see an uncanny similarity between it and *bhava-taṇhā* (Pāli: craving for existence), one of the three forms of craving, according to the Theravāda Buddhist tradition, that prevents beings from reaching true freedom.

But is the overall picture that Tsuchiya presents of relational Christianity accurate? Are the writings of Franz Kafka and Søren Kierkegaard the best comparative pointers to Christianity's message? I would suggest not. Kafka's beetle offers an almost irresistible parallel to Chuang-tzu's butterfly. Gregor Samsa, imprisoned as beetle by an unforgiving and demanding web of relationships, is the butterfly's perfect shadow image. I would contest, however, Tsuchiya's implication that Kafka's fettered beetle is a representation of Christian transcendence. As for Søren Kierkegaard, nineteenth-century Danish theologian, my misgiving here is not that Tsuchiya has got Kierkegaard wrong, but that Kierkegaard himself offers too narrow a view of the Christian narratives of salvation and faith.

With what, therefore, would I substitute Tsuchiya's choices? I would go to the Bible rather than to the nineteenth century in order to find a cosmic spirituality that is self-forgetting. From the Hebrew Bible I would choose verses such as these that situate humanity within rather than outside the natural world:

> For you shall go out in joy
>   and be led back in peace;
> the mountains and the hills before you,
>   shall burst into song,
> and all the trees of the field shall clap their hands.[1]

> Let the sea roar, and all that fills it:
>   the world and those who live in it.
> Let the floods clap their hands;
>   let the hills sing together for joy
> at the presence of the Lord. . .[2]

From the New Testament, I would choose these words of Jesus:

> Therefore I tell you, do not worry about your life, what you will eat or what you will drink, or about your body, what you will wear. Is not life more than food, and the body more than clothing? Look at the birds of the air; they neither sow

---

1 Isaiah 55.12.   2 Psalm 98.7–9.

nor reap nor gather into barns, and yet your heavenly Father feeds them.[3]

And these:

> Then Jesus told his disciples, 'If any want to become my followers, let them deny themselves and take up their cross and follow me. For those who want to save their life will lose it, and those who lose their life for my sake will find it.'[4]

These do not move Christianity away from the relational. The context of the quotes from the Hebrew Bible is blatantly theistic. The cosmos is created by God and is in relationship with God. But the important point is that this relationship is one of joy and even playfulness. Ripples of cosmic energy flow through the images. And the human is not alienated from this energy but united with it. I can imagine Chuang-tzu's butterfly in this environment.

The passages from the New Testament concentrate on the forgetting, or denying, of self, in relation to God. Although the first eventually draws a distinction between the bird and the human, it uses images from the natural world to break down anxiety-driven ego-boundaries between 'self' and 'other', 'self' and the cosmos. The self-forgetting and freedom of the natural world become spiritual teachers. The second reading places renunciation of self at the heart of relationship with God. The religious path is presented as one in which the ego, and its wish for security and self-gratification, must be left behind.

I would like to suggest that the distinction between the cosmological ego and the relational ego made by Tsuchiya, rooted in the acceptance or rejection of cosmological freedom for the self, is not as clear-cut as Tsuchiya implies. Both Buddhism and Christianity speak of a wrong concept of self. Just as Buddhism would insist there is no room for the egotistic self within the

---

3 Matthew 6.25–26.   4 Matthew 16.24–25.

interconnectedness and fluidity of the cosmos, so Christianity would say that there is no room for it within any relationship with God, however 'God' is configured. In other words, relationship and dissolution of the 'self', relationship and freedom, do not exclude each other.

Having said this, I would want to stress that Tsuchiya's paper has a message for Christians that we ignore at our peril. For what he has done is compare the best of Taoism, influenced by Buddhism, with the shadow side of Christianity, the dark side that has been present throughout Christianity's history. Christians need to hear the Buddhist view that craving for survival beyond death is not a wholesome motivation for religious faith, that it is in fact a false path leading to individualism rather than the renunciation of self that is so central to the Christian gospels. They need to be aware that dealing with religious diversity, religious dissent or religious anxiety, through closure or Christian triumphalism is dangerously myopic in a world of diverse faiths. To quote Tsuchiya, it is the '"unfreedom" that marks the end of philosophy and art'. But it is more than this. It is the prison that has led some Christians, throughout history, to persecute the 'other'. For it is when ecstasy in the face of cosmos, or God's limitless loving energy, is reduced to anxiety that persecution can be sanctioned, and freedom becomes 'unfreedom'.

5. Response to Elizabeth Harris

KIYOSHI TSUCHIYA

I am encouraged to see that both Elizabeth Harris and I begin our investigations of religion from the same starting point. We indeed agree that the problem of ego is the most fundamental problem of all. In whatever cultural and historical environment, this problem invariably leads us to question the validity of our own existence. In essence religious speculation and practice always attempt to respond to this question.

As Elizabeth Harris illustrates in her presentation, both Buddhism and Christianity are confronted with the same problem of ego, and they both offer a diagnosis and a remedy. Here 'Buddhism and Christianity touch but also diverge'. In my view Buddhism and Christianity share the same diagnosis but Christianity sets out a remedy that is radically different from the Buddhist one. Religious life as manifested in the Buddhist tradition and in the Christian tradition is indeed quite different. Our task is to present this difference clearly and to speculate, if possible, on reasons why the traditions are different. The fluidity in our contemporary society allows us to experience other religious traditions by learning about them or even practising them. A Buddhist-Christian dialogue has been one of the most frequent and fruitful of these exchanges. Our familiarity with both traditions, however, is not the same as their similarity or compatibility. As Harris says, Buddhism and Christianity also diverge. And this divergence calls for our interpretation.

My hypothesis here is that Buddhism and Christianity are different because they present slightly different diagnoses to the same problem. They present different reasonings as to why the ego is the problem. Buddhism teaches that we do not exist as ego, that our ego is merely a mistake, an appearance. Christianity, in contrast, insists that we do exist as an ego, as a selfish, sinful ego and teaches the way towards redemption. Buddhism sees the ego as 'false', while Christianity presents the ego as 'sinful'. Here lies the difficulty of any attempt of uniting the two traditions. To use the word 'real', the ego that an unenlightened Buddhist might be aware of is not real, while the sinful ego of a Christian is unmistakably real. The Buddhist remedy of liberation from the falsehood of the ego, for a Christian, is simply to dodge the problem. Similarly, Christian hope of redemption, for a Buddhist, is to cling hopelessly to the very mistake that had initiated religious practice.

In accepting that the ego is the problem, we assume that the ego is a part of the whole that nevertheless fails to partake in it properly. In this sense our awareness of ego as a problem and our assumption that there is something larger than the ego are simultaneous. This assumption remains an assumption and will never reach finality. However, it is this assumption that marks the most radical difference between Buddhism and Christianity. The Christian God is one such assumption. God with a personality and a personal will shows Christianity's basic orientation towards personifying this assumption. In contrast, Buddhism, while lacking this personal assumption, has an unshakeable cosmic assumption. The dharma that simultaneously rules the cosmos and decides our ignorance and enlightenment is the law that is above the manipulation of a person or a personal will either divine or merely human.

It is at this point of comparison that we become aware of the two distinct, possibly contradictory, religious orientations. While Buddhism assimilates itself with naturalism, Christianity shows its determined anti-naturalism. When the ego in Buddhism is merely a 'false' appearance, its resolution is the only possible orientation. It thus presents a cosmological transcendence. However, if the ego is 'sinful', it needs redemptive justification that nature cannot supply. Therefore it has to resort to personal transcendence. Elizabeth Harris's quotation of Buddha's denial of the power of prayer is particularly interesting in this context. The Buddha teaches that prayer is like an idle attempt to raise a rock from the pool.[1] If we compare this with Christ's statement of the power of faith, the contrast between the basic orientations of the two traditions becomes blatantly clear. Christ declares, 'also if ye shall say unto this mountain, Be thou removed, and be thou cast into the sea; it shall be done'.[2] If the Buddha's episode may come across as anti-humanism, Christ's statement shows his determined anti-naturalism.

There is a tendency in Christianity to drive humanism beyond nature, as well as a tendency in Buddhism, especially in Chinese Buddhism, to purge itself of any form of humanism. A Buddhist-Christian dialogue cannot bypass these radical examples from both traditions. I accept the possibility that not only the starting point but also the ultimate goal of Buddhism and Christianity could be the same. This union, however, is not authentic unless it shows a way to go beyond the theoretically contradictory and practically confrontational difference that we find in the Buddhist and Christian orientations.

---

1 *Gāmaṇisaṃyutta, Saṃyutta Nikāya* iv 312–13.
2 Matthew 21.21, KJV.

PART II

THE ULTIMATE

6. Ultimate Reality in Buddhism and Christianity:

A Christian Perspective

KARL BAIER

The Concept of Ultimate Reality and Its Relation to Religion

Before I discuss the understanding of Ultimate Reality in Christianity and Buddhism I would like to clarify to some extent the meaning of the term 'Ultimate Reality'. One might define Ultimate Reality as that which is more important than everything else in the life of individuals and communities. An understanding of Ultimate Reality is always linked to an understanding of human life and its essential purposes. One cannot conceive of Ultimate Reality without thinking of the human being for whom it is of ultimate relevance.

Moreover, it is part of the notion of Ultimate Reality that its ultimate importance is not the result of a subjective, arbitrary choice. Rather, Ultimate Reality is believed to be ultimate in light of the true nature of reality. And the meaning of Ultimate Reality is always related to some notion of its counterpart – namely, the non-ultimate realities – and the links between the two. In a similar way Ultimate Reality as *summum bonum*, highest good, is interrelated with other goods and is to be understood in relation to them.

Last but not least Ultimate Reality is connected with spirituality. The spirituality of a person or group can be defined as a project to integrate one's life by living according to the Ultimate Reality one perceives.[1] Generally implicit in a given understanding of Ultimate Reality are ways of referring to it and guidelines for integrating it into daily life (moral standards, ways of living, rituals, prayer, meditation, etc.). Spirituality also encompasses knowledge about the obstacles to a life in harmony with the Ultimate and how these obstacles can be removed.

The outline just given dovetails with Paul Tillich's formal conception of ultimate concern and faith: 'Faith is the state of being ultimately concerned. The content matters infinitely for the life of the believer; it does not however matter for the formal definition.'[2] Tillich's ultimate concern has both an anthropological and an ontological dimension. It includes a human attitude or a way of acting that takes one thing to be more important than all other things. On the other hand, it refers to the Ultimate as content that matters infinitely for the particular human life concerned with it. The formality of the term allows it to function as a category of comparison with respect to very different world-views and religions. Thus can Buddhism and Christianity, for example, be compared with respect to their understandings of Ultimate Reality.[3]

I would argue that an engagement with an ultimate concern belongs essentially to the human condition. To relate one's life to an Ultimate Reality, in the sense of viewing one thing as more important than all other things, does not necessarily entail membership in a religion or even seeing oneself as

---

1 Cf. S.M. Schneiders, 1998, 'The Study of Christian Spirituality: Contours and Dynamics of a Discipline', in *Studies in Spirituality* 8, pp. 38–57 (39f.).

2 P. Tillich, 1988, *Main Works*, vol. 5, ed. C.H. Ratschow, Berlin and New York: De Gruyter, p. 233.

3 When comparing Christianity with Islam or perhaps Vishnuism there is no necessity to introduce the category of Ultimate Reality. It is sufficient to ask how their concepts of God are interrelated. However, as Buddhism and also Taoism and secular world-views don't refer to God as Ultimate Reality, the more comprehensive category has to be used as *tertium comparationis*.

religious.[4] One may well perceive personal or social well-being, or justice for all, or the classless society or a heroic attitude in the face of universal meaninglessness, etc. as something worth living and dying for. But I would not yet call this a religious concern. It would be more precise to speak of a 'most important reality' than to call these broadly conceived horizons of meaningful life 'Ultimate Reality'. The 'most important' concern is religious (at least in the sense of the great world religions) only if it relates to a reality that is more than just a part of the world in which we are living (even though it be the most important part); it must come before us as a numinous presence that transcends everything in the world and the finite world itself.

Religions are cultural systems for dealing with that kind of world-transcending Ultimate Reality. Those who have come to know an original founding figure, such as the Buddha or Jesus Christ in Buddhism and Christianity, are sustained by the spirituality of these founders and develop further the inherent richness of their experience of the Ultimate. The efforts to transmit the message of the founders to followers in the succeeding generations has given rise to traditions lived out by communities in some organized form with codified doctrines, lineages of transmission, social hierarchies, etc. This institutionalization does not mean that the religious traditions become uniform. Religions are not monotonous highways but, as Hans Küng once said, they resemble complex and ever-changing systems of streams and rivers.

Turning now to the understanding of Ultimate Reality in Christianity and in Buddhism, it therefore should be clear that something like *the* Christian or *the* Buddhist view does not exist. Every religious tradition is internally diverse. In the case

---

4 In this respect I don't agree with W.A. Christian, 1964, *Meaning and Truth in Religion*, Princeton: Princeton University Press, p. 60, who seems to identify the relation to something more important than anything else with being religious. As Tillich speaks of 'faith' and 'believers' and being 'infinitely' concerned, it is quite clear that he refers to religious concepts of Ultimate Reality and also does not differentiate them from non-religious ones.

at hand both religions have a complex history spanning 2,000 or 2,400 years respectively. During this great expanse of time each of these religions, in the effort to understand itself and its experiences of Ultimate Reality, has developed in many and varied ways. The diversity of historical paradigms within the two religions manifests itself in a plurality of schools, orders and churches, which often disagree among themselves as to doctrines and spiritual practices. Therefore to speak of one single concept of Ultimate Reality in Buddhism or Christianity is already a simplification, though of course the different streams of understanding are interconnected and do have a common source. Needless to say, I can present here only some introductory remarks aimed at giving a first impression of a very complex field.

My description of Ultimate Reality in Christianity follows a major strand of Christian theology, one that has been influenced by Neo-Platonic negative theology. At the same time it emphasizes the non-duality between Ultimate Reality and non-ultimate reality, and also the motive of kenotic self-giving. A similar tradition strand can be found in other religions. Especially for many theologians involved in the Buddhist-Christian dialogue, including myself, it functions as a hermeneutical key to the understanding of Buddhism. Buddhism on the other hand helps us to improve our understanding of this kind of Christian thinking. So not only my understanding of Buddhism but also my view of the Christian Ultimate Reality is already to some extent a product of inter-religious dialogue. By means of transformative encounter Buddhism and Christianity cease to be independent bodies of thought. Of course I do not want to deny the existence of other legitimate traditions of Christian thought in which both negative theology and the idea of *kenosis* play a minor role, and the relation between Ultimate and non-Ultimate Reality is conceived in a more dualistic manner.

The Non-Other Beyond Being and Non-Being: A Christian Deconstruction of Ultimate Reality

There is a very simple answer to the question about Ultimate Reality in Christianity: The Ultimate Reality is God. But who is the Christian God? If we look closer we will find that the answer to this question as well as to the first one is not as simple as it might seem. I would like to begin my reflections on the Christian God by quoting a dialogue written by Nicholas Cusanus in 1444. The name of the dialogue is *De Deo abscondito*, 'On the Hidden God'.[5] As we all have certain images and prejudices in our heads concerning the Christian God it may be useful to start with a text that tries to deconstruct some of them.

Cusanus starts his dialogue by letting a pagan observe a worshipping Christian who prostrates and sheds tears of love.[6] The pagan, who does not represent one specific non-Christian

---

5 The term *deus absconditus* refers to Isa. 45.15 which in the Vulgate, the most common Latin version of the Bible, is translated as: '*Vere tu es Deus absconditus, Deus Israel salvator*', 'Truly you are a God who conceals himself, God of Israel, Saviour!'

6 I quote according to the translation of J. Hopkins, 1994, *A Miscellany of Cusa*, Minneapolis: Arthur J. Banning Press, pp. 300–05. The model for teaching the hidden God to a pagan is Paul's speech on the Areopagus, Acts 17.18ff., in which Paul proclaims the 'unknown God' to the Athenians. Paul's proclamation is connected with a critique of idols based on the Old Testament's prohibition of images of God, probably the most important biblical source of negative theology. In the beginning of *De quaerendo Deo* (1445) Cusanus explicitly refers to Acts 17.18ff. He confesses to admiring the way in which Paul explained the unknown God to the Greek philosophers by revealing to them that this God as the only true God is beyond every human imagination and insight. The philosophical and theological tradition regarding the 'unkown God' before and after Cusanus is treated by D. Carabine, 1995, *The Unknown God: Negative Theology in the Platonic Tradition. Plato to Eriugena*, Leuven: Peeters; I.N. Bulhof and L.K. Kate (eds), 2001, *Flight of the Gods: Philosophical Perspectives on Negative Theology*, New York: Fordham University Press; R. Stolina, 2000, *Niemand hat Gott je gesehen: Traktat über negative Theologie*, Berlin and New York: De Gruyter; O. Davies and D. Turner (eds), 2002, *Silence and the Word: Negative Theology and Incarnation*, Cambridge: Cambridge University Press.

view but rather any kind of superficial religiosity that wants to make a knowable thing out of Ultimate Reality, asks the Christian:

'Who is the God whom you worship?'

The Christian answers, 'I don't know.'

'How is it, that you worship so seriously that of which you have no knowledge?'

'Because I have no knowledge, I worship.'

'I marvel that a man is devoted to that of which he has no knowledge.'

Again the Christian: 'It is more amazing that a man is devoted to that of which he thinks he has knowledge.'[7]

Later in this dialogue the Christian admits a kind of Socratic knowledge about the Ultimate Reality he worships. 'I know that whatever-I-know is not God and that what-ever-I-conceive is not like God . . .'

'So is God nothing?'

Cusanus – through the Christian – answers: 'It is not the case that He is nothing, for this nothing has the name "nothing".'

The pagan: 'If He is not nothing, then He is something.'

'He is not something, either. For something is not every-thing. And it is not the case that God is something rather than everything.'

The pagan replies: 'You make strange claims: that God whom you worship is neither nothing nor something. No reasoning grasps this point. . . . Can He be named?'

'. . . That, whose greatness cannot be conceived remains ineffable.'

'But is He ineffable?'

---

7 This, at first glance astonishing, statement is a conclusion of the common Christian thought that God, who *per se* is beyond human comprehension, is the only one worthy of being worshipped. A similar approach can be found in Meister Eckhart, e.g. Sermon 42. The source of Eckhart and Cusanus is Augustinus, *Sermo* CXVII c.3 n.5, PL 38, 663: '*Si comprehendis, non est deus*', 'If you know it, it is not God.'

'He is not ineffable, though He is beyond all things effable; for He is the cause of all nameable things. . . .'

The pagan: 'So He is both ineffable and effable?'

'Not *that* either. For God is not the foundation of contradiction, but is Simplicity . . .'

'What then do you want to say about Him?'

'That it is neither the case that He is named nor is not named, nor the case that He both is named and is not named . . . Rather, whatever can be said . . . does not befit Him . . ., so that He is the one Beginning, which is prior to every thought formable of it.'

One could call this a deconstruction of the Christian Ultimate Reality – a deconstruction that intends at the same time to be an integral part of Christian theology. The dialogue neither affirms a concept of Ultimate Reality, nor tries to improve it, nor simply negates it. Cusanus demonstrates a kind of religious thinking that transcends the process of conceptualization by using advanced conceptual thinking. It starts from a certain pre-understanding of what it means to have a God whom you worship and shows that many of the meanings usually connected with this idea do not fit. But it is not the final aim of this procedure to redefine the concept of Ultimate Reality nor does Cusanus want to prove that the concept as it is is totally without sense. Rather, he is trying to make it transparent for a reality that exceeds all possible conceptualization by refuting all logical possibilities concerning antithetic attributes such as being/non-being, effable/ineffable, in relation to God.

The attempt to speak about Ultimate Reality in the religious sense of the word soon leads to the question of how it is possible to speak about it at all, and this, not only in Christian theology but also in other traditions, results in different ways of deconstruction. According to Cusanus, when we start to speak about God we are already 'wrong'. But not to speak about him also misses the point because he is not simply ineffable and unknowable. The tension between the necessity to speak of God because he reveals himself in manifold ways as Ultimate Reality and thus concerns us in an ultimate way, and not being able to speak of him because he infinitely exceeds the possibilities of human language and knowledge, is not something to be overcome but to be lived.[8] It is similar to a Zen koan, which one should not solve in a merely theoretical way but by existentially manifesting the ultimate truth; in other words, not by merely speaking or being silent *about* it, but speaking or being silent *out of* it.[9]

The revealed hiddenness or mysterious revelation that characterizes the Christian God is important for inter-religious dialogue. There is a huge difference between what is said about Ultimate Reality in Christianity and the Ultimate Reality in itself, and this difference has its place within Christianity itself. This means that there is a principle within Christianity that transcends Christianity and at the same time enables an opening towards the messages of other religions.[10]

We can also learn from Cusanus that God is not an additional thing among other things. Of course he is not the famous old man with the beard, but neither is he the invisible infinite supreme entity of theological and philosophical imagination. He is not a part of reality as an infinite among finite beings. There is no such thing as a 'God'. If we speak about Ultimate Reality we always tend to reify it and misunderstand it as one

---

8 Cf. J.M. Byrne, 2001, *God: Thoughts in an Age of Uncertainty*, London and New York: Continuum, p. 60. Traditionally this problem is discussed as the question of how 'negative' and 'positive' theology are related to one another. Cataphatic theology, *via positiva*, the 'positive path', means conceiving God by using affirmative statements like 'God is love', 'God is almighty', etc. Apophatic or negative theology, *via negativa*, the 'negative path', is the way to experience and understand God through negation of everything we know and think of him and thus finally entering silence in the presence of the Ultimate.

9 The differentiation and possible unity between speaking about and speaking out of God is elaborated by W. Schmithals, 1967, *Die Theologie Rudolf Bultmanns*, 2nd edn, Tübingen: Mohr Siebeck, pp. 23–50, especially p. 43.

10 Cusanus already took this step in his first sermon (1430), which can be found among the earliest of his surviving texts. There he first emphasizes the ineffability and hiddenness of God's name and then turns to the various names of God in the different languages of humankind finding truth in each of them.

reality among a totality of beings (albeit the last and greatest of them). Cusanus deconstructs this view by saying that God is beyond being something and being nothing. He functions as the absolute source of all nameable things and the one beginning of everything which is prior to every thought. The origin is not of the same kind as the originated things.[11] It is rather a borderless vastness that permeates and embraces everything. Of course the process of deconstruction can pick up again where the quoted dialogue ends, and can deconstruct the expressions 'origin', 'beginning, 'oneness', etc. In *De principio* Cusanus says the ineffable beginning is not called beginning, nor the One, nor by any other name. In a late dialogue he calls God *non Aliud*, the non-Other.[12] He calls him so because God is absolutely different from everything else through his non-difference.[13] As non-different, God is not somewhere else but here-hereafter. He approaches us as the transcendent depth of things, the infinite in the finite, which is transcendent as well as immanent – or, to be more precise, he approaches us as an event beyond the dualism of immanence and transcendence.[14] This general understanding

---

11 To talk about Ultimate Reality as something that is more important than anything else is also misleading, because it suggests that Ultimate reality forms the upper end of a scale that starts with things of no importance. According to Cusanus you cannot find the Ultimate on a scale, because it rather is the origin of every scale, within which the absolute minimum and the absolute maximum meet and are transcended.

12 Nicholas Cusanus, *De non aliud* (1462). The Latin text and English translation in J. Hopkins, 1987, *Nicholas of Cusa, On God as Not-Other: A Translation and an Appraisal of De li non aliud*, Minneapolis: Banning Press.

13 With this thought Cusanus refers to Eckhart's commentary to the Book of Wisdom, where Eckhart says that God is the undistinguished which is distinguished from everything else by its undistinguishedness. (*Deus indistinctum quoddam est quod sua indistinctione distinguitur*), *Expositio libri Sapientiae* n. 154, LW II, 490, pp. 7f. Cf. W. Beierwaltes, 1980, *Identität und Differenz*, Frankfurt: Vittorio Klostermann, pp. 97–104, pp. 105–43.

14 See R. Faber, 2001, '"Gottesmeer" – Versuch über die Ununterschiedenheit Gottes', in Th. Dienberg and M. Plattig (eds), *'Leben in Fülle': Skizzen zur christlichen Spiritualität. FS für Prof. Weismayer zu seinem 65. Geburtstag*, Münster: Lit Verlag, pp. 64–95.

of God provides, I think, the basis for everything else that can be
said about the Christian God.

Self-Communication of the Non-Other as Key to the Concept of Trinity

The Christian understanding of Ultimate Reality is further speci-
fied by the doctrine that the one origin of everything has revealed
itself as triune God. To explain the trinitarian understanding of
God, I introduce the concept of God's self-communication and
interpret the so-called persons of the Trinity as modes of his self-
communication. The notion of self-communication is not only
a key concept in the theology of Karl Rahner, one of the most
influential Catholic theologians of the twentieth century who
indeed introduced this idea into modern theology. It is also a
key concept for the understanding of Christian faith as a whole,
allowing us to see how the different parts of Christian doctrine,
such as the teachings regarding creation, Trinity, Christology,
soteriology and so forth, are interconnected.

The term is taken from the field of interpersonal relationships.
In the Judaeo-Christian tradition personal language is considered to be the least misleading way of referring to God and to
God's relation to creation and especially to human beings. The
loving relationships between persons (parents and children,
friends, lovers, etc.) are the deepest, most intimate and demanding relations that we are able to experience in this world, so if
anything they should be appropriate as a model for the relation between the Ultimate and us. If two persons communicate
with each other they do more than merely exchange information about other things. They always also communicate themselves. In talking to each other and living with each other, they
reveal their own being and become present for each other. To
communicate oneself means to let someone participate in one's
own life, sharing one's own world with the other. Personal self-
communication is an act of self-giving. You empty your mind of
selfish interests and allow others to participate in your being by
giving them the time and space they need to unfold their own

true being. This giving and receiving of life in human relationships is always based on a form of love that creates and sustains the openness and unity between those who are involved in self-communication.

As I said, interpersonal self-communication is the predominant paradigm for understanding the relation between the world and its divine source in Christianity. It qualifies the way in which God the Non-Other is relating to the world of otherness. In creation God does not just fabricate something outside of himself, but aims at communicating himself. By continuously letting the world emerge out of nothing, He opens up the possibility not only for all created things to be, but also for communion with himself. He reveals himself at the core of every originated being and lets the originated world participate in his divine life. This is an act of selfless love, because there is no necessity for God to share his *plērōma*, his abundance with anything or anyone. The different levels of creation are characterized by the increasing self-communication of God which comes to its fulfilment in the relation between God and the human being.

To see creation as a process of self-communication of the divine has its roots in the Jewish tradition, and Jesus Christ inspired a creative transformation of these roots. The encounter with him led the early Christians to the conviction that in the life and death of Jesus and also in his mysterious presence after death, God was revealing himself in an extraordinarily intense way: Jesus lived in such a radical openness towards Him whom he called his Father that he came to be viewed not simply as similar to God but 'of the same kind' – 'God from God'. Seen in the light of this new experience, self-communication means that God is not only present in various ways in his creation by letting everything be, but he even becomes a part of it. A new form of non-duality between God and his creation has been revealed. If Jesus in a way was God, were there now two Gods? This did not make sense to the early Christians, because they experienced not a second God, but the one and only God whom they as Jews had already worshipped, but now in a new way as human being. So instead of the assumption of two Gods a radical reconsideration of the nature of God took place. The self-communication of God in Jesus threw new light on the understanding of Ultimate Reality in and as a process of communication. 'A purely unitarian conception of God proved inadequate to contain this dynamic understanding of God.'[15] Inspired by thoughts of Neo-Platonic philosophers, who had already conceived the one origin of everything as internally differentiated, early Christian theology interpreted God as manifold unity, a unity which manifests its inner plurality in the process of self-communication, and especially in Jesus Christ. The doctrine of the triune God says that the one God exists as Father, Son and Holy Spirit.

God the Father is Ultimate Reality as primordial source, the transcendent creative ground of all being, *principium sine principio*, origin without origin. The talk of the triune God does not reflect a language of observation but of participation in an event of relationships in God.

> To refer to God as 'Father' thus does not mean to represent or objectify God as a father-figure, but to address God as Father, and so enter into the movement of a child-father relationship . . . At the same time, we find ourselves involved in a movement of self-giving like that of a Father sending forth a Son.[16]

God the Son (also *logos*, Word, cosmic Christ) means God as the one who reveals himself. 'In one word God spoke himself and everything.'[17] The term 'Word' again implies communication and communion. As a person reveals her or his character and intention through the words she or he is saying, God as the Word is the God who speaks to us in everything and thereby manifests himself. The Word is the self-opening of the Father within his creation. For Christians the aim of God's creation –

---

15 A.E. McGrath, 2003, *Christian Theology: An Introduction*, 3rd edn, Oxford: Blackwell, p. 321.

16 P.S. Fiddes, 2002, 'The Quest for a Place Which Is "Not-a-Place": The Hiddenness of God and the Presence of God', in O. Davies and D. Turner (eds), *Silence and the Word: Negative Theology and Incarnation*, Cambridge: Cambridge University Press, p. 53.

17 Anselm of Canterbury, *Monologion* 33.

the perfect non-duality between creation and creator – manifests itself in Jesus Christ. He is therefore called the Word of God made Flesh.[18]

God the Spirit is the life of God in which the created world participates. Already the Hebrew Bible uses the phrase 'spirit (*rûach*, 'breath') of God' as a name for the life-giving presence of Ultimate Reality. The Spirit is the unitive power that is renewing the world by uniting it with the Father. Most of all the renewing presence of God is a personal experience. Through God's self-communication he becomes present in our hearts and thereby unites us with himself.[19] And, as Basil of Caesarea says, human beings are able to share this divine presence with each other: 'Souls in which the Spirit dwells, illuminated by the Spirit, themselves become spiritual and send forth their grace to others.'[20]

The unity between God the Father and Jesus Christ as incarnated Son is interpreted as a unity without fusion, but also without separation. The one is in the other, as the Gospel of John lets Jesus say: 'I am in the Father and the Father is in me.'[21] This can also be said for the Spirit in respect to the Father and the Son and vice versa. The relation of the three is that of a *perichorēsis*, mutual indwelling. Each is room for the others.

Christians believe that the triune God is known throughout creation and through the history of salvation, especially in the redeeming encounter with Jesus Christ. Father, Son and Spirit are the modes of self-communication of God, but they not only determine his relation to the created world but also differentiate his interior structure. The God who appears as a Trinity in the history of human encounter with him is also a Trinity within himself.[22]

---

18 John 1.14.
19 See Ps. 51.11; Ps. 139.7.
20 Quoted in McGrath, *Christian Theology*, p. 311.
21 John 14.11.
22 For this axiom of identity between the so-called immanent and economic Trinity and the doctrine of Trinity in general see K. Rahner, 1970, *The Trinity*, London: Burnes & Oates.

Christian Ultimate Reality as Process of Interactive Self-Emptying

With this point I only sum up what I have been saying already. Again I refer to the idea of the self-communication of Ultimate Reality, now in a slightly different perspective.

A static, substantialist view places Ultimate Reality on one side and non-Ultimate reality on the other. Somewhere in between, mediators like Jesus Christ function as a bridge between the two realities. It is one of the major aims of this paper to show that this image does not correspond to a more developed Christian (or Buddhist) understanding of Ultimate Reality. In the Christian view God's Ultimate Reality does not stay within itself, as perhaps Aristotle's unmoving mover does. One could say perhaps that Ultimate Reality is distributing itself (*bonum est diffusivum sui*: 'the good naturally diffuses itself', said the Platonists) among several actors, who give it, receive it and pass it on to one other in a kenotic ('self-emptying') process.[23] Thus the original meaning of self-communication in a Christian context could be qualified as a circle of selfless self-communication. Self-emptying happens already within the triune God through the mutual indwelling of Father, Son and Spirit. Furthermore God is emptying, and in a way 'de-ultimating', himself, by giving room to creation as the place of his self-communication, finally becoming a human being (Jesus Christ as Ultimate Reality). Jesus, however, did not, as the Philippian hymn says, 'count equality with God something to be grasped', but emptied himself and shared his divine life with outcasts and sinners.[24] He finally demonstrated his humility and love when he did not flee from or resist his enemies and died on

---

23 For an outline of kenotic theology see J. Moltmann, 2001, 'God's Kenosis in the Creation and Consummation of the World', in J. Polkinghorne (ed.), *The Work of Love: Creation as Kenosis*, Michigan and Cambridge: Eerdmans, pp. 137–51; R.R. Brouwer, 2002, 'Kenosis in Philippians 2:5–11 and in the History of Christian Doctrine', in Onno Zijlstra (ed.), *Letting Go: Rethinking Kenosis*, Bern and Berlin: Peter Lang, pp. 69–108.

24 Phil. 2.6–8.

the cross. The disastrous consequences of basic distrust (sin), and their overcoming through defenceless love, were thereby forever inscribed into the flesh of the Ultimate (the Cross as Ultimate Reality). Jesus as the incarnation of God's kenotic, self-emptying love is no isolated or singular peak in the history of the encounter between God and humankind; rather, he passes on his union with the Father to all who are willing to receive it. 'God became a human being that humans may become God' was the formula of the church fathers for this, and in the Gospel of John it is said that to those who did accept Jesus as the divine Word 'he gave power to become children of God'.[25] So Ultimate Reality extends further to all who open themselves through the Son to the Father (the 'birth of God' as Ultimate Reality within everyone). Being blessed with the divine union they thankfully reaffirm the Father as Ultimate Reality mediated by the Son and testify to God's love by establishing loving relationships with their fellow beings. Thereby they anticipate and initially realize the 'Kingdom of God', the final consummation of the world and humankind, where God will be all in all (Ultimate Reality as the ultimate future of self-communication). Thus Ultimate Reality is on the move. It circulates between the Father, Son and Spirit, creation, sinners and believers. I suggest that this self-emptying flow of life within a cosmic play is what should be called the Christian Ultimate Reality and not 'just' God alone.

Difficulties Concerning a Christian Interpretation of Buddhist Ultimate Reality

As Lambert Schmithausen and others have shown, Buddhist theory should primarily be understood as an interpretation of Buddhist spiritual practice and the experiences which are made along this path.[26] For Buddha the priority was to understand

---

25 John 1.12.

26 Cf. L. Schmithausen, 1973, 'Spirituelle Praxis und philosophische Theorie im Buddhismus', in *Zeitschrift für Missionswissenschaft und Religionswissenschaft* 57, pp. 161–86.

what makes people suffer and to find the skilful means (*upāya*) of liberation from that suffering. Of course this enterprise has also led Buddhist thinkers to cosmological and metaphysical reflection, not least because they had to explain their religion to other schools of thought in India and elsewhere. But Buddhist theory always focused mainly on interpreting Buddhist forms of life and meditative experience, trying to defend them as practices that correspond to the nature of reality.

Buddha and his followers described the Buddhist path to salvation without speaking of God. Of course Buddha knew of the gods that were worshipped in the Indian civilization at the time, and he explicitly confirmed their existence. But they carry no ultimate meaning for the liberation of human beings. Moreover the gods are finite beings too, who long for liberation and have to be reborn as humans to gain freedom from suffering.

One can find theistic tendencies or variations within Buddhism that might, to a Christian theologian, seem closer to the Christian understanding of Ultimate Reality than do others; for example, the Lotus Sūtra's theology of an eternal Buddha, which became important in Japanese Nichiren Buddhism, or the faith in the boundless compassion of Amida Buddha, or the concept of an Ādi Buddha ('Original Buddha') that is developed in some Tantras (for instance, the *Kālacakra Tantra*, which is probably influenced by theistic religions). However, I will not be going into that for now.

In any event, Buddhism in general has no concept of God comparable to the Christian God as an almighty creator who redeems and consummates his creation through his love. The absence of a concept of God has caused any number of problems for Christian interpreters of Buddhism, from the sixteenth-century Jesuits in China, then especially from the nineteenth century onwards until the present day. For those who followed the method of a direct comparison between Buddhism and Christianity the lack of the concept of God was considered to be as important in Buddhism as the existence of such a concept is in Christianity. If you see things that way then Buddhism looks like an atheistic world-view. But, as Perry Schmidt-Leukel has pointed out, this is a misunderstanding of the type that arises when one takes the comparative category from one's own tradition, presuming that what is determinative in one's own faith must be of equal importance in the other.[27] To illustrate the hermeneutical problem concerning the absence of God-talk in Buddhism, let us imagine that your car is the only vehicle you know. If you then see an aeroplane for the first time, you might think that it must necessarily be a vehicle of inferior quality compared with your car, because it has only very small and comparative weak wheels.

Indeed influential philosophers and theologians misunderstood Buddhism as a form of nihilistic atheism. If there is an Ultimate Reality in Buddhism then according to this interpretation it is the ultimate negation of life as painful. Buddhist spirituality was considered to be pessimistic and weary of life. And Buddhist meditation was thought of as a kind of slow suicide.[28]

Nowadays no serious scholar would uphold these views. Many studies have made it clear that Buddhism is a real religion that recognizes an Ultimate Reality in the religious sense of the word explained above.[29] To present my understanding of Ultimate Reality in Buddhism I will first consider two terms used to designate it in early Buddhism. Afterwards I will turn to a Mahāyāna view of Ultimate Reality, especially as presented in Nāgārjuna's *Mūlamadhyamakakārikā*.

27 See P. Schmidt-Leukel, 1993, 'Christliche Buddhismus-Interpretation und die Gottesfrage', in *Münchener Theologische Zeitschrift* 44, pp. 349–58.

28 For the history of Christian reception of Buddhism see P. Schmidt-Leukel, 1992, '*Den Löwen brüllen hören': Zur Hermeneutik eines christlichen Verständnisses der buddhistischen Heilsbotschaft*, Paderborn: Schöningh; W. Lai and M. von Brück, 2001, *Christianity and Buddhism: A Multi-Cultural History of Their Dialogue*, Maryknoll: Orbis.

29 See E. Steinkellner, 2000, 'Buddhismus: Religion oder Philosophie? Und: Vom Wesen des Buddha', in A. Bsteh (ed.), *Der Buddhismus als Anfrage an christliche Theologie und Philosophie*, Mödling: Verlag St. Gabriel, pp. 251–62.

Ultimate Reality in Early Buddhism: *amṛta* and *nirvāṇa*

Let us look at the first section of Buddha's famous first sermon at Benares, a very early text, entitled 'Putting In Motion The Wheel Of Teaching'. Buddha arrives in the deer park close to Benares and encounters five ascetics who had formerly been his disciples. Buddha had left them because he had no longer found any sense in self-mortification, and consequently abandoned the ascetic vows. The ascetics rise and greet him: 'Be welcome, friend Gotama!' Buddha replies that they should not call him by his name nor address him as a friend anymore because he has gained complete awakening. Then he starts his sermon: 'Listen! The deathless is found (*amatam adhigatam*); I proclaim, I teach the Dharma!' After this solemn introduction he describes the Dharma ('liberating doctrine') as the 'middle path' of spiritual practice that avoids the two extremes of self-indulgence and self-mortification and leads to peace of mind, wisdom and full awakening.

In this text the term for the Buddhist Ultimate Reality is *amata* (Pāli) / *amṛta* (Sanskrit), usually translated as: 'immortality, the immortal, that without death or that without dying'.[30] In the context of the sermon the mention of the deathless has a performative, soteriological sense.[31] Buddha wants to motivate his listeners to adopt a certain form of practice that will liberate them from the painful clinging to transient things. Ultimate Reality is no mere theoretical question but becomes relevant for Buddhism primarily in the context of overcoming the ruinous interconnection of 'thirst' (desire), attachment, mortality and

---

30 Vedic myths know *amṛta* as nectar of the gods. The usage of the term in the old Buddhist sources is influenced by early upaniṣadic thought. For example, one of the prayers in *Bṛhadāraṇyaka Upaniṣad* (Br. Up. I.3.28) asks for the progress from untruth (*asat*) to truth (*sat*) or Ultimate Reality, from the darkness of ignorance (*avidyā*) to light of wisdom (*jyoti*) and from death (*mṛtyu*) to immortality (*amṛta*). Cf. S.G. Deodikar, 1992, *Upaniṣads and Early Buddhism*, Delhi: Eastern Book Linkers, p. 122, p. 131.

31 'Soteriological' is a term from Christian theology, which nowadays is also used in scholarly works on other religions. It means 'salvation-related'. 'Soteriology' is the part of theology or Buddhist theory dealing with the doctrine of salvation/liberation.

suffering. Here we have a similarity with the Judaeo-Christian tradition, for the idea of God was not developed as a theoretical hypothesis concerning the origins of the world either. Rather, the talk of a Divine Creator emerged from experiences of liberating encounters with an Ultimate Reality and thus from a soteriological context. The faith in creation developed out of the experience of a present salutary relationship between God and man in which God emerged as a reliable source of freedom, peace and justice.

As Tilmann Vetter has shown, the term *amata* means more than simply the cessation of future dying in the sense of not being reborn again.[32] In the sermon of Benares Buddha says that on his 'middle path' one is able to reach *amata* already in this life. It is something that can be directly perceived and experienced here and now. Very likely it was a mystical experience of eternity that gave Buddha ultimate release from all that makes a transient being suffer. In proper meditation a reality enters the field of awareness that is beyond death and therefore the fear of death vanishes. In a very typical way Buddha does not further describe this kind of Ultimate Reality beyond the world of finitude. The rest of the sermon deals with the kind of ethical and contemplative practice that leads to the experience of *amata*.

Like *amata* the much more popular *nibbāna* (Pāli)/*nirvāṇa* (Sanskrit) is a word for Ultimate Reality in early Buddhist thought as well as in later times.[33] In older passages of the Pāli Canon it is sometimes a metaphor for *dukkhanirodha* ('cessation of suffering'), the 'third noble truth'. 'When it was first used, it seems to have been more a figure of speech than a concept;

---

32 T. Vetter, 1988, *The Ideas and Meditative Practices of Early Buddhism*, Leiden: Brill, p. xxix n. 10, p. xxxi, pp. 8f. See also T. Vetter, 1995, 'Bei Lebzeiten das Todlose erreichen: Zum Begriff AMATA im alten Buddhismus', in G. Oberhammer (ed.), *Im Tod gewinnt der Mensch sein Selbst*, Vienna: Verlag der Österreichischen Akademie der Wissenschaften, pp. 211–23.

33 The history of Western interpretations of *nirvāṇa* is investigated by G.R. Welbon, 1968, *The Buddhist Nirvāṇa and its Western Interpreters*, Chicago: University of Chicago Press.

a definition of the term is scarcely to be found. As a figure of speech it conveys the meaning that as craving or a wrong attitude ceases, it is like a fire which has been extinguished.'[34] Indeed, a literal translation of *nir-vāṇa* is 'blown out', as in the extinguishing of a fire. The fire that is blown out when *nirvāṇa* happens is the fire of desire, and also of hate and confusion – the basic vices that bind sentient beings in *saṃsāra*, the succession of death and rebirth, until liberation is attained. The counterpart of *nirvāṇa* as an experience of Ultimate reality is *saṃsāra*. As the sphere of non-Ultimate Reality it is understood in terms of transitoriness, mortality and suffering, whereas Ultimate Reality is primarily understood as deathless. The common existential horizon within which both *saṃsāra* and *nirvāṇa* are understood is that of mortality. In early Buddhism *saṃsāra* and *nirvāṇa* seem to be more or less opposed to each other. Where one begins, the other ends. Final attainment of the Ultimate Reality entails abandonment of the conditioned world.

In Buddha's first sermon *nirvāṇa* is mentioned in one line with a list of synonyms such as the withdrawal from earthly things, the ending of the finite, peace, insight, awakening. The experience of *nirvāṇa* is one of ultimate release. The term is used to describe the peaceful state of the human mind, but there are also passages in early Buddhist texts that relate this inner peace to a transcendent reality, such as the following, famous one: 'There is, monks, something unborn, unbecome, unmade, uncreated. If, monks, this unborn, unbecome, unmade, uncreated would not be there, then there would be no escape for what is born, has become, is made, and formed.'[35]

It is very clear from this text that early Buddhism is not interested in the simple extinction of an always painful and dissatisfying life but searches for eternity, immortality. A Christian could use the same words to speak about God as source of ultimate freedom and bliss, salvation and eternal life. They also are very similar to expressions employed in the Upaniṣads for *Brahman* as Ultimate Reality.

---

34 Vetter, *Ideas and Meditative Practices*, p. 15.
35 *Udāna* 8.3.

The text just quoted is very important because it demonstrates that early Buddhism is a religion of liberation and not just a psychology. I believe it is important to underline this, because nowadays especially in the Western world you can find Buddhists who misinterpret their path as 'a psychological technique with no metaphysical implications', as John Hick once put it.[36] Especially meditation, as the core practice of Buddhist spirituality, is often misunderstood as simply producing a state of consciousness in which wishes and anxieties created by the ego disappear and are replaced by a feeling of serenity. *Nirvāṇa* understood in that way is a mere psychological state of mind, and not an experience of Ultimate Reality that transcends the experiencing subject in a certain way. Such a secularized view is sometimes promoted as a modern, humanistic alternative to what is thought of as the concept of the Christian God. But I'm afraid that it only produces a superficial version of Buddhism as a kind of tranquillizer, which does not correspond to the real depth of this religion. The often very tacit way in which many Buddhist scriptures and teachers refer to an Ultimate Reality makes such a misunderstanding possible. On the other side the silence of the Buddha and his followers has the advantage of avoiding the danger of reifying Ultimate Reality.

Nirvāṇa as *śūnya*: Nāgārjuna's Deconstruction of Ultimate Reality

In spite of this discretion the question of how to understand *nirvāṇa* and its relation to the conditioned world of everyday experience nevertheless continued to fascinate Buddhist thinkers and was further elaborated in Mahāyāna Buddhism. Mahāyāna (the 'Great Vehicle'), as a new paradigm of Buddhism, gradually developed from the first century BCE onwards. Compared with early Buddhism Mahāyāna speaks about Ultimate Reality

---

36 Cf. J. Hick, 1991, 'Religion as "Skilful Means": A Hint from Buddhism', in *International Journal for Philosophy of Religion* 30, pp. 141–58 (148).

in a more explicit way although the incomprehensibility of the Ultimate is still emphasized. New names for it appear: *dharmadhātu* (the '*dharma* realm'), *tathatā* ('suchness') or *bhūtakoṭi* (the 'peak of reality').[37] It was a South Indian Mahāyānist philosopher who drew radical consequences from Buddha's silence as to the ontological status of the Ultimate, as well as from his refusal to describe a liberated person or even reality in general in terms of being or not-being. Nāgārjuna, who lived in the second century CE, was the most important thinker of early Mahāyāna Buddhism. From his teaching emerged the Mādhyamika School, which, along with the Yogācāra School, dominated Mahāyāna thought in India. Nāgārjuna's major work is the *Mūlamadhyamakakārikā* ('Verses on the Basic Teachings of the Middle Path', abbreviated as MMK). For our topic this book is of particular interest; in it, Nāgārjuna develops a deep and still thought-provoking way to understand Ultimate Reality.

Nāgārjuna's new approach was, as already stated, based on older Buddhist teachings. Of central importance for his thought is a passage from the *Kaccāyana Sutta*:

'All exists': Kaccāna, this is one extreme. 'All does not exist': this is the second extreme. Without veering towards either of these extremes, the Tathāgata teaches the Dhamma by the middle . . .[38]

Nāgārjuna affirms:

Those who perceive self-existence and other-existence, and an existing thing and a non-existing thing, do not perceive the true nature of the Buddha's teaching. In 'The Instruction

---

37 See E. Frauwallner, 1956, *Die Philosophie des Buddhismus*, Berlin: Akademie Verlag, p. 148.

38 *Kaccāyana Sutta, Saṃyutta Nikāya* ii 17. Bhikkhu Bodhi (trans.), 2000, *The Connected Discourses of the Buddha*, Boston: Wisdom, p. 544.

of Kātyāyana' both 'it is' and 'it is not' are opposed by the Glorious One . . .[39]

In the *Kaccāyana Sutta* as well as in Nāgārjuna's thought the Middle Way between the opposites of being and not-being is shown by the *pratītyasamutpāda*, the chain of dependent-arising. Buddha developed different forms of this chain to explain the conditions that lead to the arising and perpetuation of suffering. In later Buddhist philosophy the term denotes a theory of the universal nexus and conditional dependency between all sorts of phenomena. The inner structure and meaning of dependent-arising is a major controversial topic in Buddhist philosophy, Nāgārjuna's contribution being one of the most important and radical in this debate.

Because of the mutual interdependent arising of everything he rejects the notion of *svabhāva*, 'self-existence' or 'inherent existence' in the sense of immutability and independence from other things, and replaces it with *śūnyatā* ('emptiness') as the fundamental category. He examines various philosophical key concepts such as causality, the elements, time, actor and action, truth and falsehood – all in the effort to show that contradictions arise if one understands these concepts as referring to self-existing entities.

For our topic it is crucial that in the twenty-fifth chapter of MMK he also treats *nirvāṇa* in the same way. *Nirvāṇa* is empty, he says. It is not a discrete entity with an inherent essence. Therefore categories of being and non-being, becoming and passing are inapplicable. *Nirvāṇa* is not existing, because if it were, it would be characterized by decay and death like everything else that exists. On the other hand it is also not simply non-existing. If *nirvāṇa* would be both existing and non-existing then liberation would exist and not exist at the same time. And finally he also rejects the position that *nirvāṇa* is neither existing nor not existing, for to say that something is neither existing nor not

---

39 MMK 15.6f. I quote MMK from the translation in F. Streng, 1967, *Emptiness: A Study in Religious Meaning*, Nashville: Abingdon.

existing already presupposes that there is inherent existence
and its contrary, non-existence. To take any of these views is
incompatible with the 'Middle Way', which leads to liberation. With this fourfold negation (*catuṣkoṭi*), which in the history of logic is known as Tetralemma, he excludes all possible
metaphysical views about the Buddhist Ultimate Reality. It is
interesting to note, that Cusanus also knows the Tetralemma
and uses it in the above-quoted dialogue and again, more explicitly, in *De principio* in order to eliminate all logical possibilities
of characterizing the origin in terms of being or non-being.[40]

Nāgārjuna also rejects an understanding of *nirvāṇa* as being
opposed to the world of *saṃsāra*. It should not be conceived as
a transcendent realm of the Absolute beyond the world. Instead
nirvāṇa is indistinguishable from *saṃsāra* and vice versa.
Nirvāṇa is not a place separate from the world, nor is it a higher
sphere which one enters when the attachment to the world
ceases. It is the blissful peace that happens when *prapañca*, the
world of multiplicity, construed by ontological distinctions like
eternity and non-eternity, *saṃsāra* and *nirvāṇa*, ultimate reality
and conditioned realities, ceases.

His deconstruction should not be misunderstood as agnosti-
cism or scepticism. His point is that *nirvāṇa* as Ultimate Reality is experienced only when it is not thought of as being the
contrary of *saṃsāra*. Discriminative thinking divides reality into
opposing alternatives and is therefore not able to conceive that
which transcends all relative distinctions. The inclination to discriminative thought is a form of attachment that has to be overcome to attain liberation. The practice of the fourfold negation
is meant to change our way of thinking. It aims at a release from
the attachment to and obsession with judgements concerning
being and non-being, being identical or being different, and so
on. Even the emptiness of all things should not be objectified into
an 'absolute being'. It would be a mistake to interpret it as the

40 See G. Benavides, 1984, 'Die absolute Voraussetzung von Sein und
Nichts bei Nāgārjuna und Nicolaus Cusanus', in W. Strolz (ed.), *Sein und
Nichts in der abendländischen Mystik*, Freiburg: Herder.

central idea of a certain world-view: 'Emptiness is proclaimed by the victorious one as the refutation of all viewpoints; but those who hold "emptiness" as a viewpoint – (the true perceivers) have called those "incurable".'[41] Similar to Wittgenstein's *Tractatus Logico-Philosophicus*, Nāgārjuna's philosophy is meant as a remedy that has to leave the body after it has driven the sickening substances out of the body.[42]

Bodhicitta as Response to the Emptiness of *nirvāna* and *samsāra*

From the absence of *svabhāva* (own-being) and from the identity of *samsāra* and *nirvāna* Mahāyāna Buddhism drew the ethical and soteriological consequences of non-distinguishing love and compassion towards all living beings, along with the *bodhisattva* ideal of remaining in *samsāra*. According to the Mahāyāna doctrine of 'non-abiding' or 'active nirvāna' (*apratisthita nirvāna*), full attainment of *nirvāna* does not mean to leave the conditioned world 'but to pervade it with one's nondual awareness and one's activity for beings'.[43] The decision to become a *bodhisattva* is called *bodhicitta* ('thought of enlightenment') and forms the basic spiritual attitude that corresponds to the Mahāyāna vision of Ultimate Reality. The *bodhisattva*

> can tirelessly work to aid 'suffering beings', sustained by the idea that *Nirvāna* is something already present in *samsāra*. As an advanced bodhisattva, he directly experiences the nonduality of *samsāra* and *Nirvāna*.[44]

---

41 MMK 13.8.

42 The image of the remedy is used in the *Ratnakūta*, an early Mahāyāna text. Cf. Schmidt-Leukel, '*Den Löwen brüllen hören*', p. 541. In *Tractatus Logico-Philosophicus* 6.54 Wittgenstein compares his philosophy with a ladder, which one should throw away, after having climbed it.

43 J. Makransky, 1997, *Buddhahood Embodied: Sources of Controversy in India and Tibet*, Albany: SUNY, p. 346.

44 P. Harvey, 1992, *An Introduction to Buddhism*, Cambridge: Cambridge University Press, p. 104.

From a Christian theological point of view one could perhaps
interpret this as meaning that the bodhisattva lives the non-
duality between a present- and future-oriented eschatology.[45]
Ultimate Reality as a goal of human existence is already fully
present and at the same time it always has this future aspect of
coming into the world of suffering and transforming it with the
help of human beings who practise a non-distinguishing love.

> Because dharmas have no own-being, there is nothing bound
> in *saṃsāra*, nothing freed in *nirvāṇa*, nothing is observed to
> arise, nothing observed to cease. There are no beings to save
> from *saṃsāra*, and yet the *bodhisattva* remains firm in his vow
> to save all beings.[46]

The *trikāya* Doctrine

Another important Māhāyana doctrine concerning Ultimate
Reality that should be mentioned before attempting some
conclusions about the relation between the Buddhist and the
Christian view of Ultimate Reality is the idea of *trikāya*, the threefold embodiment of the Buddha. *Trikāya* is usually translated as
'three bodies'. I follow the proposal of Makransky, who

> chose not to translate *kāya* [. . .] as 'body' since three *kāyas*
> would then connote three 'bodies' – which in ordinary English
> usage would refer to three distinct entities. Instead *kāya* is
> translated here as 'embodiment': three *kāyas* connoting three
> 'embodiments', referring to three functional expressions of
> one ontic reality; the purified dharma realm that all Buddhas
> realize.[47]

---

45 Eschatology is that part of Christian theology which deals with 'last
things', such as the final consummation of the world, resurrection, hell and
eternal life.
46 R.H. Robinson and W.L. Johnson, 1997, *The Buddhist Religion: A
Historical Introduction*, Belmont, CA: Wadsworth, p. 81.
47 Makransky, *Buddhahood Embodied*, p. 56.

According to this doctrine there are three embodiments of the realm of Ultimate Reality. The *dharmakāya* is the fullest, supramundane realization of Ultimate Reality in a non-dual, undivided awareness. It pervades the universe with its communicative and transformative powers. Buddhahood thus shares the enjoyment of the *dharmakāya* in heavenly worlds with its closest community of disciples, the great Bodhisattvas. This is called *saṃboghakāya*, the embodiment with respect to the sharing of the enjoyment of the *dharmakāya*. Through the *nirmāṇakāya* the embodiment of Ultimate Reality occurs in its widest possible scope of manifestation so as to teach vast numbers of beings, especially here on earth. I will come back to the *trikāya* doctrine in the conclusion of this paper, which now follows.

Concluding Reflections on the Relation Between the Christian and Buddhist Understanding of Ultimate Reality

I began my reflections on Ultimate Reality in Christianity with a Christian deconstruction by Nicholas Cusanus. The second part of this article highlighted a Buddhist deconstruction of Ultimate Reality as developed by Nāgārjuna. A comparison of the two thinkers reveals a number of points of agreement with respect to the basic approach to Ultimate Reality in two important strains of the Buddhist and Christian traditions: Mādhyamika and negative theology.

Both know the fourfold negation. Both employ it in the recognition that an existential approach to Ultimate Reality is only possible if we change our habits of thinking and open ourselves to a kind of non-positional awareness. In Christian negative theology as well as in Buddhist thought one finds the insight that it is necessary to leave behind a way of thinking that is affirming or negating, identifying or discriminating, if one wants to gain a knowledge of the Ultimate based on experience. Both understand the Ultimate as transcending the contraries of the conditioned world and the ordinary way of thinking corresponding to this world. Both Mahāyāna philosophy and the

Christian tradition of God as the 'non-Other' point to a non-duality between Ultimate Reality and the relative realities.

However, Cusanus and Nāgārjuna develop their insights against quite different backgrounds. Nāgārjuna starts with the *pratītyasamutpāda* understood as a theory of interdependent being that enables him to understand the impermanence of everything and how suffering arises out of the attachment to a transient reality. He criticizes positional thinking as not being able to describe a reality that is without self-existence. In the end he is applying the result of his investigation even to *pratītyasam-utpāda*, thus deconstructing even it. Finally he shows that *nirvā-ṇa* and *saṃsāra* are the same, and the peace of Ultimate Reality is attained if one perceives reality without positional thinking.

Cusanus on the other hand is reflecting on the absolute origin of everything and its relation to the originated world. He under-stands the origin as the presupposition of every being and non-being, the one beginning that is beyond being something or being nothing. This infinite ground is hidden and ineffable, but as the foundation of every reality that can be known and can be named, it is not just irrational and unknown but functions as the superrational source of all knowledge and language.

If you compare this approach with the Mādhyamika philosophy it is significant that Nāgārjuna does not think in terms of the origin and the originated, except when he discusses problems of innerwordly causality. Buddhism in general hardly understands Ultimate Reality as a creative ground of being. I don't know of any text suggesting that *nirvāṇa* creates *saṃsāra*, or that the world of forms derives from emptiness. Some texts of the Pāli Canon even explicitly reject the idea of a (anthropomorphic) creator God. If, however, creation is not conceived in a simplis-tic way as the fabrication of the world by a supreme Being but rather as a grounding of the conditioned in the unconditioned and undescribable non-Other, then perhaps the Buddhist and the Christian views are not so far away from each other as it seemed. There are structures at least in Mahāyāna thought that possibly allow an interpretation of the Buddhist Ultimate Real-ity as creative ground. As Robert Cummings Neville points out:

despite the identity alleged by Mahayana Buddhism in each case, emptiness and nirvana are both the more fundamental truths, and form and samsara by themselves are derivative and illusory without reference to emptiness and nirvana. I submit as an hypothesis for further investigation that Buddhists could reinterpret their classic expressions to say that the contingency of form on emptiness and samsara on nirvana is contingency upon a creative ground.[48]

Another difference lies in the significance of a language of interpersonal relationships for interpreting the relation between Ultimate Reality and the non-ultimate, especially human beings. Although philosophically oriented Christian theologians may also use an impersonal terminology in this context without hesitation, nevertheless the relationship is predominantly conceived as a personal tie. In Buddhism this way of experiencing the Ultimate does not come to the fore, except in some traditions like Amida Buddhism, which one could interpret as believing in Ultimate Reality as undifferentiated love and compassion. What one can find in Buddhism is an Ultimate Reality as an omnipresent redeeming realm transcending mortality and described at times as a kind of infinite essence of everything. This does not necessarily contradict a personalistic view but also does not stress it.

Modern Buddhist thinkers like Keiji Nishitani and Masao Abe, who are familiar with Christian theology, have shown that in both religions one can find a kenotic understanding of Ultimate Reality that results in similar spiritualities. According to Nishitani the Buddhist way of life as well as its way of thought are permeated with kenosis. He interprets the *trikāya* as kenotic process:

Buddha, being originally 'empty' and 'without form' takes the Form of the thus-come, whether as the simple Form of Buddha, as in *saṃbhogakāya*, or as the double Form of man-

---

48 R.C. Neville, 1991, 'Creation and Nothingness', in R.C. Neville, *Behind the Masks of God: An Essay Toward Comparative Theology*, Albany: State University of New York Press, pp. 100–01.

Buddha, and is revealed as such. Essentially this means an *ekkenôsis* ('making oneself empty') . . . The transition from being without Form to being in Form means non-ego and compassion, like a schoolmaster playing with children. In any case, throughout the basic thought of Buddhology, especially in Mahāyāna tradition, the concepts of emptiness, Compassion, and non-ego are to be inseparably connected.[49]

In both religions the effects of a life lived in view of Ultimate Reality are similar: the self-emptying of Ultimate Reality is answered by a spirituality of selflessness and compassion, undifferentiated love.[50] This, I think, is not the weakest sign supporting the view that both religions listen to a universal call for holiness, and thereby contain a deep knowledge of the same, indivisible Ultimate.

---

49 K. Nishitani, 1982, *Religion and Nothingness*, Berkeley: University of California Press, p. 288, n. 4. See also M. Abe, 1990, 'Kenotic God and Dynamic Sunyata', in J. Cobb and Ch. Ives (eds), *The Emptying God: A Buddhist-Jewish-Christian Conversation*, Maryknoll: Orbis, pp. 3–69; Ch. Ives, 1995, *Divine Emptiness and Historical Fullness: A Buddhist-Jewish-Christian Conversation with Masao Abe*, Valley Forge: Trinity Press International. Nishitani's interpretation of the *trikāya* is in a way christianized, or at least Christian-influenced. On the other side, inter-religious dialogue also leads to buddhized forms of Christian theology. As I already said in the beginning of this paper, both parts transform themselves through encounter.

50 For a comparison between a Christian *kenosis*-centred theology/spirituality and the philosophy/spirituality of emptiness in the Kyoto School see D.W. Mitchell, 1991, *Spirituality and Emptiness: The Dynamics of Spiritual Life in Buddhism and Christianity*, New York: Paulist Press.

7. Ultimate Reality in Buddhism and Christianity:

A Buddhist Perspective

MINORU NAMBARA

Awakening in India

What is the 'ultimate reality' in the Indian tradition? The Vedas (the word *Veda* means 'holy knowledge' and refers to the fundamental scriptures of the Aryan people who invaded the north-west Punjab around 1500 BCE) offered a distinct answer: It is *Ātman* and *Brahman*. *Ātman* is the nucleus of the self – its life, soul, essence and body. *Brahman*, meaning the mysterious power arising from Vedic knowledge, is the nucleus of the universe and the fount of all things. These two are difficult to distinguish; together they are the ultimate truth, the ultimate reality.

In an eternal return, the great bird flies from *Ātman* to *Brahman* and from *Brahman* to *Ātman* until it tires and falls into a sleep embraced by this *Ātman* and *Brahman*. It dreams. It awakens from the dream. Once again the bird rises up into the void and draws an arc between the two shores of sleeping and waking until, at last, it tires of this journey of flight and spirals down into a fathomless hole in which there are no dreams of any type and from which there is no waking. It enters profound sleep.

I cannot speak of the ultimate reality of Buddhism without referring to the profound dreamless sleep of which the Vedas sing, for it is out of this profound sleep that the Awakened One, the Buddha, has awakened. The nocturnal nadir of this profound sleep where neither *Ātman* nor *Brahman* exists any longer is the eternal high noon of him who has awakened. His eyes will never again shut and there will never again be awakening when his eyes open. This is the other side of sleep. The two sides form a front and back that share one surface and can never meet. The sun neither rises nor sets. Nowhere is a shadow cast. For him who has awakened it does not matter whether the world exists or does not exist, both *Brahman* and *Ātman* are no more.

To what has the Buddha awakened? Indo-Aryan culture was permeated with religious feeling. Not tied to tribal divisions, this deep religiosity also evidenced a high level of knowledge and developed detailed and elaborate rituals. Already in very ancient times, however, it had become difficult to maintain a balance between simple religious feeling and these complex rituals. Increasingly fine distinctions were artificially drawn among rituals. Further, this unfortunate process became wholly entangled in the rise of the priestly class. This development must be acknowledged as enormously important for the course of spiritual history. Rituals and the authority of the religious administration came to control the fate of the gods. The living gods then withdrew. It was at this stage – when the gods had departed – that the godless religion arrived, the one that Schopenhauer called a 'profoundly originative and sublime philosophy'.

What was most highly sought in Aryan culture for the soul was 'the sacred'. The quest suggested that incorporeal freedom was to be attained by spiritually breaking free from this world and from the body enslaved with chains. This effort towards spiritual freedom required exceptionally high levels of knowledge.

The enlightenment of Buddha under the Bodhi tree was a very intellectual type of meditation; in fact, in the earlier sutras the word 'enlightenment' is rarely used. One would do better to describe his act beneath the Bodhi tree as *contemplatio*. It was an opening of the eyes to total truth, discernment achieved by observing and surveying truth in its totality. Salvation, enlightenment and bliss – these comprised the ultimate knowledge of penetration, clear sight into the law of causation. All specific instances of an individual sadness, anxiety and suffering were generalized, conceptualized, and seen as universal phenomena. This 'knowledge' was called *bodhi, sambodhi* and *samyaksam-bodhi*; which is to say, 'to awaken to truth', 'to know truth' and 'to know clearly and completely with nothing left to know'. Through this knowledge, one was liberated from this world into enlightenment. Enlightenment did not mean that one entered peace; rather, that complete knowledge in and of itself, the wisdom called *sarvājñāna* – this was liberation and bliss.

He who is in *contemplatio* seeks no religious practice or technique of consciousness; he has no need for self-assertion or self-protection. Purified in knowledge, transcending individual fate, *contemplatio* is not something to be gained through transformation or effort. One is at peace in this pure and high knowledge, distanced from attachments of this world, not beclouded by cares. From emptiness, from limitless void, the eye sees all with clarity. With regard to emptiness – distanced from both being and nothingness, transcending both being and nothingness – there is no more denial.

By sinking into the depths of *contemplatio* I lose neither myself nor the world. This *contemplatio* is I. In this *contemplatio* I see that the world that I regard, the world that is regarded by me, is not truth. It is void. This me that is void, this world that is void, is not denied. Nor does it disappear. It continues to exist as a void detached from truth.

Eyes that see the void as the void see the true principle of truth as the truth. There is no asking, as Pilate is said to have done, 'What is Truth?' Those with the courage to stand before the Truth that transcends this world cease to ask what the true principle is because all desires have already been relinquished. He who sees the true principle will be no prisoner to the desire to ride upon religious teaching or change the world. He is in the emptiness that is detached from this world, and, alone, he finds bliss and peace.

A Creator or Supreme God, a mysterious darkness that preceded the lucid intelligence of a shadowless, bright, high-noon knowledge based on principles and the *dharma* – all this was disregarded from the outset as nonsense, as a mere shadow.

Escaping the suffering of life and the anxiety of ageing and death, Indian Buddhists were removed from their selves. Or perhaps their belief that God was truly residing, hidden, in the self's spirit was simply too uncertain. All the irregularities and illogic of the occurrences of reality were lucidly analysed and conceptualized within a linked circle of knowledge: The wheel turns to the left – and when this is, this also is and this occurs, and when this occurs this also occurs; now the wheel turns to the right – and when this is not, this also is not and when this disappears this also disappears. Everything was organized in exacting, logical, consequential order. To establish this chain of cause and effect, each term in the relationship was itself conceptualized and clearly distinguished from other concepts. Such were their lines of logic.

If religion, *religio*, is a fear of God or something that exists by its relationship to God (as with Augustine), then one can ask if the teaching of Buddha, with its absolute liberation from theories and gods, can be called 'religion'. Is it possible for there to be godless religion? Some hundreds of years after the death of Buddha, the concept of emptiness that is the heart of what is called Mahāyāna Buddhism, and the central concept of Buddhist wisdom, cause and effect, or karma, joined in sweeping away all gods.

Indeed, about Buddha's life we know nearly nothing. In the Dīgha Nikāya we read:

> his father is King Suddhodana, his mother was Queen Māyā, and his royal capital is Kapilavatthu. Such was the Lord's renunciation, such his going-forth, such his striving, such his full enlightenment, such his turning of the wheel.[1]

In these many places where 'such' is written, numerous ver-

---

1 *Dīgha Nikāya* ii 52. Quoted from: M. Walshe (trans.), 1996, *The Long Discourses of the Buddha: A Translation of the Dīgha Nikāya*, Boston: Wisdom, p. 220.

sions of Buddha's life have been recorded. We have no simple biography that would tell us of him as an individual. Compared to what has been recorded about the life of Confucius or the Greek philosophers before Socrates, or even Jesus, the amount of information regarding Buddha is exceedingly slim.

There are several possible reasons for this:

- Perhaps the texts that recorded information about his personality or life have been lost, or never existed.
- Perhaps Buddha's life had no outstanding events, or his personality lacked appeal.
- Perhaps, when carefully considered, the knowledge he gained and the import of the principles he expounded appeared far more relevant than Buddha himself, who was the product of one limited, random fate.
- Perhaps Buddha's disciples did not come to understand Buddhism by the charisma of a man called Buddha but rather by an encounter with clear teachings. Buddha is just a name. Buddhism, the religion without a god, is also the religion without a patriarchy.
- Finally, perhaps, in the context of traditional Indian philosophy, there was a greater interest in principles and knowledge transmitted by words than in specific, concrete events.

Certain fundamental tendencies within Indian religion shaped Buddhism: the severe limiting of confrontation with reality, the elimination of that which did not conform to proper principles – in particular, desire, and the perfection of knowledge. This epoch-making agenda was realized through Buddha. In terms of clarity and accuracy, knowledge reached a high point.

What occurs in this world is conceptualized as suffering, as life, as old age, as sickness, as death and so on. These are ascribed to the order of the cycle of cause and effect and are caught up in that cycle and, truly, as the sūtra holds:

... When ... liberated ... He understands: 'Destroyed is birth, the holy life has been lived, what had to be done has been done, there is no more for this state of being.'[2]

One who has attained enlightenment is forever beyond historical events that are of time and space. For Buddha, Oldenberg writes, 'truly occurrences (*Geschehen*) do not exist; suffering no longer exists.'[3]

Without history, words follow words, conceptualized and systematized. Further, the self multiplies itself, running in circles. This is because emptiness, no matter how buried, cannot be buried. Emptiness, even when emptied is not empty because its retrogression is infinite.

Buddha, the one who walked alone and free, beyond time and space like the horn of the rhinoceros,[4] appears in the sprawling expanse of the past and future and is one with the thousands of hundreds of millions of Buddhas. This peerless accomplishment that was brilliant in its pureness spiralled down into a swollen body of difficult Indian religious teachings that grew heavy with pretentiousness through textual analysis, modification and reconsideration. Truth became hidden on the other side of an endless 'story'. To see truth one must peer beyond the wall of gathered information or knowledge. But such an effort suggested even more knowledge. The wall grew all the more insurmountable. With the rhetoric of concepts and theories, the brilliant and magnificent discipline that is called Buddhology, though raised to the sublime, was trouble-ridden – as the 'bitter science' (*scientia acerba*) in contrast to the 'Gay Science' (Nietzsche). As for the truth, it had no choice but to reside in this glory and misery, in this comedy and tragedy.

---

2 *Saṃyutta Nikāya* iii 68. Quoted from Bhikkhu Bodhi (trans.), 2000, *The Connected Discourses of the Buddha: A Translation of the Saṃyutta Nikāya*, Boston: Wisdom, p. 903.

3 H. Oldenberg, 1910, *Aus dem alten Indien*, Berlin: Verlag Gebrüder Paetel.

4 See *Sutta Nipāta* 35–75.

Chinese Transitions

Many religions have entered China – Manichaeism, Zoroastrianism, Christianity and so forth – but they have not found a permanent place there. Only Buddhism became rooted in the country. One reason for this is simply the historical circumstances of the time. About the time of the advent of Buddhism, Chinese civilization started to decline. Confucianism and Taoism, which had set the framework for society for centuries, had no satisfying response to the increasing spiritual malaise of the Chinese people.

With the massive and confused immigration in which the Han tribes lost the heartland of China in the latter portion of the Western Ch'in dynasty, the idealized world where, as Confucius described it, one should 'Be stimulated by the Odes, take your stand on the rites and be perfected by music',[5] fell completely apart. The Chinese soul searched for a religious grounding for scholarship, ethics and the arts – for something primordial that preceded cognitive knowledge, practical ethics and beauty. It was in this context that China encountered Buddhism and that Buddhism encountered China.

Things that have absolutely no relationship to one another do not truly encounter one another. Additionally those things of just the same qualities have no real encounter either. For there to be an encounter, there must be areas of difference as well as areas of commonality. One such pair of things was the Indian concept of 'emptiness' (*śūnyatā*) and the Chinese concept of 'nothingness' (*wú*). The meeting of the two civilizations was the meeting of 'zero' and 'one'.

In India nothingness – conceived as non-being (*asat*) – stands opposite to being (*sat*). Their relationship is one of mutual dependence. There is nothingness because there is being, and the opposite is equally true. Nothingness does not transcend being, and that world, the beyond, does not transcend this world. There is no *act* that can transcend nothingness *and* being, or that world

---

5 *Lunyu* 8:8.

and this world because, according to the Indian conception, each depends on the other.

The possibility of transcendence inheres in the knowledge that concepts have mutual dependence. This knowledge opens a dimension that then has no relationship to the concept of mutual dependence. Knowledge that opens a transcendent dimension sees both being and nothingness, this world and that world, as void and having no relationship to truth.

The Chinese could not appreciate this knowledge in its pure form as the pleasure of a transcendent *contemplatio*. The Chinese were far too dynamic and practical for that. They were too human and too committed to the natural world. The 'emptiness' (*śūnyatā*) of India was placed within the traditional Chinese term *wú*. The concept of *wú* found in such nouns as 'non-action', 'no-name', 'no-limit', was split and elevated to the point where it independently represented the whole of ultimate reality in its emptiness (*śūnyatā*).

The Chinese character used to write the word *wú* suggests something concealed in a thicket of grass. It is a pictograph representing a thing. Hidden in the shadows of this thicket of grass is a profound and subtle mystery. The emptiness that is neither being nor nothingness is being and is nothingness. It is an abundantly powerful chaos, a power of hidden origins from which all things gain their existence.

Those Chinese who renounced the world for religious reasons were also called 'secluded ones' or 'hidden ones'. From ancient times, mountains free of any human traces were thought to be the locations most endowed with overflowing secret power. 'Secluded ones' who retreated deep into the rising foothills of these mountains became one with ultimate reality and the power of the beginning of existence of all things. They became not supernatural humans but rather those who have gone to the end' (*zhí-rén*) or 'true individuals' (*zhēn-rén*), adepts who mastered this mysterious power. Endowed with 'no-mind' they strolled through this polluted world.

Aristocratic, proud intellectualism revelled in a transcendent contemplation where, through deep insight, one realized that being and nothingness, this world and that world, were all void. Thus the Indian Buddhist became detached from both. Such an aristocratic attitude ran counter to the fundamental character of the Chinese. They could not accept that knowledge would occupy such a high and noble realm. I live just here. What was important was this *now*, this empirical reality. The Chinese were interested not simply in salvation through wisdom. Unless salvation included helping everyone who sought salvation, it was not true salvation. Thus, unlike India, for East Asian countries like China and Japan the traditions of salvation-oriented Pure Land Buddhism and Zen Buddhism flourished.

For the Chinese, committed as they were to empirical reality, existence was not a *Vorstellung* (representation) or an image generated by a subject. The world as the world has phenomenological existence beyond all concepts, unrelated from beginning to end to any cognitive thought. Buddhism brought radical changes to this world-view, freeing the Chinese heart from the phenomenological world so as to gain the absolute subjectivity. The subject is not caught up in its objects; the object has been caught up in the swollen subject. There, the hidden true world comes to itself, as it was, as it is, and as it will be. Negation turned towards the object. All objects of conscious thought, and consciousness itself, had to be negated.

There was nothing to be searched for either outside or inside. There was no need for religious practice, nor was there a need for enlightenment. It was meaningless to debate with words the *dharma* which was beyond words. One should not seek the Buddha; one should not seek the *dharma*; one should not posit the Buddha as supreme. These acts were like a lavatory, a place for relieving oneself; they enslaved people, shackling the arms and legs of the *bodhisattvas* and *arhats*. And the 'I' who says such things must also be negated. Still to be confronted was the one Chinese character *wú* in its ultimate negativity, in its emptiness emptied even of emptiness.

Meeting the Buddha, kill the Buddha; meeting a Master, kill the Master. The great freedom gained in standing on the precipice between life and death was not the opening of some deep well that would invite the full reversal of all values, announcing the arrival of a not yet known reality.

While a Chinese term *zé* indicates the link between a cause and effect, namely, the natural or logical 'therefore', as in: 'A *therefore* B', the Chinese term *jí*, pronounced like this *zé*, indicates the unchanging subject where affirmation and negation, the briefest moment and the eternal, or all such contrary concepts, are in and of themselves instantly viewed in the same light, without recourse to any temporal, rhetorical or logical relationship.

The term 'emptiness' (*kōng*) in the Chinese Tendai phrase, 'Emptiness itself is bodily form' (*kōng-jí-shì-sè*), is the absolute subject that has no object whatsoever, a subject that could also be called 'no-mind' (*wú-xīn*) or 'true mind' (*zhēn-xīn*) or 'soul' or 'spirit'. It permeates and rules all of its own. This 'of its own' is the 'no-mind' of the work of the absolute subject because this 'soul' or 'spirit' lies at the root of all things giving them their life and unity.

In this way, the phrase: 'Emptiness itself is bodily form' is also: 'All bodily form itself is emptiness' (*sè-jí-shì-kōng*). 'All bodily form itself is emptiness' – this is the phenomenological world in its unadulterated reality. This means that this very world is, in and of itself, the ultimate subject, the ultimate reality. To say that the ultimate subject rules everything is to say that it follows with no-mind the *dharma*, the principle and power of all things. This view entirely satisfied the Chinese.

The Chinese were unable to transcend this world in its phenomenological actuality as preserved by the debate surrounding *jí*. Even if they could break out of this world, there would be no new world awaiting them. The old world just as it is would be waiting for them. The old world *was* – as it is (*jí*) – the new world. The new world *was* the old world. Pain and suffering *were* salvation; this world of impurity *is* the Pure Land; all sentient beings *are* Buddha essence. In this way, it is not that Buddha is hidden within you. You, as you are, are Buddha.

'God' and 'Ultimate Reality' as Seen from a Japanese Perspective

Between China and India lay the great barrier of the Himalaya Mountains, so difficult to cross. Between China and Japan was a dark and difficult sea. This sea glowed with the long slanting rays of the autumn of Buddhism, hiding suffering in its depths.

The undersized inhabitants of these islands were connected neither to the high and noble knowledge of the proud Aryans nor to the wilful power of the Chinese adepts who moved through the sky and the depths of the abyss. They did not gaze upon great deserts. They were not oppressed by massive glaciers. They lived blessed by the wealth of the mountains and the sea. They did not seek a metaphysics that would transcend nature (like the Aryans) or magical powers (like the Chinese). In every aspect, relying on their instincts, they distrusted what was made by man. They put nature neither first nor last; they tried to be neither its master nor its slave. They lived as friends with nature.

By the end of the nineteenth century the inhabitants of our lonely island were torn out of their familiar rhythm, out of the recurring succession of quiet leisure and incisive catastrophes: the good news from the West came to them.

The Jewish God Yahweh arrived. He is hostile to nature by essence. This is the basic feature that a Japanese will note when comparing him with his own gods who, like the Greek gods, more or less live by and with nature and often even are nature itself. By insisting on the one and only God who is to be held as holy and superior to the world, nature is made into an object. Created by God, it is degraded to a creature. It lies in his hands. He makes it and he destroys it (the Flood!). Also, the word of the Lord 'And it was good', spoken on the days of creation, splits the one nature up into the good nature that he created and into the rest: chaos, nothing, *privatio*, the evil nature.

As seen through Asian eyes – and in relation to Christianity – 'ultimate reality', the final unconditioned that is independent of all subjective conditions of the epistemic process and that escapes all discursive rational thought or idealization, seems to be nothing else than the Jewish-Christian God 'Yahweh' who, as the one and only God, calls himself the 'being of all beings'.

The originally Latin word *real* is rendered in German as *wirklich*, thereby acquiring a peculiar meaning that is alien to the Latin *res* or *realitas*. While *realitas* (thingness, being) primarily expresses a substance-metaphysical aspect, *Wirklichkeit* or *Wirkung* implies actuality pure and simple. Actuality is neither the first cause nor the final principle, but that which presses itself upon us as 'real', in contrast to appearance. Hebrew words like *hāyā* (being) or *heyeh* (I am, or: I will be) indicate that God is not a conceptual being or 'being' in the abstract but reality in the eternal now, the mysterious power to create, the one who causes to be.

More than with this Jewish God surrounded with this specific aura, we sympathize with the spirit of the late Hellenistic mind as it flourished in the Eastern Mediterranean coastal areas before the rise of Islam and the establishment of the Holy Roman Empire of the German nation. At that same time, Buddhism was experiencing a rebirth in India. And in China, with the death of the old Lord of Heaven and under the influence of the new Buddhism, the high culture of the T'ang was established, whose afterglow extended as far as Japan.

In late antiquity, the great syncretistic epoch, two important events occurred – important for the whole of humanity, not only for the Western but also for the Eastern soul:

1. The birth of Jesus Christ in Nazareth.
2. The encounter of the Western with the Eastern mind.

The West comes into contact with the Eastern world – which is marked by negative thought – and learns that 'ultimate reality' is not 'being', nor is it the 'being of all beings'; rather, it is non-being, the nothingness or emptiness that transcends being.

Being is incarcerated within the cycle of transmigration. Origen knows this ancient Indian doctrine and disputes it from a Christian perspective. Plotinus too believes that the souls change their lives and enter constantly into new forms. As in Buddhism the process of liberation from '*saṃsāra*' is of intellectual nature. But for Plotinus salvation from sensual-bodily existence consists in renouncing the diversity of being. It occurs in three stages:

1. After the separation from all carnal sensuality through death, the soul flies back to its home. This archaic-shamanistic belief in the immortality of the soul – which spread as far as the eastern end of Eurasia – is expressed in Plotinus in strongly intellectualized form as the renunciation of everything exterior and the return to a spiritualized interior 'I'.

2. This is raised to the next stage of what Plato propounded with his idea of the universal soul: The individual ego-souls (unique, distinct, self-conscious, immaterial) are elevated to the mind. The soul (*psyche*) becomes mind (*nous*); its interior spiritualized being is transformed into an intellectualized being, an idea, an archetype actualized through thought. In mind the departure from bodily-sensual being is made permanent. Thought takes control of being. Knowledge (*epistēmē*) takes the place of perception (*aïsthesis*). Thought takes being under its wings. The priority of thought over being is obvious. Having become dependent on thought, impoverished being is now abstracted into pure being and finally into beinglessness.

3. In terms of the German word '*Geist*', the transition to the highest stage is then brought about by a superhuman, vitalizing divine power that reveals itself through *ekstasis*. The quest for 'ultimate reality' comes to an end in the all-comprehensive vision. Mind liberated from thought and being liberated from being are beheld, that is, realized in their limits, and transcended.

In Buddhism there is no transcendence: The absolute that encompasses everything and dissolves everything in itself is sometimes called nothing, sometimes everything, and sometimes suchness (*tathatā*) – such as being is – because there is neither nothing nor being.

The transcending of the totality of being, including even Divine being (Proclus), the breakdown of all concepts, the bursting of all metaphors – these are neither Greek nor Christian. Since Plotinus, the quest for this sort of transcendence formed – within the primarily positive thinking of the West – a separate theological tradition beyond the ordinary, the so-called '*theologia negativa*'. Through Dionysius the pseudo-Areopagite, Augustine, Scotus Eriugena and Maimonides it was handed down, with all its various faces, to Meister Eckhart.

Meister Eckhart strives towards 'ultimate reality' far beyond nature:

1. The 'created' world cannot be the 'ultimate reality'. The soul is not satisfied with its own stained being. One needs to 'break through' it, 'break' it, 'transcend' it.
2. One even needs to 'break through' or 'beyond' the Creator God as the correlate of the created world.

Both of these two 'destructive' ways lead to the very same word 'nothing', even if one might identify in it two contrary meanings:

1. All creatures are nothing but 'nothing'.
2. God is nothing but 'nothing'.

By way of negation – the 'no' being put forth by the intellect (*intellectus*) – the soul rises higher and higher. By the grace of God the human is overwhelmed and overcome in 'humanity'; and God is broken through towards the 'Godhead'. God and human being meet in this intellectual elevation. The soul's advance towards God is at the same time God's advance to the soul which is and becomes equal to God. God cannot be without the soul, and the soul cannot be without God. The abyss calls to the abyss. Reason or intellect, the highest faculty of the soul, discloses the abyss and pushes the Creator God into the desert. The union (*unio*) happens neither in God nor in the soul, but in the abyss, in the desert.

Meister Eckhart's mysticism has met with interest from the

godless Zen mystics in modern Japan, but also led to some misunderstandings. Buddhists thought to recognize in this 'solitude' or 'desert' – also called 'nothing' – their Mahāyāna Buddhist *kōng* (emptiness, relativity). Basically, nothing is more alien to the Asians than the dualistic separation of the world into the personal Creator God on the one hand and the created world on the other hand. Their interest is in a ground, unknown to rational logic, that underlies both the exterior phenomena, as stable, self-existent objects, and the purely subjective-logical epistemic process as well. With a meditational practice that distrusts and prohibits any sort of conceptual-logical articulation Buddhists seek to break through to a disclosure of this ground. Then the ground will show itself as *kōng*, as the absolute nothing beyond any articulation in words. The ground is dissolved in its own bottomlessness. Nothing in, or of, or for itself is left.

Kōng, empty, content-less, pure activity with neither goal nor cause, is experienced in giving up any attempt to penetrate deeper into actual, real human existence and real, finite beings. Zen Buddhism is not a philosophy. It is the way and nothing but the way, and on the way no metaphysical flowers blossom. It is the method for relativizing our conceptions of reality so that the way can work. With or without the aid of gods or humans, the way works and runs in its emptiness-power. Nothing can 'opt out' of the course of nature. Everything is 'natural', and 'in accordance with nature'; everything is the coming and going of the eternally alike. In the Taoist traces of *wú*, all problems are dissolved, even the ultimate things, without being solved.

In Buddhism, the beings are just there, without reason, without asking about a reason. The beings are the different faces and colours of the eternally alike. Being is appearance and nothing else. In this light, to ask about an 'ultimate reality' is here nonsense.

For Meister Eckhart the 'desert' or 'abyss' is full of efficacious actuality. It is not dissolution but completion. The absolute end is the Ur-beginning. The abyss 'grounds' the soul (the 'ground of the soul') as well as God (the 'ground of God'). Absolute emptiness 'is' fullness. The desert wells up; the light shines (John) in the dark abyss of the Godhead. The transformation occurs in timeless immediacy. God gives birth to the Son and the Son to God. This 'giving birth' is neither natural nor spiritual. It is the '*actus purus*' (pure actuality) of the mind, the intellectualized 'I'. Everything that God gave to his Son he also gives to the soul.[6] God and human (the soul) coincide without any intermediary in a timeless eternal 'I'. This 'I', as the ground of myself, God and all things, absorbs God, human and world and – in the immediate presence of the eternal continuously procreating itself – it wants to create the world anew, bursting forth and rising out as 'God works in all his power'.[7] Neo-Platonism is long forgotten. Reality is no longer the actuality of an idea in itself. It becomes the 'modern', the eternal new creation.

Vis-à-vis the Godhead mysticism of Meister Eckhart stands the new mysticism of Jacob Boehme, the Jesus mysticism.

1. This Jesus mysticism does not search for the 'ultimate reality', but remains within the harmony of the Trinity. Jacob Boehme, son of a poor peasant and himself a humble shoemaker, later a trader, received his mystical experience in the midst of nature. His mystical world was developed in a powerful relation to nature – we might even say alchemically.

2. This autodidact is not a child of '*scientia*' (science) but of '*sophia*' (wisdom) who learned his ABCs in the 'school of the Holy Spirit'. He calls himself a 'theosophist'.

3. A number of like-minded peasants and townsfolk gathered around Jacob Boehme and copied down his writings. Many of them had their own mystical experiences, sharing and deepening them through 'telling and listening'. Such like-minded circles spread throughout Germany and even beyond, to the Netherlands, England, Scandinavia, Eastern Europe, Russia and France.

---

6 Cf. *Sermon* 5.   7 Cf. *Sermon* 52.

4. The vocabulary of the new mysticism departed from the learned language of the scholastics. Almost all the Boehmists used their own mother-tongue, which was so much closer to living experience and united people far more intimately.

The basic differences between the two kinds of mysticism, Eckhart's and Boehme's, can be traced back to the two events of global importance which occurred in late antiquity and which I mentioned before: Jesus Christ and Plotinus.

The event of 'Jesus Christ' who was hated by 'this world' and wandered about with a few disciples not knowing where to lay his head – this unique world-event, lost in the secret abyss of memory, is resurrected in the ground of the souls of the new mystics: 'Our hearts are burning within us, while Christ is speaking to us' (Zinzendorf).

The Japanese word *dekigoto* means 'occurrence'. *Deki* is derived from *idekuru*, which means 'comes out'. The syllable *-ru* is a suffixed auxiliary verb that shades the verb neither with the passive nor with the active voice but endows it rather with the meaning of spontaneity. This action that arises from within something might be expressed in English as 'spontaneous' ('of one's own accord'), derived from the Latin word *spons* (free will). Etymologists believe that at the root of this auxiliary verb that indicates spontaneity – i.e., this *-ru* (or also: *-raru*) – is the verb *aru*, meaning 'to be', but in very early Japanese written with the Chinese character *shēn*, meaning 'life'. Therefore, 'to be', or 'to live', is associated with the auxiliary verb that gives Japanese verbs the sense of spontaneous self-arising.

Dekigoto can fall from the sky, as in the German word *Würfelfall* or the Latin *casus;* it can also well up from the ground as in the Latin word *eventum* or in the English word 'outcome'. Occurrences transcend the imagination and break out of the realm of contemplation. They 'open', as in the German word *Ereignis*, derived from *Eräugnis*. In Japanese the verb *okiru* is used. The verb means 'to happen' but is derived from the old pronunciation of *oku* (now pronounced *iki*), the word for 'breath'. Thus etymologically, the verb *okiru* means 'to begin to breath' or 'come to life'. This real thing is concrete, a word derived from the Latin prefix *con-* ('with' or 'together') and *crēscere* (meaning 'to grow'). *Dekigoto* and events, unlike the products of the imagination or ideas, well up and appear from the bottomless abyss without explanation. They are impenetrable to understanding either by reasoning or by passion.

If we were to consider *dekigoto* with respect to the two poles of human artifice on the one hand, and nature on the other, then *dekigoto* would be found close to nature. And a human's existence could be called an occurrence within an occurrence. *Dekigoto* become *dekigoto* with a human's existence.

While a concept is one link in a chain of established relationships, a *dekigoto* stands uniquely alone as a 'miracle', with the entirety of what has not occurred trailing behind. The unexpected, the single occurrence, the random event and wholeness – these possess this special characteristic. Visible, they are unseen. Audible, they are uncannily wrapped in silence. Hidden, they appear; upon appearing, they are hidden. The relativity of subject and object and principle and law are drawn into a dark well and their significance is pressed on humans. The sky might fall and the earth might rupture but if there is no one to experience these, then nothing 'happens', nothing 'comes to life'. *Dekigoto* presume a self in humans. When humans act inattentively to the challenge of opaque reality, of impulse, of resistance, *dekigoto* do not happen.

According to the new mysticism of Boehme the resurrection of Jesus Christ means at the same time the resurrection of nature. It is not about the immortality of the soul after its separation from the flesh. Rather the separation of mind and flesh itself is meant to be revoked and uplifted to the 'eternal' flesh, thereby restoring the primordial state as it was before Adam's fall. The 'eternal' nature, the unitary ground that encompasses everything and brings every individual back to itself as itself – this unity is not 'the One', pure and simple, which is 'left over', as it were, once diversity and attributes have been eliminated. Nature loses its truth if it breaks away from the all-encompassing unity. The breakdown of unity can be traced to the ego-centred desire of the human being in 'this' world. According to this new view of nature it is crucial to understand the difference between 'natural' desire and 'ego-centred' desire. Thus shall the opposition between the 'natural, old man of the flesh' (Luther) and the 'new man of the spirit' be rendered irrelevant.

From this follows a further insight: 'Ego-centred' desire constructs and organizes 'this' world where the devil is at work – a devil not of flesh and blood. This world hates and kills Jesus Christ, who is not from 'this' world. Hence *imitatio Christi*, the imitation of Christ, does not mean to strive at the perfection of virtue, to purify the soul by its segregation from the flesh, but rather to live in 'this' world: to take upon oneself the suffering in this fallen world and to empty the bitter cup to the dregs.

Hunger and thirst are quenched. Sickness is healed. Tears are wiped away. Healing is given to humans as miracle and 'model'. The deaf hear and the blind receive sight. But following the 'model' (*imitatio Christi)* is not the only way. One follows one's own way, a parallel way, in the gentle moonlight.

Concluding Thoughts

Hunger and thirst – this desire is neither a unitary, blind fundamental desire, nor is it a high-level desire that seeks the fulfilment of a goal, nor is it a volition. It is neither active nor passive but instead stands between these. It is *jihatsu*, naturally arising: that is, nature in its rising to life. It is different from the desire or volition which consciously works towards a clearly determined goal such as that caused by thirst or hunger. Hunger and thirst can be satisfied. These are related to the measures of sufficient and insufficient, and when balance is restored, these desires cease. The activity of filling ends of its own.

The naturally arising desire is also different from the blind and unitary desire. It ends when the need is fulfilled, has within itself a clear beginning and end, and proceeds along in a predetermined direction. It bears a self-goal oriented towards itself and residing in itself. Desire finds its sufficiency and ceases; this is self-sufficiency. Desire again awakens. However, there is no searching for the next thing or running about blindly to just anywhere. Unlike the prideful sense of achievement or victory that occurs when one gains a set goal, this natural fulfilment bestows a deep sense of contentment.

In contrast to this, desire linked to volition necessarily connotes the tendency to move ceaselessly from one identified goal to the next. In a way very similar to that of blind desire, it connotes the danger of being swept along. When the hunted game is caught, the next game is hunted, for volition establishes itself in the setting up of a purpose. The attainment of one goal means a new deficiency, a new unfulfilled state. One reason for this is the pleasure and discomfort of modern life, the stress associated with the pursuit of pleasure, and so forth. Another reason is found in the fact that the equation of volition with desire has been imbued with a positive ethical status, and been fully incorporated as a formula demanded by society to maintain its vigour. On the other hand, with regard to naturally arising desire, it is neither necessary nor possible to internalize or codify it because naturally arising desire is dimensionless with no possibility of possessing an inside or outside.

The unprecedented global dominance of the West, embracing a fearlessness towards the gods and God, and an unshakable faith in the advancement of the frontal lobe of the cerebral cortex, is superficially nearing its end. The Japanese are pushing aside in less than a hundred years the trials and tribulations experienced in the garden of a pleasure which knew neither hunger nor thirst, as they successfully pursue the tracks of modernizing cultures, throwing to the winds the old Asia which valued so highly the harmony of the whole.

Religion or, I would suggest, the imitation of religion, has been made ill by civilized man; it has been fatigued by him. Living intensely in order to please the spirit stimulates desire but does not end hunger. Neither science nor civilization quenches its thirst nor heals its ills. True religion has direct relevance to living truth. It operates within life in its nakedness.

There is no doubt that the human race has struggled and

grown over these thousands of years thanks to religion, which has garnered the fruit of the flowers of the pure and simple soul whose roots lie deep in the heart of nature. It is as certain that, in the future, religion will even more perform such important work. There are many people everywhere across the surface of this globe who in their poverty are just barely managing to live, who know nothing of the comforts of civilization. Before we who live in our unprecedented garden of gluttony and gaudy display can debate whether there is a future for religion or whether religion remains a necessity, we must first experience this 'reality' of the poor and the meek.

Note

Nambara's chapter was written in English and German. The German parts were initially translated by Perry Schmidt-Leukel and the entire text was revised by Carolina Weening.

8. Response to Minoru Nambara

KARL BAIER

Nambara points out the complex changes that Buddhism underwent on its journey to East Asia. He describes the historical path of Buddhism from India to Japan as a hierarchy of growing insights into the nature of reality. Buddha's enlightenment bringing 'liberation from all theories and gods' appeared in India as 'high and noble knowledge of the Aryans'. Perhaps the cognitive and elitist character of early Buddhism and Indian Mahāyāna is a little overemphasized here. Did Buddha's contemplation under the Bodhi tree reveal only a rationalistic 'high noon knowledge' that lacks the dimension of divine mystery? My impression is that the Four Noble Truths (which are already a later attempt to systematize the original insight) try to explain as precisely as possible the shadow of suffering and the laws of its emergence and disappearance. But the light that shines forth when this shadow withdraws remains surrounded by solemn silence. One should also not forget that not only the somewhat elitist ideal of the arhat but also the ideal of the bodhisattva had already been developed in India.

According to Nambara, Indian Buddhism constitutes a transcendent dimension reached through meditation which culminates in a blissful state of total detachment from the world. This 'otherworldliness' of earlier Buddhism was then overcome by Chinese Buddhism, which emphasized the importance of living here and now within the realm of empirical reality and of helping others to gain salvation. It was also less intellectual (at least, I would add, in the beginning, considering the elaborate metaphysics of the later Hua Yan school, for example) and assimilated important Taoist concepts. It seems to me that Nambara is favouring a kind of Taoist version of Buddhism combined with a friendly 'down to earth' relationship to nature, which does not seek for magical powers as did the old Taoists, and which he thinks is best represented by indigenous Japanese piety.

What then is Ultimate Reality and its relation to the non-Ultimate as Nambara perceives it through his Japanese Buddhist understanding? His symbol for the Ultimate is the Mahāyānic emptiness (*śūnyatā*) understood in the light of Taoist nothingness (*wú*). Emptiness is neither being nor nothingness. But at the same time it is emptied of its own emptiness and therefore it is nothing else but being and nothingness.

With this concept he rejects all views that regard Ultimate Reality as something or someone outside the world. The very world is, in and of itself, Ultimate Reality. Both are identical. But which kind of identity is meant here? Is it a complete and literal identity, or an identity that is accompanied by a certain difference? In the first case, Nambara would support a kind of naturalism and indeed, some of his statements give the impression that Ultimate Reality means nothing more for him than the course of nature – the Universe which encompasses all and lets the Thusness (*tathatā*) of every individual being happen.

On the other hand, Nambara interprets the Japanese *dekigoto* ('occurrence') ontologically as a mysterious, spontaneous self-arising 'from the bottomless abyss'. All that is – being in general – has the event-structure of *dekigoto*. Hence, the experience of the Universe is connected with the experience of a bottomless abyss. Nature in itself is open towards a dimension of mystery, an infinite depth within every finite being. It seems to me that this approach is not so far from the dynamic and differentiated unity (or non-duality) between the world-transcending Ultimate and the non-ultimate world that I suggested in my paper. Perhaps Nambara associates the pure immanentistic view with Chinese Buddhism, and the *dekigoto* view with Japanese thought. However, it has been impossible for me to come to a final conclusion about what his paradoxical identity-discourse chooses to opt for. Perhaps the meaning of this kind of discourse is to avoid choosing, in addition to any other sort of discriminative thinking.

On one point he is unambiguous. Nambara sharply criticizes a monotheistic understanding of Ultimate Reality, underlining that in Buddhism a creator or supreme God 'was disregarded from the outset as nonsense'. He rejects the division of the world into a personal creator on the one hand and created beings on the other. This kind of God would be inimical towards nature. Nature would become a mere object and thus be degraded.

I share his criticism of certain questionable concepts of the creator God in the Abrahamic Religions from the Old Testament onwards. Although the insight that God can only be spoken of analogically was always present, several motives created the tendency in popular belief as well as in theology to think of God as a particular being, beyond the mundane, who rules his creation in a way that humiliates nature and human beings. Symbolic language that calls God 'Lord', 'King' or 'Being of beings', etc., as well as the concept of God's almightiness have led to false views about the relationship between God and creation. Furthermore the inclination towards a substantialist ontology, which conceives the individual thing as the paradigm of what it means to be real, reinforced the tendency to objectify God. In modern theology (and in several older traditions as well) this kind of God-talk has been criticized very often. The dialogue with Buddhism has also made us aware of the impossibility of thinking of God in terms of an invisible superior being.

Nevertheless, I believe it is historically wrong to say that the God of the Old Testament is generally conceived as an obstinate ruler of the world who does with his creation whatever he wants to do. The different myths of creation in the Hebrew Bible all agree that creation means bringing the world into being and maintaining it as an ordered space that enables life to flourish. The story of the flood, for instance, which Nambara offers as an example of God's arbitrary rule, is part of a longer tale concerning the mythical origin of the world. Its theological focus is the message that God remains merciful in spite of repeated disruptions of the harmoniously ordered nature caused by human beings. The story ends with the blessing of humankind and the promise of God to uphold the rhythms of nature as long as the earth endures.

In spite of the tendency towards a dualism between creator and creation, already the church fathers, as well as many later theologians, understood creation not as an act establishing distance between God and the created world but primarily as a call to enter God's presence. 'You made us for yourself, and our hearts are restless until they find their rest in you' (Augustine). In my paper I argued that from a Christian point of view creation could be understood as the initial opening of God's self-communication. As this self-communication is a selfless ('kenotic') giving of divinity, it implies that the created nature participates in God's divinity and (at least according to some theologies) is given the power of co-creatorship.

For Nambara, two historical events in late antiquity changed the Yahweh concept of Ultimate Reality and brought it closer to the Buddhist view: The first is connected with the life and teachings of Jesus Christ; the second concerns the development of Eastern-influenced Neo-Platonic philosophy, which led to the development of negative theology. Nambara exemplifies the significance of these events for the understanding of Ultimate Reality with Meister Eckhart's Godhead mysticism and Jakob Boehme's Christology.

Whether Neo-Platonism is influenced by Eastern thought at all and, if so, to what degree, is still completely uncertain due to the lack of any historical proof. Be that as it may, is this kind of negative thinking un-Greek and un-Christian per se, as Nambara says? At any rate – if the hypothesis of its Eastern origin is true – it did indeed become Greek and Christian (Jewish and Muslim as well). Neo-Platonic thought thus proved its power to elucidate from within the experiences and beliefs of several religions; it did not simply remain a foreign factor. As I tried to show in my paper, even certain biblical notions of God may well reveal a negative theology, albeit the specific terminology and methodology is a product of Neo-Platonic thought.

Nambara rightly points out that Meister Eckhart has

functioned as an important bridge between a Christian and a Buddhist understanding of Ultimate Reality. At this point I regret that I am unable to start a discussion of his interpretation of the famous medieval theologian. For Nambara, Eckhart (like Indian Buddhism) is a representative of the lofty transcendent heights of an intellectual *vita contemplativa*. However, one should not forget how Eckhart developed the priority of the *vita activa* – for instance in his '*Reden der Unterweisung*' and in the famous Sermon 86 on Mary and Martha.

According to Nambara, Jakob Boehme is closer to Chinese and Japanese Buddhism than Eckhart because Boehme's christocentric mysticism is strongly related to the resurrection of nature as a whole. Following the path of Jesus Christ means living within the fallen world, participating in its suffering and in its healing. Egocentric desire, which disturbs the primordial unity of nature, is overcome by natural desire, which Nambara compares with *jihatsu*, nature in its rising to life. I find these analogies drawn by Nambara fascinating. Clearly they are worth exploring more closely and I would like to thank Nambara for indicating this line of possible future research, which appears to be very rewarding.

I totally agree with Nambara when he finds in Jesus Christ and in Christology a kind of emptiness and compassion both of which love the earth. They do not seek an otherworldly bliss but manifest a resurrected harmony of the whole universe. If we Christians really believe in the life and death of Christ as the revelation of the unity between Ultimate Reality and the world, we should definitely leave behind the image of God as a sovereign ruler in a distant Hereafter – a conception that is so alien not only to Nambara's East Asian thought, but also to many people in today's Western societies.

After all, how do the Buddhist and the Christian understanding of Ultimate Reality relate to one another? Is not Christ for me the final revelation of Ultimate Reality? Do I think the best that I can learn from a Buddhist is that there are already traces of Christ's truth in Buddhism? Is not Zen for Nambara the ultimate peak of wisdom, the unbeatable perception of things as they really are? Does he believe the best that he can learn from a Christian is that there are already traces of the Buddha Dharma in Christianity? But if we were to think like that, would we be able to have a real, transformative dialogue with each other? I can only speak for myself here. The more I am involved in the encounter with Buddhism the more I am convinced of the fundamental parity between the two religions and their liberating revelations of Ultimate Reality.

9. Response to Karl Baier

MINORU NAMBARA

In his paper Karl Baier emphasizes the human, anthropological dimension even with respect to 'ultimate reality'. Christianity, with an experience of transcendence different from Buddhism's, has developed a different anthropology as well. While Baier tries to give 'a first impression of a very complex field', I see my own task primarily as an exploration of *where* a meeting of two so very different religions – the god-less Buddhism and the love-full Christianity – might be possible. To complete this task I don't want to get lost in details. It is crucial to recognize as clearly as possible just what is essential and decisive.

Only with the global changes in the political and economic state of the world about a hundred years ago did Buddhism begin to come to terms with the other major religions and with Christianity in particular. The sweeping developments in science and technology that took off at roughly the same time undermined, with similar speed, the religions. Religions became history, past cultural phenomena, objects of study, each one different from the other and each one as much the other. Only the spiritual vacuum that was thereby generated provides a bird's-eye view, an overview to those who dare to place themselves at the edge of the abyss of nothing.

For a long time now, Buddhists have befriended nothingness, for it lends them a clear sight or vision. To this end the gods and the demons, the juggler of truth, must all die. Sensual desires as well as the intellectual greed for knowledge of 'truth' must come to an end. Lofty concepts need to withdraw. When seeing and contemplating in peaceful freedom, life ceases, and death with it. In *nirvāṇa* the soul attains the 'bird's-eye view of immortality'. This is contrary to Christian 'resurrection' and 'incarnation'. The Buddhist is free from death because he is not of life. The Awakened One peacefully dwells apart from life and death. Christian terminological constructs like 'Creator God and created world', 'God as the consummation of history', 'the human as the image of God (*imago dei*)', 'liberty and evil', 'crucifixion of the Son of God', or 'justification' are all alien and unintelligible to a Buddhist. Love, the closest bond between God and human, or human and human, would only disturb a Buddhist. It is too narrowing and too exciting. He only accepts the general love toward the most remote – that is, the supra-individual 'compassion' falling like a shower of blossoms not knowing anything of itself. And the Christian? He would like to love the Buddhist as his neighbour – but there is no one, there is nothing. Christian anthropology, so human and warm, is undergirded by a specific experience of transcendence. The absolute is a personal God who is closely connected with the human. God is not a concept and cannot be grasped even by the concept of 'ultimate reality'. He who created the universe in love and wrath is not a principle, nor is he something like a 'First Cause' ('*Ur-Sache*').

All this developed quite differently, however, in that process of depersonalization that started already in Hellenism. With it philosophy entered religion, and religion was transformed into philosophy, or theology. God, the Father, had to let himself be grasped as the First Cause. This new spirit was of eminent and enriching importance for the further development of Christianity – also in view of its encounter with Buddhism.

- The process of Hellenization disengaged Christianity from its Jewish prehistory and elevated it to a world religion.
- The release of God from the fetters of regional and confessional bonds and an association with the Greek philosophical spirit set free new strengths: A domain was opened up where humans could not only, and not necessarily, walk by faith or simple confession but where they could also stroll about in philosophical thought.

- By the concept of the 'seeds of the logos' (*logos spermatikos*) a new idea became thinkable, namely, that the *logos* who had appeared in Jesus Christ was revealed among all people and cultures. The historical event acquired a metaphysical dimension.

In this regard the event was also important for the encounter with Buddhism: Yahweh and '*to hen*' ('the One') entered into a momentous covenant. In its shade the Holy Trinity – Father, Son and Holy Spirit – was transferred to the conceptual level. It became a trinity of 'power, wisdom, goodness' (*potentia, sapientia, bonitas*) or – on the mathematical level – of 'unity, equality, relation'. This new spirit transcends itself through intuition and contemplation, and dares to go even beyond being. In that nothing where there is no *ne plus ultra*, no assimilation nor approximation, the distinctions between the religions recede; Buddhists abandon their Buddhist-ness and Christians their Christian-ness and open themselves, without changing or renouncing their faith. Only the complete relinquishment of being leads to a new, hitherto unknown unity.

During the Hellenistic period a similar encounter between religious traditions took place in the East – between Buddhism and the Chinese religions of Confucianism and Taoism. The adaptation of Buddhism in East Asia can be compared to the process of Hellenization. But as opposed to developments in the West, the rebirth of Buddhism in the East implicated a rehabilitation of nature – neglected by Indians and Europeans alike – with all its holy forces, a process that even today has not yet come to its end.

In conclusion I would like to add a few remarks on the role of 'ultimate reality' within the tradition of 'negative theology' as Karl Baier addresses it in his paper.

'Negative theology' – a curious, alien element within the theological tradition of Europe – searches 'by negation' (*via negativa*) for an 'ultimate reality' that does not reveal itself and that transcends every human understanding. All human interpretations and definitions are unmasked as misunderstandings and distortions generated by an optimistic human greed for knowledge. In this regard 'negative theology' works to liberate Christianity and Christian theology from its inclination towards the human, all too human, and at the same time from its claim to absoluteness as well. Buddhists too try to define truth negatively. This truth complies with their efforts and discloses itself in their religious experiences. Each one of these experiences is real – a mystical realization of truth. For the whole reveals itself only in the individual experience: the whole in the particular, the undetermined in the determined.

Negative propositions do not refer to some determined 'vis-à-vis' – God or the Absolute, which would stand 'vis-à-vis' the human as the Other or as the great Thou and would thus be declared the Ineffable. Rather, negative propositions disclose a dimension hitherto unknown to humans: the unidentified, completely new, which eternally was before every beginning and beyond all opposites, appearing and yet always escaping all souls, whether Buddhist or Christian.

Towards the end of his life Nicholas Cusanus arrived at his utmost concept of God, the '*non aliud*'. God is 'non-other' than God. The 'non-other' is the underlying precondition of everything and at the same time the precondition of the total difference from everything: God is 'non-other' than God, but equally so wood is non-other than wood, and you too are non-other than you. God, wood and you, are all different from one another. Hidden creative forces of language awake, forming and shaping a linguistic unity in their freedom, limited only by the limiting whole, the ineffable. Remaining within these limits, the finite hints at the infinite. The name is neither the designation, nor is the definition the essential nature. Language determines itself. Language is the revelation. It acts, co-enacts and actualizes reality.

Note

This chapter was written in German, translated by Perry Schmidt-Leukel and revised by Carolina Weening.

PART III

THE MEDIATORS

10. Buddha and Christ as Mediators of the Transcendent:

A Christian Perspective

PERRY SCHMIDT-LEUKEL

Should you ever go to Chiang Mai, the beautiful capital of Thailand's North, be sure not to miss the Buddhist temple *Doi Suthep*, built high into the slope of Suthep mountain, north-west of Chiang Mai. In former times one had to climb more than 300 steps for the final part of the way to the top, but today one can take a modern elevator to the plateau of the temple area: a wide plain of shining polished stone offering a marvellous view over Chiang Mai and the whole valley below. If you turn around, you find yourself surrounded by several smaller and bigger stupas, all covered with gold, dazzlingly reflecting and radiating Thailand's bright sunlight. Due to the enormous height, the temple plateau is at times hemmed with tattered clouds, and so you can't help thinking that you stand in the middle of a celestial palace, an effect that was probably intended by the building masters. Next to the stupas there are various Thai salas, open temple constructions and colonnades with numerous Buddha statues – the large ones in the very same dazzling gold as the stupas, the smaller ones partly in a darker, almost mystical glow of jewels and jade. No doubt everything in this place proclaims the supramundane, not to say 'divine' nature of the Buddha. On the inner side of the wall that circumscribes the core of the temple area you see a series of highly poetic wall-paintings depicting the Buddha legend. The picture that shows the Buddha or, more precisely, Prince Gautama, moving from home into homelessness, does not show Gautama riding on his faithful horse Kanthaka, as the text of the legend has it. Rather, it depicts Gautama flying on the back of his horse over a deep valley out of the world into the realm where heaven, earth, humans and here even animals meet – as if he were attracted by a powerful, invisible force.

What a difference between the presentation of the Buddha within the genuine context of religious veneration, as in this Theravāda temple, and the image of the Buddha – currently so widespread in the West – according to which the Buddha was simply a human being, free from all divine features![1] Indeed this modern view does not at all correspond to the description of the Buddha in the classical Buddhist scriptures. In the Pāli Canon, for example, it is told how the Brahman Dona discovered the Buddha's footprints with the sign of the thousand-spoked wheels that were under Buddha's soles. Amazed by these footprints, the Brahman thought: 'How wonderful and marvellous – it cannot be that these are the footprints of a human being.'[2] Dona followed the track until he met the Buddha. Respectfully approaching him, Dona asked the Buddha what kind of being he was and received the answer that the Buddha cannot be described as a celestial being, nor as a ghost, nor as a human being. These are all forms of *samsāric* existence – that is, beings that are still

1 Cf. Geoffrey Parrinder, 1997, *Avatar and Incarnation*, Oxford: Oneworld, p. 246: 'modern apologists . . . say that Gautama was a man with nothing supernatural about him, and his teaching was a simple ethic which should be acceptable to the rationalistic western world. The trouble is that this is not how the Buddha is viewed, or ever has been viewed, in any of the eastern schools of traditional Buddhism, Theravāda or Mahāyāna. The Buddha is not a god, a *deva*, but he is superior to all exalted human and divine beings . . .' For an early, but largely neglected critique of a reductive portrayal of the Buddha see also Hsueh-li Cheng, 1981, 'Buddha, Man and God', in *Dialogue* (N.S.) 8, pp. 54–68.

2 *Anguttara Nikāya* iv 36. Translation from: Edward Conze (ed. and trans.), 2000, *Buddhist Texts Through the Ages*, repr., Oxford: Oneworld, p. 104.

caught in *saṃsāra*, the net of constant rebirth. But the Buddha is a being who has transcended all this:

> Brahmin, those outflows whereby, if they had not been extinguished, I might have been a deva (celestial being) . . . or a human being – those outflows are extinguished in me . . . although born in the world, grown up in the world, having overcome the world, I abide unsoiled by the world. Take it that I am Buddha, brahmin.[3]

The view that the Buddha *as a Buddha* embodies or incarnates a reality that is above gods and humans, that is, a reality that essentially transcends the world of *saṃsāra*, is by no means just a later fabrication of Mahāyāna Buddhism, even if it is true that on a doctrinal level the Mahāyāna has elaborated this view more than the Theravāda has. In what follows, I would like to draw a very brief and selective sketch of this development and relate the Buddhist understanding of incarnation to its Christian parallel. Thereby I will explore the possibility of seeing Buddha and Christ as incarnations of that transcendent reality which is the basis of our salvation.

On the Buddhist Belief in Incarnation

It is told in the Pāli Canon that the Buddha, after his Enlightenment, was hesitant at first to proclaim the insight he had received.[4] But then god Brahmā intervened and showed the 'Exalted One' that the sentient beings would be lost if they were deprived of the help contained in the Buddha's teaching. The Buddha felt compassion with the beings and so he decided to preach the Dharma, the Buddhist teaching. According to another version, also told in the Pāli Canon, it was Māra, the evil tempter, who tried to prevent the Buddha from teaching.[5] Māra declared to the

---

3 Conze, *Buddhist Texts*, p. 105.
4 See *Majjhima Nikāya* i 168–9.
5 See *Dīgha Nikāya* ii 112–13.

Buddha that, since he had now completed the path and attained the highest goal, it would be appropriate to leave the world. But the Buddha replied that he would not depart this world until holy conduct is solidly established – that is, until the Dharma is well taught and the Buddha's followers are able to pass it on.

In both of its versions this narrative emphasizes the point that the Buddha had achieved through his Enlightenment everything he could aspire to for himself; thus all his activity *after* the Enlightenment was entirely and exclusively motivated by altruism. Only for the sake of the sentient beings, out of perfect compassion, the Buddha proclaimed the *Dharma*, the eternal truth he had found. I suppose that behind this tradition stands the well-documented ancient Indian conviction according to which a sage or an enlightened one maintains silence.[6] Therefore someone like the Buddha who spent forty-five years as an itinerant preacher could by no means be regarded as enlightened. In any event, as late as the seventh century the Buddhist philosopher Dharmakīrti still found it necessary to take issue with this objection. He replied with what had already been the point in the two narratives of the Pāli Canon, namely, that the Buddha was perfect in wisdom *and* in compassion, and that the perfection of compassion had been the sole motivation for his preaching.[7]

However, the Buddhist tradition went even further and this already at an early stage. The story wherein Māra tempts the Buddha to depart from the world after his Enlightenment probably alludes to religiously motivated suicide, a practice not unusual in the Buddha's day.[8] Hence, not only Buddha's preaching activity

---

6 See *Saṃyutta Nikāya* i 206.

7 Cf. *Pramāṇavārttika* II, 142–6, 280–2. Cf. Tilman Vetter (ed. and trans.), 1984, *Der Buddha und seine Lehre in Dharmakīrti's Pramā-ṇavārttika*, Wien: Arbeitskreis für tibetische und buddhistische Studien. Universität Wien pp. 50–2, 169–71.

8 This is testified to in e.g. *Saṃyutta Nikāya* i 121; v 320; *Majjhima Nikāya* 145 (iii 269).

but the whole of his existence following his Enlightenment must be seen as an expression of his compassion and his propagation of the *Dharma*. And this means the whole of his existence as a 'Buddha', because Gautama became a 'Buddha' (a 'fully awakened one') only through his Enlightenment. Thus in the Pāli Canon the Buddha is repeatedly identified with the *Dharma*: 'Seeing the *Dharma*', says the Buddha, 'one sees me, seeing me one sees the *Dharma*.'[9] It is worth noting that at least in some places the tenor is that the Buddha thereby points away from himself and towards the exclusive significance of the *Dharma*.[10] But precisely this significance is manifested in the lives of those who are seized by the *Dharma*. The 'visible *Dharma*' – says the Pāli Canon – is the life of a person who has become entirely and lastingly free from greed, hatred and delusion. And, the text continues, the life of such a person is the 'visible *nirvāṇa*'.[11] The lives of the enlightened ones are, so to say, '*nirvāṇized*'. They have 'plunged into the deathless, have achieved it completely, have taken it for free and enjoy the highest peace'.[12]

In this context one needs to bear in mind that according to the traditional Buddhist view *nirvāṇa* is not merely a mental state, the state of the enlightened one. *Nirvāṇa* is rather understood as an 'unconditioned' (*asaṃskṛta*), 'transcendent' (*lokottara*) reality,[13]

---

9 Cf. *Saṃyutta Nikāya* iii 120, *Itivuttaka* 92.

10 On this, see the relevant remarks of Lambert Schmithausen, in A. Bsteh (ed.), 2000, *Der Buddhismus als Anfrage an christliche Theologie und Philosophie*, Mödling: Verlag St. Gabriel, p. 263.

11 Cf. *Aṅguttara Nikāya* 3.54–6 (i 157–9).

12 *Khuddaka Pāṭha* 6:7.

13 The point has been very clearly made in some excellent recent studies as, for example, Moti Lal Pandit, 1993, 'Nirvāṇa as the Unconditioned', in Moti Lal Pandit, *Being as Becoming: Studies in Early Buddhism*, New Delhi: Intercultural Publications, pp. 312–39. John Makransky, 1997, *Buddhahood Embodied: Sources of Controversy in India and Tibet*, Albany: SUNY, particularly pp. 85–108. Steven Collins, 1998, *Nirvana and Other Buddhist Felicities*, Cambridge: Cambridge University Press, pp. 161–85. Peter Harvey, 2004, *The Selfless Mind: Personality, Consciousness and Nirvāṇa in Early Buddhism*, repr., London and New York: RoutledgeCurzon, pp. 180–97.

whose existence is the condition of the possibility of salvation. Thus it is said in the Pāli Canon:

> There is, monks, a not-born (*ajātaṁ*), a not-brought-to-being (*abhūtaṁ*), a not-made (*akataṁ*), a not-conditioned (*asaṅkhataṁ*). If, monks, there were no not-born, not-brought-to-being, not-made, not-conditioned, no escape would be discerned from what is born, brought-to-being, made, conditioned. But since there is a not-born, a not-brought-to-being, a not-made, a not-conditioned, therefore an escape is discerned from what is born, brought-to-being, made, conditioned.[14]

In this sense two of the most influential works of traditional Theravāda Buddhism, the *Milindapañha* and Buddhaghosa's *Visuddhi Magga*, present the following argument: In order to be a deathless reality, *nirvāṇa* needs to be unconditioned. For everything that is subject to conditioned origination is also subject to death and decay. And since it is unconditioned, *nirvāṇa* cannot be merely a mental state. For as the mental state of the enlightened one, it would be conditioned, that is, it would arise as the result of completing the Buddhist path. Therefore the state of the enlightened one must be understood as the attainment of a transcendent reality that exists independently from this achievement. Hence it is the existence of this unconditioned reality that makes Enlightenment, which is the liberation from the world of conditioned existence, at all possible.[15] With this in mind, the concept of the 'visible *nirvāṇa*' could be interpreted as follows: The enlightened one, freed from the roots of all evil and motivated exclusively by perfect compassion, is imbued with, and hence transparent to, the unconditioned reality of *nirvāṇa*, which in itself transcends all conditioned reality and all human understanding.

These beginnings of a Buddhist belief in incarnation were further developed with the rise of Mahāyāna Buddhism. In the

---

14 *Udāna* 8:3; and *Itivuttaka* 43; cf. John Ireland (trans.), 1997, *The Udana and Itivuttaka*, Kandy: Buddhist Publication Society, pp. 103, 180.
15 Cf. *Milindapañha* 269f., *Visuddhimagga* 507–09.

still relatively early, but at the same time extremely influential *Lotus Sūtra*, which became formative for all of East Asian Buddhism, the earthly Buddha is portrayed as the temporally limited manifestation of a supra-mundane and virtually eternal[16] Buddha-reality. In the *Lotus Sūtra* this reality is named the 'Father of the World' who for the sake of the deluded beings manifests or incarnates among them in order to show them the path towards Enlightenment.[17] Obvious are the parallels to the *avatāra* concept of the *Bhagavadgītā*, which was composed at about the same time as the *Lotus Sūtra*.[18]

The Buddhist belief in incarnation is fully developed in the later mahāyānistic doctrine of the 'Three Buddha Bodies'

---

16 The *Lotus Sūtra*, chapter 15 (in Kumārajīva's version: chapter 16), is slightly ambiguous as to the Buddha's eternity. On the one hand, it still speaks of an attainment of the Buddhahood. On the other hand, it says that this 'attainment' took place in an immeasurable past and that the Buddha's life is never-ending. In East Asian Buddhism it was and is taught that the Buddha of the *Lotus Sūtra* is in fact eternal. Cf. Paul Williams, 1989, *Mahā yāna Buddhism: The Doctrinal Foundations*, London and New York: Routledge, pp. 151f.

17 *Saddharmapuṇḍarīka Sūtra* (Sanskrit version) 15:21–23: 'So am I the father of the world, the Selfborn, the Healer, the Protector of all creatures. . . . What reason should I have to continually manifest myself? When men become unbelieving, unwise, ignorant, careless, fond of sensual pleasures, and from thoughtlessness run into misfortune, Then I, who know the course of the world, declare: I am so and so, (and consider): How can I incline them to enlightenment? How can they become partakers of the Buddha-laws?' H. Kern (trans.), 1963, *Saddharma-Puṇḍarīka or The Lotus of the True Law* (SBE XXI, 1884), repr., New York: Dover Publications, pp. 309f.

18 See *Bhagavadgītā* 4:6–8: 'Though I am unborn, and My self is imperishable, though I am the lord of all creatures, . . . I come into (empiric) being through My power (*māyā*). Whenever there is a decline of righteousness and rise of unrighteousness, . . . then I send forth (create incarnate) Myself. For the protection of the good, for the destruction of the wicked, and for the establishment of righteousness, I come into being from age to age.' S. Radhakrishnan and Ch. A. Moore (eds), 1989, *A Source Book in Indian Philosophy*, ppb. repr., Princeton: Princeton University Press, p. 116. The parallels between the *Lotus Sūtra* and the *Bhagavadgītā* have already been pointed out by H. Kern, cf. *Saddharma-Puṇḍarīka or The Lotus of the True Law*, pp. xxvf.

(*trikāya*).[19] 'Body' (*kāya*) refers here to the respective form or level of reality or effectivity within the complex reality of the Buddha. The earthly Buddha represents the 'Transformation Body' (*nirmāṇakāya*) – so-called either because of the imperma-nence of this form of reality or because of its relative unreality, which is to say, a form of existence that in comparison with the unconditioned ultimate reality resembles an illusion. Following the track traced by the *Lotus Sūtra*, the earthly Buddha of the *nirmāṇakāya* is further regarded as the manifestation of a supra-mundane Buddha whose form of reality is designated as 'Enjoy-ment Body' (*saṃbhogakāya*). The name 'Enjoyment Body' probably refers on the one hand to Buddhahood as it is enjoyed by the Buddha as the fruit of his own striving and on the other hand to Buddhahood as an enjoyment for the others in so far as the Buddha's existence is basically understood as an altruistically motivated pro-existence.[20] However, the ultimate basis (*āśraya*) of the human and the supra-mundane Buddha is the inconceiv-able, ineffable transcendent reality, which in the context of the 'Three Buddha-Bodies' is called the 'Dharma Body' (*dharmakā-ya*, also called *svābhāvika-kāya* = 'Essential Body'). In contrast to the two other bodies, the *dharmakāya* is not a 'form' of existence, but a 'formless' (*arūpa*) reality. The 'Transformation Body' and the 'Enjoyment Body' are both called 'Form Bod-ies' (*rūpakāya*) because they are conceivable and even visible – the human Buddha through human eyes, the supra-mundane Buddha through meditational vision. But the *dharmakāya* is in a radical sense inconceivable and ineffable. It is the ultimate true

---

19 On the *trikāya*-doctrine see Gadjin Nagao, 1991, 'On the Theory of Buddha-Body (*Buddha-kāya*)', in Gadjin Nagao, *Mādhyamika and Yogācāra: A Study of Mahāyāna Philosophies*, Albany: SUNY, pp. 103–22; Helmut Tauscher, 1998, 'Die Buddha-Wirklichkeit in den späteren Formen des mahāyānistischen Buddhismus', in P. Schmidt-Leukel (ed.), *Wer ist Buddha? Eine Gestalt und ihre Bedeutung für die Menschheit*, Munich: Diederichs, pp. 93–118, 247–51; Paul Griffiths, 1994, *On Being Buddha: The Classical Doctrine of Buddhahood*, Albany: SUNY; Makransky, *Buddhahood Embodied*.

20 Cf. Nagao, 'On the Theory of Buddha-Body', p. 108.

reality transcending, underlying and permeating everything,[21] accessible only through the two form bodies.

The dynamics of the 'Buddha-Bodies' doctrine can be interpreted as the twofold movement of ascent and descent.[22] The ascent begins with the human Buddha through whom an understanding of the divine Buddha as his supra-mundane ground is won. And this supra-mundane Buddha needs to be transcended too towards its ultimate ground, the ineffable, truly eternal or timeless[23] reality of the *dharmakāya*. But at the same time this

---

21 Paul Harrison (1992, 'Is the Dharma-kāya the Real "Phantom Body" of the Buddha?', in *Journal of the International Association of Buddhist Studies* 15, pp. 44–94) has warned strongly against an understanding – or, as he thinks, misunderstanding – of the *dharmakāya* as 'a kind of Buddhist absolute' (p. 44). Harrison has produced impressive philological evidence that at least in pre-Mahāyāna, early Mahāyāna and partly middle Mahāyāna usage '*dharmakāya*' should be understood as either Buddha's embodiment in his teaching or as the Buddha's equipment with the 'body', i.e., with the full range, of those attributes and features which are particular to a Buddha. However, Harrison seems to interpret the *dharma as teaching* in a quite modern, purely propositional sense, and not in the traditional sense according to which the *dharma* is an eternal truth or law discovered by the Buddha and reflected or mediated in his teachings. Moreover, Harrison seems to neglect the fact that the attributes of the Buddha are traditionally understood along the lines of the idea of the 'visible *dharma/nirvāṇa*' and hence as expressive of an ultimate, unconditioned reality. For a critique of Harrison's interpretation of the early Mahāyāna usage of the term *dharmakāya* see Makransky, *Buddhahood Embodied*, pp. 373–5, n. 12 (see fn. 13). For Makransky the 'study of Buddhist understanding of *dharmakā ya* could instigate rewarding new lines of inquiry into the nature of God; and I believe the reverse to be equally rewarding' (*Buddhahood Embodied*, p. 370).

22 Cf. G. Nagao, 'The Bodhisattva Returns to this World', in Nagao, *Mādhyamika and Yogācāra*, pp. 23–34.

23 See, for example, the *Ch'êng-wei-shi-lun* (chapter 14): 'The pure realm of the Dharma is said to be eternal because it is devoid of origination, . devoid of cessation, and by nature unchanging.' Francis H. Cook (trans.), 1999, *Three Texts on Consciousness Only* (BDK English Tripitaka 60–I, II, III), Berkeley: Numata Center for Buddhist Translation and Research, p. 359. While the eternal or timeless nature of the *dharmakāya* is undisputed, the eternity of the *saṃbhogakāya* is similarly ambiguous as the eternity of the Buddha in the *Lotus Sūtra* (see fn. 16 above). Sometimes the eternity of the *saṃbhogakāya* is affirmed (as e.g. in the *Ch'êng-wei-shi-lun* 14, cf. *Three*

movement of ascent can also be seen as a movement of descent. That is, the human Buddha is a manifestation or incarnation, an *avatāra* (literally 'descent') of the supra-mundane Buddha, and the supra-mundane Buddha, the Buddha of the 'Enjoyment Body', is a manifestation, a concretizing or an 'outflow' (*niṣyanda*)[24] of the absolute Buddha, the *dharmakāya*.

The motif of descent has played a significant role in the ideas of some Buddhist thinkers, as for example in the work of T'an-luan who lived in China from 476 until 542. In accordance with the Indian Mahāyāna tradition T'an-luan understood the formless *dharmakāya* as the true basis and ground of the two form bodies. But he interpreted this distinction as two different modes of the one *dharmakāya*. The '*dharmakāya* as suchness' is the *dharmakāya* in its inconceivable, absolute reality. And the '*dharmakāya* as skilful means' is the *dharmakāya* as it is manifest in the two form bodies in order to make itself accessible. According to T'an-luan, these two modes of the *dharmakāya* are different, but not separable, are one, but not identical.[25] In the thirteenth century, this idea was adopted by Shinran Shōnin (1173–1262), the founding figure of the Japanese Jōdo-Shin

---

Texts on Consciousness Only, p. 361), sometimes eternity is attributed genuinely only to the *dharmakāya*, while the *saṃbhogakāya* is somehow expressive of this, as for example in *Mahāyānasaṃgraha*, chapter 10 (cf. John P. Keenan (trans.), 1992, *The Summary of the Great Vehicle by Bodhisattva Asaṅga* (BDK English Tripitaka 46–III), Berkeley: Numata Center for Buddhist Translation and Research, p. 120). Nagao has rightly said of the *saṃbhogakāya* that it 'has the two aspects of being at once transcendental and phenomenal, and at once historic and super-historic.' Nagao, 'On the Theory of Buddha-Body', p. 110.

24 Cf. Nagao, 'On the Theory of Buddha-Body', p. 110 and p. 250, n. 17 (with references).

25 See T'an-luan's Commentary on Vasubhandu's Treatise on the Pure Land (Ching-t'u lun) as quoted in Shinran's *Kyōgyōshinshō* part IV (Gutoku Shaku Shinran, 1973, *The Kyōgyōshinshō* trans. D.T. Suzuki, ed. The Eastern Buddhist Society, Kyoto: Shinshū Ōtaniha, pp. 189f.). See also the translation in: *The Collected Works of Shinran*, 1997, vol. 1, Kyoto: Jōdo Shinshū Hongwanji-ha, p. 165.

Shū.[26] According to Shinran, the inconceivable '*dharmakāya* as suchness' manifests itself as the '*dharmakāya* as skilful means' in the form of Amida Buddha, the supra-mundane Buddha of limitless, all-encompassing compassion; in turn, Amida Buddha is manifested or incarnated as Gautama Buddha, in order to guide the beings towards their salvation. In other words, the inconceivable transcendent reality is revealed to us as the mind of infinite loving-kindness finding its meta-historical expression in the figure of Amida and its historical expression in Gautama Buddha. Thus despite the inconceivability of the ultimate in itself, it can be determined in the mode of revelation as 'great compassion' (*mahākaruṇā*). 'The aspiration for Buddhahood', says Shinran:

> . . . is the aspiration to save all beings. The aspiration to save all beings is the mind that grasps sentient beings and brings them to birth in the Pure Land of happiness. This mind is the mind of ultimate equality. It is great compassion. This mind attains Buddhahood. This mind is Buddha.[27]

From this vantage point let us look back on the portrayal of Gautama Buddha in the Pāli Canon:[28] In his proclamation of the *dharma* Buddha indiscriminately embraced everyone, whether brahman, king, prince, merchant, farmer, or servant, whether

---

26 See Hee-Sung Keel, 1995, *Understanding Shinran: A Dialogical Approach*, Berkeley: Asian Humanities Press, pp. 154–82; Perry Schmidt-Leukel, 'Gautama und Amida-Buddha: Das Buddha-Bild bei Shinran Shonin', in Schmidt-Leukel (ed.), *Wer ist Buddha?*, pp. 119–39, 252–9 (see fn. 19), and Schmidt-Leukel, 1992, '*Den Löwen brüllen hören': Zur Hermeneutik eines christlichen Verständnisses der buddhistischen Heilsbotschaft*, Paderborn: Schöningh, pp. 605–54.

27 'Passages on the Pure Land Way (*Jōdo monrui jushō*)', in *The Collected Works of Shinran*, vol. 1, p. 314.

28 I refer here to the image of the Buddha as sketched in the canonical scriptures, not to the character features of the historical Buddha, about whom we have no certain knowledge apart from his reflection in the mirror of faithful veneration. The same needs to be said with regard to the character features of Jesus.

high, low or outcast, wealthy or poor, man or woman. He publicly honoured the leper Suppabuddha by offering him the seat on his right-hand side.[29] He did not turn down the invitation to dinner in the house of the prostitute Ambapālī, even as some noble-men tried to hold him back.[30] He spoke highly of the drunkard Sarakāni as of someone who had attained the first stage of holi-ness.[31] And he did not even hesitate to seek a personal encounter with the cruel mass-murderer Aṅgulimāla. After he succeeded in converting him, he admitted him to the order despite the public displeasure this caused.[32] The Buddha rejected the caste system and proclaimed that people should be judged only by their spiritual and moral achievements, not by their descent.[33] He confirmed that women are on principle spiritually equal to men and established as a result the order of nuns.[34] When he met Panthaka, a man expelled from house and home, the Buddha put his arm tenderly around him, comforted him with kind words, gave him a linen cloth for washing his feet and admitted him to the community.[35] With his own hands the Buddha washed and tended a monk who suffered from fatal diarrhoea and was neglected by his fellow monks. They were admonished by the Buddha with the words: 'Whoever, monks, would wait upon me . . . should wait upon the sick.'[36] He instructed the children not to harm animals[37] and rejected the Vedic animal sacrifices as cruel and useless.[38] He taught a loving-kindness that does not exclude anyone, a loving-kindness that is forbearing and for-giving and includes even the worst enemy.[39] When a war once

29 See *Udāna* 5:3.

30 See *Dīgha Nikāya* 16 (ii 96–102).

31 See *Saṃyutta Nikāya* v 375–8.

32 See *Majjhima Nikāya* 86.

33 Cf. *Sutta Nipāta* 116–42, 594–656; *Dhammapada* 383–423; *Majjhima Nikāya* 84.

34 See *Cullavagga* 10:1.

35 See *Theragātha* 557–66.

36 *Mahāvagga* 8:26,1–4.

37 See *Udāna* 5:4.

38 Cf. *Dīgha Nikāya* 5; *Sutta Nipāta* 284–315.

39 Cf. *Sutta Nipāta* 1:8; *Majjhima Nikāya* 21.

threatened to break out over a shortage of water, the Buddha actively intervened and managed to reconcile the hostile tribes thereby preventing the pending carnage.[40] What real love means, he said, can be seen from a mother who protects her child with her life.[41] The image of the Buddha in the Pāli Canon is summarily stated in the words of the lay-follower Jīvaka: 'I have heard that Brahma lives with love. But I saw with my own eyes that the Venerable One (the Buddha) is always living with love.'[42]

On the Christian Belief in Incarnation

The portrayal of Jesus in the gospels bears some strikingly similar features to the image of the Buddha. Jesus, too, addressed his message of the forthcoming Kingdom of God to people from all strata of society, to men and women, to Jews and non-Jews, to the scribes and to the simple, to the rich and to the poor, to the insiders and to the outsiders of society such as tax-collectors, prostitutes and drunkards. He accompanied his message of the saving and liberating reign of God by symbolic acts of healing and exorcism, and lived a life in service of others, again symbolically expressed by the washing of his disciples' feet. He encouraged a life of non-violence, and as the central rule of God's kingdom he proclaimed and practised forgiving love, which includes even one's enemies and finds its highest expression in sacrificing one's life for one's friends.

Jesus' life, as portrayed in the gospels, was entirely determined by his understanding of and his complete dedication to the Kingdom of God. But Jesus did not put himself in God's place. Wolfhart Pannenberg summed up what is nowadays an uncontroversial view in serious biblical scholarship:

At the heart of the message of Jesus stood the Father and his coming kingdom, not any dignity that Jesus claimed for his

---

40 See *Jātaka* 536.
41 See *Sutta Nipāta* 149.
42 *Majjhima Nikāya* 55 (i 369).

own person that would thus make himself equal to God (John 5:18). Jesus differentiated himself as a mere man from the Father as the one God. He thus subjected himself to the claim of the coming divine rule, just as he required his hearers to do. He could even reject the respectful title 'good Master' (Mark 10:18 par.), with a reference to God alone as good.[43]

Quite early and rather quickly, however, the professions of faith went beyond Jesus' own self-understanding, such that the Gospel of John could already speak about Jesus as the 'word' or *logos* 'made flesh'. One decisive reason for this may have to do with Jesus' own message of the Kingdom of God. Jesus, as Joachim Gnilka says, 'did not merely proclaim the coming reign of God; it also became an event in him, linking his message, his work, and his person.'[44] In principle this view is corroborated by the Jewish historian Geza Vermes. In Jesus' understanding, says Vermes, God's rule on earth is realized in that humans fulfil the divine will. Hence the two petitions of the Lord's Prayer must be seen in close conjunction: God's kingdom comes by letting God's will be done.[45] According to Vermes, the guiding idea behind Jesus' understanding of God's kingdom was the imitation of God – to be merciful to one another, just as God is merciful to us (Luke 6.36).[46] In this sense Jesus' life reflected the love of God. To quote Vermes:

> The 'neighbours' he is to love as himself often turn out to be the outcasts of society, whose company he does not merely accept but positively seeks. . . . He treats them as friends . . . But his behaviour should cause no surprise. He is simply

---

43 Wolfhart Pannenberg, 1994, *Systematic Theology*, vol. 2, Grand Rapids: Eerdmans, p. 372.

44 Joachim Gnilka, 1997, *Jesus of Nazareth: Message and History*, Peabody: Hendrickson Publishers, p. 255.

45 See Geza Vermes, 1981, *The Gospel of Jesus the Jew: The Riddell Memorial Lectures*, Newcastle: University of Newcastle upon Tyne, part II.

46 See Geza Vermes, 1993, *The Religion of Jesus the Jew*, London: SCM Press, pp. 157ff., 200ff.

imitating in his personal conduct what he understands to be the conduct of the Father towards those of his children who return to relation with him from a state of irrelation.[47]

It is not difficult to see how from this the following conclusion, as expressed by Gnilka, can be drawn:

> Since the kingdom of God denotes God establishing God's gracious reign, the presence of the future reign of God in Jesus' ministry ultimately means that God is actually at work in him and that in Jesus God's love itself could be experienced.[48]

In this light the metaphor of the divine word made flesh makes good sense: Jesus embodies in his life and work what God is to us. In Jesus it becomes clear that 'God is love', as declared in the first letter of John (1 John 4.8). The word that is metaphorically spoken to us by God gains a concrete, relevant, perceptible, or even – as also said in the first letter of John (1 John 1.1) – 'tangible' form in the life and person of Jesus.

This is, however, precisely what prohibits a simple identification of Jesus and God, demanding instead a dynamic, high-contrast correlation that retains both the real representation of God in the life of Jesus and, at the same time, the genuine difference between Jesus, the human, and God. This has found a startling expression in the paradoxical word of the letter to the Colossians calling Jesus 'the image of the invisible God' (Col. 1.15). That is, God remains the 'invisible' reality that transcends all our finite perception and conception, and yet what God is to us finds in Jesus a visible and conceivable image.

---

47 Vermes, *The Gospel of Jesus the Jew*, p. 44.

48 Gnilka, *Jesus of Nazareth*, p. 254 (translation amended). The German original reads: 'Weil Gottesherrschaft besagt, daß Gott seine gnädige Herrschaft aufrichtet, bedeutet die Gegenwärtigkeit der zukünftigen Gottesherrschaft im Wirken Jesu letztlich, daß Gott unmittelbar in ihm wirkt, die Liebe Gottes selbst in ihm erfahrbar wurde.' J. Gnilka, 1990, *Jesus von Nazaret*, Freiburg: Herder, p. 258.

As Christian belief in incarnation developed further, this tense correlation was clearly in danger of being dissolved for the sole benefit of its divine pole. It is therefore important and should not be underestimated that the theological development did not come to a halt when the Council of Nicaea (325) exclusively emphasized Jesus' substantial unity with God. Indeed, it led to the Council of Chalcedon (451), which balanced and in a sense amended Nicaea by adding that Jesus is not only of one substance with God but also of one substance with humans.[49] However, the question of how one should understand the relationship between the divine and the human natures of Jesus, and in particular, how it would be possible to affirm Jesus' divine nature without denying his true humanness, was left unanswered.

Pluralist Perspectives

To be sure, there are a number of differences between Jesus and Gautama, differences regarding the context, the content, and in a sense the grammar of their life and their teachings, and, of course, differences between the faithful interpretation of their person as the Christ, the 'Anointed One', and as the Buddha, the 'Enlightened' or 'Awakened One'. But there are also some startling structural parallels in the formation of the Buddhist and Christian belief in incarnation, as in the interpretation of the Buddha and the Christ as mediators of transcendent reality: Gautama embodies the Dharma he taught, and Jesus embodies the Kingdom of God he proclaimed. Seen from the perspective of their followers, both Jesus and Gautama are actual expressive figures of that ultimate reality to which they refer through their message, their work and their life. The Buddha appears to his adherents as the 'visible *nirvāṇa*' and the Christ appears to his adherents as the visible 'image of the invisible God'. In both cases, this seems to provide the starting point for the further

---

49 See J.N.D. Kelly, 1977, *Early Christian Doctrines*, 5th rev. edn, London: Adam & Charles Black; Frances Young, 1983, *From Nicaea to Chalcedon*, London: SCM Press.

development of the respective concepts of incarnation. In this context I would like to underline two things:

(1) The immediate foundation for the incarnation belief does not consist in a corresponding self-understanding of Jesus or Gautama. Jesus did not understand himself as the human incarnation of the second person of a trinitarian God[50] any more than Gautama saw himself as the 'Transformation Body' (*nirmāṇakāya*) of a three-bodied Buddha-reality or cosmic *trikāya*. Rather, both were pointing beyond themselves: Jesus to the Father whose coming reign he lived and proclaimed, and Gautama to the *Dharma* he lived and proclaimed. In both cases the formation of incarnation belief begins with the religious experience of those for whom Jesus and Gautama became the decisive mediators of their own respective relation to transcendent reality. It was the disciples of Jesus who experienced Jesus as the mediator of God's presence, and it was the disciples of Gautama for whom he became the personified Dharma and the 'visible *nirvāṇa*'. Belief in incarnation is thus grounded in the principle of a real-symbolic mediation, that is, the symbol pointing away from itself to the symbolized from which it is different, while at the same time making the symbolized present through the symbol itself. This is, as Roger Haight rightly emphasizes, the crucial and lasting core of the incarnation idea.[51]

(2) What enabled Jesus and Gautama to become mediators of a salvific relation to a transcendent reality for their disciples was

---

50 As Reinhard Hübner has shown, the doctrine of the Trinity was neither implicitly nor explicitly characteristic for the origins of Christianity, and did not develop before c. 150 CE. Moreover, its first proponents were accused of the heresies of ditheism and tritheisms. See R. Hübner, 1996, Ἐἷς Θεὸς Ιησους Χριστός Zum christlichen Gottesglauben im 2. Jahrhundert – ein Versuch', in *Münchener Theologische Zeitschrift* 47, pp. 325–44. For an outline of the development from the monotheism of Jesus to the later Christian doctrine of the Trinity, see Karl-Heinz Ohlig, 1999, *Ein Gott in drei Personen? Vom Vater Jesu zum 'Mysterium' der Trinität*, Mainz: Matthias Grünewald Verlag.

51 See Roger Haight, 1992, 'The Case for Spirit Christology', in *Theological Studies* 53, pp. 257–87; Roger Haight, 1999, *Jesus: Symbol of God*, Maryknoll: Orbis.

of course the fact that Jesus and Gautama lived their own lives out of such a close relationship with transcendence: in Jesus' case, his complete self-surrender to the Father and his will; in Gautama's, his utmost striving for *nirvāṇa* and his loving, selfless, *nirvāṇized* life after his Enlightenment. However, the logic of incarnation-belief entails that this was not merely Jesus' and Gautama's own achievement, but something that originated in the transcendent reality *itself*. Within the Christian context this is expressed by the affirmation of the full divinity of the Spirit with whom, according to scriptural testimony, Jesus was filled and who lay at the foundation of his work. Within Buddhism the doctrine of the Buddha Nature or Buddha Germ (*tathāgata-garbha*) fulfils a similar function.[52] In the face of the question as to how it is possible at all that a deluded being enmeshed in greed and hatred could become a Buddha, Mahāyāna Buddhism responds with the belief in a potentiality or inclination within every being: an embryonic Buddha Nature, rooted in nothing else than in the unconditioned reality of the 'Dharma Body' (*dharmakāya*) itself.

Inevitably, this now confronts us with the issue of the uniqueness of incarnation. The Buddha Nature of all beings enables

---

52 For a brief overview over the doctrine of Buddha Nature see Paul Williams, 1989, *Mahāyāna-Buddhism: The Doctrinal Foundations*, London: Routledge, pp. 96–115. For a more comprehensive treatment see David Seyfort Ruegg, 1969, *La Théorie du Tathāgatagarbha et du Gotra*, Paris: École Française d'Extrême Orient; David Seyfort Ruegg, 1989, *Buddha-Nature, Mind and the Problem of Gradualism in a Comparative Perspective*, London: SOAS; Sally B. King, 1991, *Buddha Nature*, Albany: SUNY; S.K. Hookham, 1991, *The Buddha Within*, Albany: SUNY. A translation of the short, but highly influential *Tathāgatagarbha Sūtra* is offered by W.H. Grosnick, 1995, 'The Tathāgatagarbha Sūtra', in D.S. Lopez (ed.), *Buddhism in Practice*, Princeton: Princeton University Press, pp. 92–106. Perhaps the most important scripture on Buddha Nature, the *Ratnagotravibhaga*, has been translated in: Jikido Takasaki, 1966, *A Study on the Ratnagotravibhāga (Uttaratantra) Being a Treatise on the Tathāgatagarbha Theory of Mahāyāna Buddhism* (Serie Orientale Roma 33), Rome: Istituto Italiano per il Medio ed Estremo Oriente, and more recently in: R. Fuchs (trans.), 2000, *Buddha Nature: The Mahayana Uttaratantra Shastra by Arya Maitreya*, Ithaca: Snow Lion Publications.

them fully to unfold this and become Buddhas. Could something similar be said within Christianity about the divine Spirit? According to Romans 8.14, 'all who are being led by the Spirit of God, these are sons of God'. In a modern theological anthropology, as for example in the thought of Karl Rahner, the gift of the Spirit is not understood in a particularist manner but as the gracious presence of God in the life of *all* people. The perfect way in which Jesus resonated with the Spirit therefore represents, as Rahner said, the '*highest* instance of the actualization of the essence of human reality, which consists in this: that man is in so far as he abandons himself to the absolute mystery whom we call God.'[53] Given such a conception, the idea that Christ had two natures can no longer jeopardize his true humanity. On the contrary, the universal presence of the divine Spirit in the depth of everyone's existence is exactly the precondition for the full actualization of what it means to be truly human. This, however, allows for the possibility of something like a 'gradual incarnation', according to which everyone incarnates or embodies the presence of God, in so far and to the degree that he or she resonates in his or her life with the divine Spirit. But why should we then not seriously reckon with the possibility that there are several 'highest instances' of such an 'actualization of the essence of human reality', that is with the possibility of several incarnations so conceived?[54]

Concretely: What impact does the Christian belief in the divine incarnation in Jesus have on Christians' response to the Buddhist belief in Buddha as the 'visible *nirvāna*' or the incarnation of the 'Dharma Body' (*dharmakāya*)? Will the belief that God was in Christ help Christians to accept or even affirm the Buddhist

---

53 Rahner's emphasis. Karl Rahner, 1978, *Foundations of Christian Faith*, London: Darton, Longman & Todd, p. 218.

54 See also Paul Knitter, 1985, *No Other Name? A Critical Survey of Christian Attitudes Toward the World Religions*, Maryknoll: Orbis, pp. 186–94, where Knitter raises similar questions regarding Karl Rahner's Christology. For an example of a clear version of a gradual understanding of incarnation see John Hick, 1993, *The Metaphor of God Incarnate*, London: SCM Press, particularly pp. 99–111.

belief in incarnation, or will it oblige them to deny that Buddha embodied the *dharmakāya*? The answer to this question depends not only on what type of incarnation concept is presupposed and whether this allows in principle for the possibility of several incarnations or not. It will also depend on whether Christians can identify the reality that they see embodied in Jesus with the reality that Buddhists see embodied in the Buddha. Is it possible, from a Christian perspective, to identify the reality called 'God' with the reality called '*dharmakāya*'?

First of all, it needs to be stated soberly that historically and phenomenologically 'God' and '*dharmakāya*' are not identical. The connotations they carry within their respective systems and their historical genealogies are simply too different. But despite those undeniable differences they can be seen as 'functional equivalents'. Within their own and different contexts they both serve as pointers towards an unconditioned, transcendent reality that is the ultimate source of salvation or liberation. Whether this entails that they are pointing towards the *same* ultimate reality, can not be established in any objective and unquestionable sense, of course. The response to this question can only be given by the members of the respective religious communities themselves on the basis of specific criteria prescribed by their own traditions. From a Christian point of view the two most important criteria may be that any functional equivalent to God can be seen as genuine, (1) if it does not entail idolatry, that is, if it does not confound the ultimate with any finite and man-made reality (Ex. 20.4); and (2) if it is intrinsically linked to the evocation of selfless love, as stated in 1 John 4.7: 'Everyone who loves . . . knows God'. I suggest that the *dharmakāya* complies exceptionally well with these two criteria and that therefore Christians can and should regard it as a genuine equivalent – that is, as a concept which points indeed to the very same transcendent reality known to Christians under the concept of 'God'. Again, this does not mean that *dharmakāya* and God are the same, but that they refer in different ways to the same reality that transcends them both.

Could such a view meet with consent from Buddhists? Can

Buddhists identify the Christian God as a genuine equivalent to the *dharmakāya* and hence see Jesus as an authentic incarnation? José Cabezón has argued that what is objectionable from a Mahāyāna Buddhist perspective is not 'the claim that Jesus is the incarnation or manifestation of a deity' but rather 'the Christian characterisation of the deity whose manifestation Jesus is said to be'.[55] According to Cabezón, this could neither be the God of the Hebrew Bible, who has too many morally objectionable features,[56] nor 'the God of later Christian theological speculation', since from a Buddhist point of view such a God does not exist.[57] Alternatively Jesus could be understood along the lines of the 'Three Bodies' doctrine as 'a *nirmāṇakāya* – that is, as the physical embodiment of an enlightened being.'[58] But this, says Cabezón, would still leave us with the question as to how to

---

55 J.I. Cabezón, 2000, 'A God, but Not a Savior', in R.M. Gross and T. Muck (eds), 2000, *Buddhists Talk about Jesus: Christians Talk about the Buddha*, New York: Continuum, pp. 17–31, here p. 24. Additionally, Cabezón rejects 'the claim that Jesus is unique in being such a manifestation' (p. 24). This criticism has been frequently advanced by Buddhists (cf. Perry Schmidt-Leukel (ed.), 2001, *Buddhist Perceptions of Jesus*, St. Ottilien: EOS-Verlag, p. 29), and coincides with the view of those Hindus who accept Jesus as an *avatāra*, but not as the only one. However, as I tried to show, incarnation can also from a Christian perspective be conceived such that it no longer entails an inevitable claim to uniqueness.

56 'The God of the Hebrew Bible is a jealous one that demands the undivided loyalty of its followers, it demands of them blood sacrifice, it is partial and capable of seemingly malevolent actions, to the point of even engaging in violent reprisals against those who refuse to obey its will. . . . Those who would identify Jesus with the God of the Hebrew Bible make him heir to a divine legacy that is, from a Buddhist viewpoint, at the very least of questionable worth.' Cabezón, 'A God, but Not a Savior', p. 25.

57 'There is no god who is the creator of the universe, who is originally pure and primordially perfected, who is omnipotent and who can will the salvation of beings. Jesus, therefore, cannot be the incarnation of such a God.' Cabezón, 'A God, but Not a Savior', p. 26. For the attempt to show that those traditional Christian ideas have far more in common with the Buddhist understanding of ultimate reality than Cabezón admits, see my essay 'The Unbridgeable Gulf? Towards a Buddhist-Christian Theology of Creation', in P. Schmidt-Leukel (ed.), 2006, *Buddhism, Christianity and the Question of Creation: Karmic or Divine?*, Aldershot: Ashgate.

58 Cabezón, 'A God, but Not a Savior', p. 26.

explain the contradictions between the teachings of Jesus and the traditional Buddhist doctrines. Nevertheless Cabezón indicates that this problem might be solved with recourse to the Buddhist doctrine of 'skilful means' *(upāya)* – the idea that in face of the inconceivability and ineffability of ultimate reality all teachings are at best only provisionally or relatively true if and in so far as they can be used to guide people to Enlightenment.[59]

A similar approach has been adopted by three other Buddhist thinkers. Alfred Bloom,[60] Masao Abe,[61] and John Makransky[62] have, each in his own way, argued that, as Bloom says, the 'Gods, Buddhas, and spiritual beings or symbols are manifestations from the *Dharmakāya* . . . in order to guide beings to Enlightenment'.[63] Hence, 'other religions, each in their own historical and spiritual development', could be interpreted 'as means' in the Buddhist sense of *upāya*. Makransky states, quite similarly, that

> (v)iewed from within the Mahāyāna doctrine of skilful means, non-Buddhist traditions *do* originate in or fully express, in their own ways, the Absolute realised on the Buddhist path . . . Buddhahood is speaking through the world, and through the various religions.[64]

Abe too employs the 'Three Bodies' scheme in order to provide a Buddhist interpretation of religious diversity. He assigns to the

---

59 Cf. Michael Pye, 1978, *Skilful Means: A Concept in Mahayana Buddhism*, London: Duckworth; J.I. Cabezón, 1994, *Buddhism and Language: A Study of Indo-Tibetan Scholasticism*, Albany: SUNY.

60 See A. Bloom, 1992, 'Shin Buddhism in Encounter with a Religiously Plural World', in *The Pure Land*, New Series, nos. 8–9, pp. 17–31.

61 See M. Abe, 1985, 'A Dynamic Unity in Religious Pluralism: A Proposal from the Buddhist Point of View', in J. Hick and H. Askari (eds), *The Experience of Religious Diversity*, Aldershot: Gower, pp. 163–90, 225–7.

62 See J. Makransky, 2003, 'Buddhist Perspectives on Truth in Other Religions: Past and Present', in *Theological Studies* 64, pp. 334–61.

63 Bloom, 'Shin Buddhism in Encounter with a Religiously Plural World', p. 26.

64 Makransky, 'Buddhist Perspectives on Truth in Other Religions', p. 358.

level of the *nirmāṇakāya* any 'historical religious figure that is the center of faith', such as Gautama, Krishna, Jesus, Muhammad or Moses; and to the level of the *saṃbhogakāya* any 'personal God who is supra-historical but has a particular name and virtue', such as Amida, Ishvara, Yahweh or Allah.[65] The level of the *dharmakāya* is represented by what Abe calls 'formless emptiness' or 'boundless openness'. This is linked to the other two levels or 'bodies' as their 'ultimate ground', and 'dynamically reveals itself both in terms of personal "God" and in terms of "lords", that are historical religious figures.'[66]

I wish to highlight two observations with regard to these Buddhist proposals. First, each of the three Buddhist thinkers uses a conceptuality specific to his own particular sub-tradition in order to give a clearer profile or specification to the understanding of the Ultimate or *dharmakāya*. For Alfred Bloom, who is a Pure Land Buddhist, the *dharmakāya* is primarily qualified as Amida Buddha,[67] while the Zen Buddhist Masao Abe qualifies the *dharmakāya* as 'boundless openness', a term that is specific to the Zen Buddhist tradition and is reminiscent of Bodhidharma.[68] Makransky speaks about the *dharmakāya* more generally (but again typically for the Tibetan tradition to which he belongs) as 'Buddhahood'.

Second, all three point out that ultimate reality is beyond all concepts, and that therefore, even their tradition-specific conceptuality needs to be transcended. But this is precisely what the idea of 'skilful means' entails, so that it is again their Mahāyāna Buddhist background that enables and encourages such a view. The Buddhist affirmation that all language is at best only 'an approximation of the highest truth' might be, as Bloom indicates, the specific Buddhist contribution to inter-religious dialogue in face of those 'traditions which may be more literalist or objectivist

65 Abe, 'A Dynamic Unity in Religious Pluralism', pp. 182–7.

66 Abe, 'A Dynamic Unity in Religious Pluralism', p. 184.

67 See Bloom, 'Shin Buddhism in Encounter with a Religiously Plural World', pp. 26f.

68 See Heinrich Dumoulin, 1994, *Zen-Buddhism: A History. Vol. I: India and China*, New York: Macmillan, Simon & Schuster, pp. 90ff.

in character.'[69] Makransky says explicitly that Buddhism is not superior in having the better concepts for the absolute, but quite the contrary because it displays 'a fuller knowledge of the ways that persons mistake their representations for absolute reality . . .'[70] Hence, Buddhism is provided with 'a fuller awareness of how its representations (all of which are relative, conceptual constructs) may be used to undercut, rather than reinforce, the human habit of absolutising what is not absolute and clinging to it.'[71] Similarly, Abe insists that his designation of the ultimate as 'Boundless Openness' should not be misread as the affirmation of a conceptual superiority, but as the invitation to all religions to go beyond their specific traditional forms of representing the ultimate, so as to be able to accept all forms as manifestations of 'formless emptiness'.[72]

As can be seen from these statements, some Buddhists are indeed prepared to identify the reality that Christians see incarnate in Jesus as a manifestation of the *dharmakāya* if and in so far as the Christian God can be understood along the lines of 'skilful means' (*upāya*) – which is to say, if the Christian God serves the purpose of leading to Enlightenment as understood by Buddhists by fostering the process of non-attachment, whether on the existential level of transcending self-centredness or on the epistemological level of transcending all clinging to concepts. Given that Mahāyāna Buddhism understands its own concepts too as 'skilful means', this entails – as it seems – a conditioned acceptance of the Christian God as functionally equivalent to Buddhist concepts of the ultimate.

It may be true that Mahāyāna Buddhism, more than any other religious tradition, has affirmed the need for transcending all concepts. And while it is certainly true that Christianity has

69 Bloom, 'Shin Buddhism in Encounter with a Religiously Plural World', p. 29.

70 Makransky, 'Buddhist Perspectives on Truth in Other Religions', p. 359.

71 Makransky, 'Buddhist Perspectives on Truth in Other Religions', p. 359.

72 See Abe, 'A Dynamic Unity in Religious Pluralism', pp. 184–90.

always had a strong and influential tradition of apophatic or negative theology, affirming that God is beyond everything that humans can conceive of, this has hardly functioned as a criterion in the assessment of other religions. But I think that the old criterion of non-idolatry, that is, of making no image of God, could and should be understood as referring to our conceptual and theological images of God as well.[73]

In any case, the fact that the criteriological emphasis of Buddhism and Christianity in their assessment of other potential mediators of transcendence is different, does not necessarily entail a claim to superiority.[74] For the Buddhist emphasis on the fostering of non-attachment and the Christian emphasis on the fostering of love can be seen as complementary and mutually qualifying.[75] Detachment without loving involvement would not be a sign of liberation but at best a form of indifferent complacency. And loving involvement without detachment seems but a barely concealed form of self-centredness.[76] If therefore detachment and loving involvement are indeed complementary and mutually qualifying, then both the Buddha and the Christ can be recognized by Buddhists and by Christians as authentic mediators of salvific transcendent reality – a recognition that would transform and enrich the followers of both.

---

73 This has been forcefully argued in Wilfred Cantwell Smith, 1987, 'Idolatry: In Comparative Perspective', in J. Hick and P. Knitter (eds), *The Myth of Christian Uniqueness: Toward a Pluralistic Theology of Religions*, Maryknoll: Orbis, pp. 53–68.

74 I agree with Alfred Bloom that one 'does not necessarily intend the denigration of another faith if one's understanding of the ultimate and essential unity of faith is seen through the prism of one's own faith.' Bloom, 'Shin Buddhism in Encounter with a Religiously Plural World', pp. 26f.

75 See P. Schmidt-Leukel, 2003, 'Buddhism and Christianity: Antagonistic or Complementary?', in *Studies in World Christianity* 9, pp. 265–79.

76 Something similar has already been expressed by Buddhaghosa (4/5th century CE) in the *Visuddhimagga* IX (p. 325), where he describes the 'great beings' (*mahāsatta*) as combining unswerving love (*mettā*) with perfect equanimity (*upekkhā*).

11. Buddha and Christ as Mediators of the Transcendent:

A Buddhist Perspective[1]

JOHN MAKRANSKY

Can the Buddha and the Christ both be viewed as mediators of transcendent reality from a Buddhist perspective? And if so, how? These are the questions I have been asked to address.

My response should be contextualized. I am a scholar trained in Buddhist studies by the Western academy and a Buddhist trained in Tibetan traditions that are Mahāyāna and Tantric. Mahāyāna Buddhism emphasizes the ultimate undividedness of *saṃsāra* (conditioned life) and *nirvāṇa* (the unconditioned dimension of freedom). Tantric Buddhism enacts that basic view in vivid forms of ritual and meditation. I first met and fell in love with Buddhism during my studies in college. After serving in the US Peace Corps in Asia I travelled to Nepal and India in 1978 to meet, study and practise with Tibetan lamas. I have continued my study and practice of Tibetan (Mahāyāna, Tantric) Buddhism under the guidance of those and other lamas ever since, a programme that has included daily practice of Buddhist meditation and ritual for the past twenty-six years.

1 This article owes much to deeply thoughtful input I received this past year from several colleagues to whom I am immensely indebted: Fr. Michael Himes, Mark Heim, Francis Clooney, S.J., Catherine Cornille, Pheme Perkins, Richard Kearney, Robert Magliola, Luis Roy, O.P., Thomas Cattoi, Lisa Cahill, Fr. Robert Imbelli, Perry Schmidt-Leukel, John Riches. Any errors here are, of course, just my own.

Introduction

In some of his recent writings, theologian Perry Schmidt-Leukel begins his analysis of Buddha and Christ as mediators of the transcendent by focusing upon the historical persons of Gautama and Jesus, understanding each as a human being who became so receptive to the liberating power of transcendent reality as to become the 'visible face' of the transcendent (the face of God or the face of *nirvāṇa*).[2] I must agree with Schmidt-Leukel that Buddhists revere Gautama Buddha not just as someone who had especially profound thoughts *about* reality, but as someone who became *perfectly transparent* to the unconditioned reality, *nirvāṇa*, so as to fully embody its qualities of unconditioned freedom, all-inclusive love and penetrating insight and to disclose the means for many others to realize them. My response, then, to the first opening question of this essay is yes, Buddhists have viewed the Buddha as a mediator of the transcendent, unconditioned reality, *nirvāṇa*.

Yet if Christianity and Buddhism are similar in viewing their central figures as the face of ultimate reality, they have historically differed in their understanding of the soteriological roles of those figures, their roles in saving or liberating persons. Many Christian theologians have understood Christ to be the one who redeems persons from the crushing burden of their sin, a burden possessed by real, sinful selves whose disordered emotions and sufferings express their sinful condition. This seems to contrast sharply with how Buddhists have understood the Buddha's soteriological role: the one who provides means for persons to discover the lack of intrinsic reality of any such self, thereby undercutting the root of self-grasping that underlies personal suffering. To put it another way, Christ's passion and death has been understood as an atonement for the sins of persons, which takes the burden of sin from the self. But the Buddha's activity

---

2 Perry Schmidt-Leukel, 'Buddha and Christ as Mediators of the Transcendent: A Christian Perspective', Chapter 10 in this volume; Perry Schmidt-Leukel, 2002, 'Buddha and Christ as Mediators of Salvific Transcendent Reality', in *Swedish Missiological Themes* 90, pp. 17–38.

is understood to trigger a recognition in persons that there is no such self to grasp or defend, hence no real basis of 'sin'.

To further explore these questions, I want to focus particularly on practices of Christian and Buddhist communities that bring people into an experience of Christ or Buddha as the living presence and power of ultimate reality, not just as a cherished figure remembered from a distant past, but as a continuing presence and liberating power in the present – in Christian terms, communing with God in Christ and through that with God's creatures; in Buddhist terms, communing through perfect forms of Buddhahood (*rūpakāya*) with the transcendent qualities and powers of Buddhahood (*dharmakāya*) and thereby with all beings.

A Mahāyāna Buddhist's Experience of Christian Communion

Since I began teaching Buddhism and comparative theology at Boston College, which is a Jesuit Catholic University, I have often attended weekly Eucharist, the liturgical enactment of communion with God in Christ. I have deeply appreciated elements of the Christian rite in their fundamental structure and power, not in spite of my Mahāyāna Buddhist training but apparently *because of that training* – seemingly sensitized to Christian liturgy by decades of daily practice of Buddhist liturgies that invoke the liberating power of Buddhahood. It seems that the patterns of religious receptivity in me formed by such daily Buddhist practice meet, at least to some degree, the patterns of Christian liturgy: prayer, repentance, blessing, listening receptively to revealed truths, opening to receive the purifying and transforming power of divine life, being offered into deep communion with transcendent reality ('God') through its perfect embodiment ('Christ') in utmost receptivity and trust, the inwardly liberating power of which ('Spirit') links one's heart to many others (like 'one body') in unconditional love ('agape').

My inner response, prepared it appears at least in part by Buddhist practice, has been twofold. On the one hand, there is a sense of vivid recognition and appreciation of analogous patterns; and on the other hand, perhaps paradoxically, a wonder at so much difference. First, I found the Christian rite inspiring in ways similar to my inspiration from Buddhist liturgies, which triggered reflections back upon Buddhism regarding analogous forms whose implicit elements of communion and ecclesiology, recognizable in light of the Christian communion ritual, have not received as much theological development in Buddhist commentaries.[3]

On the other hand, I also experienced much wonder at difference. The Christian rite is embedded in a Christian narra-

---

3 'Communion' here, is broadly understood as one's sharing in the life of the other, e.g. sharing in the life of God and God's sharing in your very life, or becoming receptive to the qualities, energies and liberating powers of Buddhahood and participating in them. Implicit elements of communion and ecclesiology in Buddhist traditions to which I refer include:

(a) Meditation practices from early Buddhism that bring the Buddha vividly to mind to experience the inspiration and power of his qualities and presence (*buddhānusmṛti*). See Kevin Trainor, 1997, *Relics, Ritual and Representation in Buddhism*, Cambridge: Cambridge University Press, pp. 184–7. As explained later in this chapter, such practices are further developed in Mahāyāna Buddhist liturgies, where Buddhist devotees commune with the qualities, energies and radiant blessings of Buddhahood as a transforming and liberating power; also: John Makransky, 2000, 'Mahāyāna Buddhist Ritual and Ethical Activity in the World', in *Buddhist-Christian Studies* 20, pp. 54–9, and John Makransky, 'Tathāgata', in the new revised *Encyclopedia of Religion*, ed. Robert Buswell, New York: Macmillan (forthcoming).

(b) The perfected form of Buddhahood, referred to as *saṃbhoga-kāya* in the three Buddha-body scheme of Mahāyāna treatises, is understood not just as the fruition of an individual bodhisattva's path to enlightenment, but also as a 'body of communion in the joy of the Dharma', a supramundane Buddha form communing with advanced bodhisattvas in the Dharma qualities of boundless love, gnosis and joy which spread out to all beings. This is pictured in Buddha realm scenes of Mahāyāna scriptures and in Asian Buddhist art, contributing to the development of the tantric mandala. See John Makransky, 1997, *Buddhahood Embodied: Sources of Controversy in India and Tibet*, Albany: SUNY, chapters 4, 5 and 13; John Makransky, 2004, 'Buddhahood and Buddha Bodies', in *Encyclopedia of Buddhism*, vol. 1, New York, Macmillan, pp. 76–9; David McMahan, 2002, *Empty Vision,* London: RoutledgeCurzon, chapters 4 and 5.

(c) Implicit bodhisattva ecclesiologies in Mahāyāna scriptures include scenes in which bodhisattvas are not functioning merely as isolated individuals on individual paths to enlightenment, but as communal expressions of Buddha activity, many bodhisattvas performing enlightened

tive radically different from the Buddhist – creation of all by
God, renewal of a prior historical covenant of a chosen people,
a unique incarnation of God among that people as Messiah
(Christ), his passion, death and resurrection redeeming humankind from its burden of sin. And that narrative, in turn, frames
much difference in doctrinal understanding: human beings irre-
ducibly distinct from God in their communion with him (versus
complete oneness with Buddhahood in non-dual gnosis), Jesus'
sacrifice and resurrection unleashing the power that redeems and
frees (versus the Buddha's pointing persons to the inmost nature
of their own experience, the liberating power of aware emptiness), the Spirit of God as active in and through Christian community (versus the inner powers of enlightened resolve, karmic
accumulation and Buddha nature as what energizes the community of bodhisattvas). It was as if my formation in Tibetan
Buddhism conformed me *both* to recognize a real liberating
power within Christian communion *and* to be challenged by its
radically different understanding of the sources and implications
of that power.

   This returns us to the other key question I was asked to
address. Is Christ a mediation of the transcendent from a
Buddhist perspective? My formation in Tibetan Mahāyāna

activities throughout many realms as one community (*bodhisattva saṃgha*),
becoming part of the Buddha's body (*nirmāṇakāya*) through the power
of their prior vows and merit, the blessings of the Buddhas (*adhiṣṭhāna*,
radiance) and the emergent qualities of Buddha nature (*tathāgata-garbha*).
Though understood through distinctive Buddhist doctrines, analogies can
be drawn to Christian ecclesiological understandings of faithful persons
pulled communally into participation in the body of Christ through the
activity of God's spirit. For examples of bodhisattvas depicted in Mahāyāna sutras as a communal, ecclesiological expression of liberating Buddha
activity, see Makransky, *Buddhahood Embodied*, pp. 183–4; Edward
Conze (trans.), 1979, *The Large Sutra on Perfect Wisdom*, Delhi: Motilal
Banarsidass, pp. 573–643; Burton Watson (trans.), 1993, *The Lotus Sutra*,
New York: Columbia University, pp. 190–5; Robert Thurman (trans.),
1986, *The Holy Teaching of Vimalakīrti*, London: Penn State University
Press, pp. 69–71; Etienne Lamotte (trans.), 1998, *Śuraṃgamasamādhisūtra:
The Concentration of Heroic Progress*, London: Curzon, pp. 159–61; Cecil
Bendall, W.H.D. Rouse (trans.), 1981, *Śikṣā-samuccaya*, compiled by Śā-
ntideva, Delhi: Motilal Banarsidass, pp. 290–306.

Buddhist practice seems to have opened channels of receptivity to the Christian rite and its trinitarian power, to recognize some of its liberating functions, and to receive light from it back upon my own tradition in unexpected ways, all of which would seem to confirm, at least anecdotally, that the Christ of Christian communion indeed functions somehow as a mediation of ultimate reality as I, a Buddhist, understand that reality. But if this is so, given the differences in narrative frame and doctrinal understanding, how am I, a Mahāyāna Buddhist, to make sense of that?

Christian Understanding of Communion as Liberating Power of the Transcendent

In the liturgy of Eucharistic communion, as understood not only in Catholic and Orthodox traditions but also by Luther and Calvin, participants are not merely reminiscing about the historical Jesus long gone, but are entered into communion with the transcendent God through the living presence and power of Christ in the Spirit, which flows out into communion with creatures, drawing them into the Body of Christ. This is what many Christians have understood, in part, as their ongoing encounter with the 'resurrected Christ', not merely with the historical Jesus.[4]

Doctrines of atonement for sin, redemption through Christ's

---

4 See, e.g., J.M.R. Tillard, 2001, *Flesh of the Church, Flesh of Christ*, Collegeville, MN: Liturgical Press; Pierre-Marie Gy, 1987, 'Sacraments and Liturgy in Latin Christianity', in Jill Rait (ed.), *Christian Spirituality: Origins to the Twelfth Century*, New York: Crossroad, pp. 365–81; James McCue, 2001, 'Liturgy and Eucharist II. West', in Jill Rait (ed.) *Christian Spirituality: High Middle Ages and Reformation*, New York: Crossroad, pp. 427–38; Marc Lienhard, 2001, 'Luther and the Beginnings of the Reformation', in Rait (ed.), *Christian Spirituality: High Middle Ages and Reformation*, pp. 268–99; William Bouwsma, 2001, 'The Spirituality of John Calvin', in Rait (ed.), *Christian Spirituality: High Middle Ages and Reformation*, pp. 318–33; Mark Heim, 2001, *The Depth of the Riches: A Trinitarian Theology of Religious Ends*, Cambridge, MA: Eerdmans, pp. 65, 69–71, 76; Nicholas Lash, 1993, *Believing Three Ways in One God*, Notre Dame, IN: University of Notre Dame Press, pp. 72–82, 88–90, 94–103; Thomas Merton, 1963, *Life and Holiness*, New York: Image Books, pp. 60–9.

passion, death and resurrection were formulated in part to account for the experience of such liberating power in communal Christian practice. Trinitarian doctrine was the product of centuries of struggle by Christian thinkers to discern the proper doctrinal form for their communal experience of the ever-present liberating power of Christ as mediation of God. Perry Schmidt-Leukel, drawing upon Roger Haight, has noted that for early Christians, Christ functioned as symbol through which God, the symbolized, became vividly present.[5] This is precisely the sacramental principle that Christian liturgy re-enacts.

Communing with the ultimate, unconditioned reality ('God') by means of its perfect incarnation or form ('Christ') through an inner liberating power (of 'Spirit') that re-creates or restores one's inmost being in the image of the ultimate – with qualities of unconditional love, joy, patience, self-control, spiritual wisdom, unleashing a liberating power of love and goodness that radiates to many other beings – from a Mahāyāna Buddhist perspective the basic structure of such trinitarian communion and its liberating power is recognizable, although the explanation for what it is and how it functions is different.

How Buddhist Analogues to Christian Communion Developed

Numerous scriptural accounts depict Gautama Buddha devotedly as a figure of tremendous liberating power. There is the sense, in such accounts, that the Buddha had such deep knowledge of the inmost psyches' of persons, and such liberating power in his compassionate relation to them, that even a brief communication, gesture or merely his presence could trigger deep states of reverence or stages of awakening among those who were receptive to him. Each bodily gesture, look and word, it is believed, expressed the liberating power of his mind, his direct awareness of the unconditioned reality, *nirvāṇa*. The liberating power

5 See Schmidt-Leukel, 'Buddha and Christ', Chapter 10 in this volume, p. 167.

of his mind, the *nirvāṇic* realization that came to be known as '*dharmakāya*' (body of Dharma attainment) replete with qualities of all-inclusive love, compassion, spiritual insight and power, communicated itself through his physical body, '*rūpakāya*', by gesture, word and the inspiring energy of his physical presence.[6]

The ritual and meditation practices of Buddhist communities after Gautama's physical passing maintained and developed this paradigm of relating to the Buddha as the embodied power (*rūpakāya*) of transcendent awareness (*dharmakāya*). Special symbolic forms that stand in for the Buddha's physical body (*rūpakāya*) have provided ways for laity and monastics to continue to offer themselves ritually to the liberating power of the Buddha's *nirvāṇic* attainment (*dharmakāya*). At reliquary mounds with relics of the Buddha inside (*stūpas*), devotees have re-enacted the offering of themselves to the Buddha and his teaching (*dharma*) through the ritual forms reported in early Buddhist scriptures: circumambulating and bowing to the stūpa reliquary (as Gautama's followers had reverenced him), offering beautiful flowers, incense, lamps, foods (as they had offered to Gautama), praying for fulfilment of mundane and supra-mundane needs, receiving inspiration and energy from the reliquary whose consecrated relics (representing *rūpakāya*) are believed to be saturated with the power of the Buddha's transcendent attainment (*dharmakāya*). In Buddhist chronicles

---

6 See, e.g., John Makransky, 2003, 'Buddhist Perspectives on Truth in Other Religions: Past and Present', in *Theological Studies* 64, no. 2, pp. 334–61; Makransky, 'Buddhahood and Buddha Bodies', pp. 76–9, and Makransky, *Buddhahood Embodied*, pp. 23–8; Peter Harvey, 1990, *An Introduction to Buddhism*, Cambridge: Cambridge University Press, pp. 22–6; Bhikkhu Nyanamoli (trans.), 1964, *The Path of Purification (Visuddhimagga) by Buddhaghosa*, Colombo: Semage, pp. 221–30; Edward Conze (ed.), 1964, *Buddhist Texts Through the Ages*, New York: Harper, pp. 104, 110–11; Bhikkhu Bodhi (trans.), 2000, *The Connected Discourses of the Buddha (Saṃyutta Nikāya)*, Boston: Wisdom, pp. 1143, 1846–7; Maurice Walshe (trans.), 1995, *The Long Discourses of the Buddha (Dīgha Nikāya)*, Boston: Wisdom, pp. 124, 141, 178–9, 185, 334.

there are stories of devotees whose practice at such reliquary mounds has led to spontaneous visions of the Buddha or radiant blessings that evoke in them deep tranquillity, bliss, faith or spontaneous realization of stages of the Buddha's path. Thus the liberating power of *dharmakāya*, Buddha's *nirvāṇa*, is mediated ritually through his *rūpakāya* to those caught in the bondage and suffering of *saṃsāra*, so beings in this world may continue to encounter the transcendent, liberating dimension of reality through its perfect form.[7]

Buddhanusmṛti ('recalling the Buddha') meditation has been an important Buddhist practice from early Buddhism to the present. It has involved bringing the Buddha to mind, vividly envisioning the beauty of his form together with his qualities of all-pervading love, compassion, penetrating wisdom and spiritual power, bathing in those qualities, and being offered up to them. Meditators accomplished in this practice were said to experience the Buddha's qualities and powers as vividly present in their world, freeing them from anxiety, taking their minds toward the Buddha plane of awareness, and transforming them into holy beings worthy of reverence.[8] Such practices also supported the emergence of images and statues of the Buddha that functioned as *rūpakāya*, a real manifestation of Buddhahood in the world, when they were ritually consecrated with the presence and power of the Buddha's *dharmakāya*, the power of his *nirvāṇic* awareness.[9]

Conservative schools like the Theravāda and Sarvāstivāda

7 Trainor, *Relics, Ritual and Representation in Buddhism*; John Strong, 2002, *The Legend of Ashoka*, Delhi: Motilal Banarsidass.

8 Paul Harrison, 1992, 'Commemoration and Identification in Buddhānusmṛti', in Janet Gyatso (ed.), *In the Mirror of Memory: Reflections on Mindfulness and Remembrance in Indian and Tibetan Buddhism*, Albany: SUNY; Paul Williams, 1989, *Mahāyāna Buddhism*, London: Routledge, pp. 217–20, 255–6; Trainor, *Relics, Ritual and Representation in Buddhism*, pp. 184–5.

9 Trainor, *Relics, Ritual and Representation in Buddhism*; Donald Swearer, 2004, 'Consecration', in *Encyclopedia of Buddhism*, vol. 1, New York: Macmillan, pp. 178–81; Donald Swearer, *Becoming the Buddha*, Princeton: Princeton University Press.

systematically formulated *nirvāṇa* and *saṃsāra* as a duality in their Abhidharma literature. To fully attain *nirvāṇa*, the unconditioned dimension of freedom, was to cut the defiled roots of conditioned life, of *saṃsāra*, ultimately to leave conditioned existence behind altogether. One who has attained *nirvāṇa*, it was said, had cut the causes for further rebirth, so that physical death puts a final end to his conditioned mind and body, an end to any further participation in conditioned life.[10] But according to what many Buddhist communities were practising, ritually, meditationally, a Buddha's *nirvāṇa* was being engaged *not* just as a Buddha's cessation of defilement and consequent freedom *from* the world but *also* as his manifestation of liberating power *for and in* the world. This seems to have been given earliest doctrinal expression in some of the Mahāsāṃghika school's doctrines of Buddhahood, and was much further developed in Mahāyāna scriptures and treatises of early centuries CE.[11]

Like early Christians struggling to give doctrinal formulation to their communal experience of the liberating power of Christ, which eventually developed into trinitarian form, Mahāyāna Buddhists struggled to reformulate the relationship of *nirvāṇa* and *saṃsāra* in line with their communal experience that the liberating power of a Buddha's *nirvāṇic* attainment manifests within *saṃsāra* in special symbolic forms and through means of practice passed down by tradition. The doctrinal reformulation of the *nirvāṇa* of the Buddhas as an unending, all-pervasive, liberating power in the world took diverse expression in Mahāyāna scriptures and treatises of the first to sixth centuries CE (as in the *Lotus Sūtra* quoted by Schmidt-Leukel), gradually coalescing around the concept of the Buddhas' 'unrestricted' or 'active *nirvāṇa*' (*apratiṣṭhita-nirvāṇa*): a Buddha's *nirvāṇa* understood as an

---

10 Etienne Lamotte, 1988, *History of Indian Buddhism*, trans. Sara Webb-Boin, Paris: Institut Orientaliste, pp. 23–52; Makransky, *Buddhahood Embodied*, pp. 28, 320–3.

11 Andre Bareau, 1989, 'Hīnayāna Buddhism', in Joseph Kitagawa and Mark Cummings (eds), *Buddhism and Asian History*, New York: Macmillan, pp. 197–204; Hajime Nakamura, 'Mahāyāna Buddhism', in Kitagawa and Cummings (eds), *Buddhism and Asian History*, pp. 215–40.

attainment of freedom so profound that it triggers the liberation of countless other beings through inconceivable radiant blessings, manifestations and activities.[12]

Mahāyāna Practices that Inform Buddhist Communion with Buddhahood as a Liberating Power in the World

This developing paradigm of a Buddha's *nirvāṇa* as a vast liberating power within *saṃsāra* was further informed by other Mahāyāna practices and developing doctrines described below.

Buddhist Practices of Transcendental Wisdom that Reveal the Nirvāṇic Nature of Saṃsāra in its Emptiness

The Mahāyāna *Perfection of Wisdom scriptures* (*Prajñā-pāramitā sūtras*) declared all phenomena to be empty of substantial, independent existence (*svabhāva-śūnya*), hence illusory. When bodhisattvas on the path to Buddhahood attain direct knowledge of that truth, they realize that all things in their intrinsic emptiness have always been in *nirvāṇic* peace, that *saṃsāra* is ultimately undivided from *nirvāṇa*, that *saṃsāra* itself can be re-engaged as a field of enlightened freedom and activity. The awareness that knows emptiness deconstructs the apparent boundary between sacred and profane, *nirvāṇa* and *saṃsāra*. Everything is intrinsically sacred, 'sacramental', each aspect of experience, each encounter.[13]

---

12 Makransky, *Buddhahood Embodied*, pp. 319–68.

13 See, e.g., Makransky, *Buddhahood Embodied*, pp. 324–6; Edward Conze (trans.), 1975, *Buddhist Wisdom Books: The Diamond Sutra and the Heart Sutra*, London: Allen & Unwin, pp. 81–101; Edward Conze (trans.), 1973, *The Perfection of Wisdom in Eight Thousand Lines*, Berkeley: Four Seasons, pp. 97–102, 142–8, 193–4; Conze, *The Large Sutra on Perfect Wisdom*, pp. 565–72; Thurman, *The Holy Teaching of Vimalakīrti*, pp. 73–7.

Buddhist Practices of Love and Compassion that Culminate in Unending Buddha Activity

Awareness of emptiness also deconstructs the thought-made wall of seeming difference in value between self and others to reveal an ultimate sameness, supporting an unconditional love and compassion that empathizes with other beings as one's self. Unconditional compassion, in turn, opens and empowers the mind to let go into the groundlessness of the empty, radiant nature of being.[14] Instead of the 'glue' of self-grasping that binds beings to rebirth in the conditioned world, Buddhahood is bound to the world with the 'glue' of compassion for beings, as the spontaneous, energetic expression of the wisdom of emptiness. All this reinforces the reformulation of a Buddha's *nirvāṇa* as unrestricted, active, energetic, manifesting in numerous forms the liberating power of *nirvāṇa* as the transcendent realization of compassion-wisdom.

Devotion to the Buddhas in Communion with their Qualities, Energies and Powers

In several Mahāyāna scriptures, to begin to recognize the empty, insubstantial nature of things is to deepen one's faith in the Buddhas and to open one's perception to the luminous realms of their radiant activity (pure Buddha realms) that had previously been obscured by clinging to things as substantial. Thus, to realize emptiness is not merely to stop one's existence, but to open up supernal, radiant dimensions of existence that had previously been obscured, to commune with the Buddhas there in deep faith. Some scriptures emphasize the radiant, pure Buddha realms as abodes of rebirth for beings who cultivate faith in celestial Buddhas, such as Amitābha or Akṣobhya. Other scriptures develop synergies between devotional forms of

---

14 See, e.g., Makransky, *Buddhahood Embodied*, pp. 326–9; Thurman, *The Holy Teaching of Vimalakīrti*, pp. 43–9; Conze, *Perfection of Wisdom in Eight Thousand Lines*, p. 226; Harvey, *Introduction to Buddhism*, pp. 121–5; Williams, *Mahāyāna Buddhism*, pp. 49–54, 197–203.

practice, visionary experience of celestial Buddhas and wisdom of emptiness. In these texts, devotional practice offering oneself in service to the Buddhas releases self-grasping to allow a deeper knowledge of emptiness, which opens into visionary experience of Buddhas and communion with their radiant qualities, energies and powers, leading to even stronger reverence and devotion, expressed in further service and offering, leading to deeper experience of emptiness, opening into further visionary experience and communion with the Buddhas, and so on.[15]

All such Buddhist practices of wisdom, love and devotional communion were given unified liturgical forms in Mahāyāna Buddhist scriptures from the second century CE, forms of ritual meditation practice that informed developing practices of East Asia and Tibet. An especially influential one is the seven-branch offering and purification liturgy found in the Avataṃsaka scripture, which inscribes the Buddhist devotee in the visionary world of the scripture, invoking the presence and power of the Buddhas and bodhisattvas in liturgical meditation practice, disclosing the devotee's world as a theatre of divine Buddha activity through ritual forms of reverence, offering, repentance, gratitude, prayerful requests and reception of radiant, purifying blessing that opens the devotee's heart and mind to the love, compassion, wisdom and liberating power of the Buddhas so as to participate in their divine activity through works of service to spiritual preceptors and beings and through dedication of spiritual power (merit, *puṇya*) for universal enlightenment.[16]

15 See, e.g., Makransky, *Buddhahood Embodied*, pp. 329–34; Williams, *Mahāyāna Buddhism*, pp. 120–7, 215–30; G. MacQueen, 1982, 'Inspired Speech in Early Mahāyāna Buddhism', in *Religion* 12, pp. 49–65; Harvey, *Introduction to Buddhism*, pp. 258–69; D. McMahan, 2002, *Empty Vision*, London: RoutledgeCurzon, pp. 143–74.

16 See Thomas Cleary (trans.), 1993, *The Flower Ornament Scripture: A Translation of the Avataṃsaka Sūtra*, Boston: Shambhala, pp. 1510–18; John Makransky, 2000, 'Mahāyāna Buddhist Ritual', in *Buddhist-Christian Studies* 20, pp. 54–9;. Williams, *Mahāyāna Buddhism*, pp. 120–7; Richard Payne, 2004, 'Ritual', in *Encyclopedia of Buddhism*, vol. 1, New York: Macmillan, pp. 723–6; Shantideva, 1997, *A Guide to the Bodhisattva Way of Life*, trans. Vesna and B. Alan Wallace, Ithaca: Snow Lion, pp. 23–37.

Through such ritual-meditation forms, Buddhists have communed with the transcendent powers and energies of transcendent Buddhahood (*dharmakāya*) through perfect forms of it (*rūpakāya*), so as to relinquish the reifying patterns of mind that hide the radiant emptiness of things and to open their receptivity to qualities of Buddhaness awakening within themselves, qualities that include unconditional love, compassion, joy, penetrating wisdom and liberating power, envisioned and sensed as radiating out to all other beings.

Such practices informed the Buddhological doctrine of the 'Three Buddha Bodies (*kāyas*)' mentioned by Schmidt-Leukel in his chapter, the Bodhisattva devotee communing with *dharmakāya* through its perfect, radiant form, *sambhogakāya*, located in the centre of a circle of communion that radiates out liberating energy and power to beings in clouds of radiant blessing, divine activities and manifestations (*nirmāṇakāya*).[17]

How, from a Mahāyāna Buddhist Viewpoint, might Christ be Understood as a Mediation of Ultimate Reality?

Theologian Mark Heim has developed a theology of religions from a Christian point of view that can be reinterpreted from a Mahāyāna Buddhist perspective so as to provide one way to address that question. Theology of religions is the attempt from a standpoint within one religious tradition to understand the relation between different claims of salvific truth among diverse religious traditions. In his recent book, *The Depth of the Riches: A Trinitarian Theology of Religious Ends*, Heim develops a Christian, trinitarian theology of religions, which he characterizes as a theology of 'multiple religious ends'. There he argues that persons of the great religious traditions, through different religious beliefs and practices, do not accomplish just the same

---

17 Perry Schmidt-Leukel, 'Buddha and Christ', Chapter 10 in this volume, pp. 157–61; Makransky, *Buddhahood Embodied*, chapters 5 and 13; Makransky, 'Buddhahood and Buddha Bodies', pp. 76–9; Makransky, 'Tathāgata'.

religious end, but they do accomplish real ends that are related to each other within the complex ultimate reality that all such religions engage (the trinitarian God).[18]

Heim constructs his Christian theology of religions in opposition to two common options, theological exclusivism and theological pluralism. Theological exclusivism (such as that of Karl Barth) has argued that one tradition is salvifically true, the others false, ignoring the spiritual qualities embodied by persons formed by other traditions. Since other religious traditions are merely human constructs, this logic goes, but one's own tradition is based in the actual revelation of the ultimate reality (God), the others could not possibly realize the salvific goal that one's own tradition makes possible. In this way, differences of belief and practice are given central emphasis in an exclusionary way. Theological pluralism (such as that of John Hick) on the other hand, argues for the power of the one ultimate reality behind all great religions to save all persons, downplaying the specifics of difference in belief and practice. Since the great religions engage the same ultimate reality, to which they refer by different names, it is argued, then in spite of their differences in belief and practice they should all be able to lead people to the same basic realization of that ultimate reality, the same basic salvific goal.

Both, Heim argues, share a mistaken assumption, that the ultimate reality posited by religions is uncomplex. Given that assumption, if specific differences of religious belief and practice are emphasized, since the uncomplex ultimate reality presumably mirrors just one such set of beliefs and practices, only one tradition could be salvifically true while the other traditions would simply be false (the exclusivism of Barth). Or, given the same assumption of an uncomplex ultimate reality with an emphasis on its universal salvific power, then the differing religions may all be understood to lead to the same salvific end through differing means of belief and practice whose specific differences do not finally matter (theological pluralism of Hick).

---

18 Heim, *Depth of the Riches*.

But, Heim argues, the ultimate reality to which the great religions refer, which he understands as the trinitarian God posited by Christianity, is *complex*, with varied dimensions for human encounter. Hence, its complexity is mirrored in the diversity of means through which it is encountered, which results in different kinds of realization of its qualities, the attainment of different religious ends, by persons of different traditions. Since persons of different traditions are genuinely encountering God, and opening to or realizing qualities of God, they have much to learn from each other about the same God. But because their differing beliefs and practices differently mediate their encounters with God, which affects the depth and fullness of their realization of God's salvific qualities, the differences of belief and practice really do matter for religious fulfilments attained, and there is a genuine basis for friendly argument between traditions about the importance of particular beliefs and practices and about their proper integration.[19]

Since, Heim argues, neither theological exclusivism nor pluralism sufficiently uphold the complexity of ultimate reality, neither adequately accounts for the diversity of authentic religious realizations of it. As a Christian theologian, he argues that God as Trinity represents a complex ultimate reality to which persons formed by practices of different religious traditions diversely relate themselves. From a Christian perspective, then, Buddhists, Hindus and Muslims are engaging the trinitarian God that Christians engage in its complexity; but each intensively focuses uniquely upon particular aspects of that complex reality in ways that tend to delimit or exclude other aspects, resulting in realizations of its liberating qualities that differ from fullest Christian realization, 'salvation' as fullest communion with God. For Heim, Christian Trinitarian communion with God and other creatures in Christ represents the fullest integration of all aspects of engagement with the complex ultimate reality of God, while he acknowledges that a Buddhist, Hindu or Muslim might more deeply realize other aspects of relation to that reality, and

19 Heim, *Depth of the Riches*, pp. 33–8, 289–92.

therefore argue for a different integration as fullest.[20] Indeed, that is part of what I, as a Buddhist, will argue below.

Here are some of the virtues of Heim's model for my purpose here: (1) It motivates strong interest to learn *from* other traditions as other means of connection to the same liberating truth cherished by one's own tradition – a basis for reverencing others' encounters with liberating truth on a par with one's own. That is to be preferred over an interest just in learning *about* other traditions as human constructs divorced from the revealed truth of one's own tradition, the weakness of exclusivism. (2) Each tradition places great importance on its distinctive understandings and practices as constituting what it means by 'salvation' or 'liberation' (in Christianity, to be redeemed from sin by God, or, in Buddhism, to be freed from bondage to delusion and karma by one's own direct realization of emptiness). Heim's model permits us to acknowledge and learn from differences in each other's understandings of salvific principles, so that specific understandings and practices most important to each tradition are permitted to retain their importance within a dialogue of mutual learning. This avoids the weakness of theological pluralism: the difficulty it has in acknowledging how specific differences in belief and practice may make a real difference in religious ends attained.

Heim's model, if newly interpreted to fit a Mahāyāna Buddhist perspective, provides a powerful way to answer the question I posed at the start of this article – why should my trainings in Buddhist practices have opened channels of receptivity, appreciation, inspiration from the Christian communion ritual, to recognize some of its liberating functions, and to receive light from it back upon my own tradition in unexpected ways, even amidst so much difference?

This would make eminent sense if the fundamental structure of communion engaged by Christians and Buddhists is part of the structure of reality as such, both traditions practising means of communion given by the transcendent and immanent ultimate reality that make persons receptive to the liberating power of

---

20 Heim, *Depth of the Riches*, pp. 289–91.

that reality. From a Mahāyāna Buddhist viewpoint, that reality is the empty, radiant, all-pervasive, undivided ground of being (referred to as *dharmadhātu* and *dharmakāya*), the empty, lucid, intrinsic goodness of all experience (referred to as 'Buddha nature'), possessed of limitless capacity for manifestation of divine qualities, forms, symbols and liberating powers.

Heim as a Christian theologian isolated three dimensions of the trinitarian God that he understands diverse religions to engage: the 'impersonal', 'iconic' and 'communion' dimensions. The 'impersonal' is the transcendent mystery of God beyond human conception, the 'iconic' involves surrender to God as other, and 'communion' involves sharing in the life of God. From a Christian perspective, Heim argues, Buddhists and Advaitan Hindus tend to focus intensively (and more exclusively) on the first dimension (the transcendent mystery), Muslims on the second (submission to God as other), while Christians integrate all three dimensions most fully within the third dimension (communion with God in Christ). In that characterization, Heim does not pay much attention to Mahāyāna Buddhist practices of communion such as those described in the previous section.[21]

Here is how I would reinterpret Heim's model of truth among religions so as to inscribe it within a Mahāyāna Buddhist view. Suffering beings, fearing the impermanent, empty, ungraspable, nature of their experience become caught in ego-grasping patterns of thought and reaction that seek to create the impression of a concrete, autonomous, and unassailable self and world over against the tide of change, clinging to what appears to support that sense of self, fearing and hating what appears to undercut it, thus generating deluded emotions of self-grasping, aversion, and fear that drive individual and social suffering.

These, the Buddha taught, are the inmost causes of suffering which chain the minds of beings to their own self-grasping projections, shutting out the qualities and liberating powers to be found in the empty, radiant ground of being (*dharmadhātu*, *dharmakāya*). Mahāyāna Buddhist practices, through patterns

---

21 Heim, *Depth of the Riches*, pp. 174–97.

revealed by the Buddhas, provide means to release the mind from those shackles, to open persons to the empty, radiant ground of being through three basic kinds of practice: practices of wisdom, love, and devotional communion. *Practices of wisdom* are means to look into and sense directly the lack of independent reality of subjects and objects of thought, to recognize vividly their thought-madeness, emptiness, so the deepest patterns of self-grasping bondage may be released. *Practices of boundless love and compassion* open the mind to the unconditional, all-inclusive transcendent power of goodness beyond self-centred patterns of thought and grasping. *Practices of devotion to and communion* with the qualities of the Buddhas and bodhisattvas elicit a surrender of ego patterns to the unconditioned essence of experience, the ground of liberating Buddha qualities, revealing it as one's own inmost nature and capacity of enlightened goodness and freedom (Buddha nature).

From this Buddhist perspective, Christian practice can enter Christians into communion with the unconditioned reality and its liberating powers in faith through what they cherish as its perfect embodiment ('Christ'), so as to deeply relax their patterns of self-grasping and be opened to qualities of Buddhahood in the empty, radiant ground of being: qualities of unconditional love, compassion and liberating power that radiate out to many others. From this perspective, such Christian practice would represent a skilful means to be harmonized to the empty ground of being and its liberating qualities in cultures where the Buddha's teaching of emptiness is little known or too challenging yet for many to accept, but practices of unconditional love and devotional communion may be deeply engaged. Indeed, Christian practice engages *dharmakāya* so intensively in communion through Christ as *rūpakāya* that much light can shine back upon Buddhist thought and practice from Christian reflection upon Christology, communion and ecclesiology.[22]

---

22 See n. 3 above for examples of light upon Buddhism from Christian praxis of communion and ecclesiology.

Continuing to employ Heim's model of diverse religious realizations from a Buddhist perspective – Christian traditions, then, tend to focus intensively on the love and communion aspects of participation in the ultimate reality. Mahāyāna traditions that I have received, while profoundly integrating those two aspects, focus more intensively than Christian traditions upon the wisdom-emptiness aspect as the centre of soteriology, the very source of liberation. 'Emptiness' (*śūnyatā*) here is not understood merely as an emptying of self-concern, nor as an intellectual belief in the inconceivability of God, nor as an apophatic union with God attained by rare persons whose special vocation is mysticism. Rather, emptiness is here understood in Buddhist terms as the insubstantial nature of all aspects of ordinary experience, to be realized in non-dual awareness at some point by all who have entered into the bodhisattva path of enlightenment. This non-dual encounter with the empty nature of reality has been introduced to many followers of the Buddha through special means of guidance and practice from age to age, distinctively informing Buddhist understanding of love and communion earlier described.

From this Buddhist point of view, then, the ultimate reality that Christians engage in practice as 'God' is what Buddhists engage in practice as '*dharmakāya*', differently understood. But, because Buddhists and Christians are taught to focus most intensively upon different aspects of that reality, they would tend to realize different qualities of it more fully, or realize similar qualities of it differently.

For example, Buddhism teaches that bondage is created by patterns of thought that construct, reify and cling to an autonomous sense of 'self' and 'other'. Therefore, it is taught, to cut the deepest layers of such bondage and fully purify the mind, one must realize the emptiness of all such patterns within a stable non-dual, non-conceptual awareness. Furthermore, Indo-Tibetan and Zen traditions explain, although the Buddhas can inspire and guide the awakening of beings, Buddhas can not give persons a stable non-dual awareness of emptiness just through grace. For that reason, these traditions have exerted much effort to provide clear direction to enter practitioners into the wisdom of emptiness and non-duality in their own experience.[23]

Buddhist teachings of unconditional compassion and love, in turn, are profoundly informed by that specific kind of wisdom. Deep Buddhist compassion, it is taught, is compassion elicited by the wisdom of emptiness that understands how beings suffer through bondage to a duality that is created by their own minds. Deepest compassion is non-dual awareness suffused with a tone of compassion that has transcended even the distinction of 'self' and 'other'.[24]

In Christian understanding, because the ultimate reality (which I call 'dharmakāya' and Christians call 'God') is differently understood, and also the human problem, so is the posited solution and praxis. The problem is sin, a broken relationship with God, which is to be redeemed mainly through the power of God's grace in communion. Restored relationship as a salvific goal implies distinctions that define trinitarian relationships within God and between God, oneself and other creatures. A sign of restored relationship is deep participation in God's unconditional love (*agape*) that pervades all creation. But such love is a love within relatedness, mirroring the relations of the Trinity, involving distinctions between poles of relatedness that are irreducible, not non-dual.[25]

---

23 See, e.g., Thrangu Rinpoche, 2003, *Pointing Out the Dharmakaya*, Ithaca: Snow Lion; Ken McLeod, 2001, *Wake Up to Your Life*, New York: Harper, chapters 9 and 10; Dzogchen Ponlop, 2003, *Wild Awakening: The Heart of Mahamudra and Dzogchen*, Boston: Shambhala; Thich Thien-an, 1975, *Zen Philosophy, Zen Practice*, Berkeley, CA: Dharma Publications; Peter Gregory, 1986, *Traditions of Meditation in Chinese Buddhism*, Honolulu: Kuroda Inst.

24 See, e.g., Makransky, *Buddhahood Embodied*, pp. 326–8; Gampopa, 1998, *Jewel Ornament of Liberation*, trans. Khenpo Konchog Gyaltsen, Ithaca: Snow Lion, p. 130; Ringu Tulku, 2001, *Path to Buddhahood: Teachings on Gampopa's Jewel Ornament of Liberation*, Boston: Shambhala, pp. 60–1; Reginald Ray, 2000, *Indestructible Truth*, Boston: Shambhala, pp. 324–6.

25 Heim, *Depth of the Riches*, pp. 179, 195–6, 202–4, 212, 216–17, 246, 286–9.

Such love, as an unconditional, all-inclusive willing of the good of all creation seems similar to the all-inclusive and unconditional love and compassion of Mahāyāna Buddhism. But it would also be different – Christians such as Heim would not extrapolate the deepest realization of unconditional love or compassion to complete non-duality. Indeed they might have compassion for Buddhists who do so, for losing relationship with God and other creatures in their deconstruction of relations as ultimately empty. Mahāyāna Buddhists, on the other hand, might have compassion for Christians for grasping to duality without realizing how their own minds have reified it, holding themselves back from a fuller realization of the empty nature of reality (in other words, holding back from fuller realization of *dharmakāya*).

Similarly, Mahāyāna and Tantric devotional communion with the Buddhas ultimately leads to dissolution even of the seemingly separate poles of 'self' and 'Buddha' within a non-dual realization of *dharmakāya* beyond such distinctions. Indeed, that non-dual realization is understood as the deepest form of devotion in Indo-Tibetan Buddhism.[26] Christian theologians such as Heim, on the other hand, identify communion with God within relationship as the essence of salvation, maintaining the separate poles of that relationship as fundamental for salvation and irreducible.[27]

In Mahāyāna traditions of India and Tibet and in Zen traditions of East Asia, the power of inmost liberation is not something understood to come supernaturally from beyond the natural order of persons and their experience as many Christian theologians have argued. Rather, inmost freedom and unconditional goodness are found in the very essence of ordinary experience. In addition, Christian understanding of God as omnipotent

---

26 See, e.g., McMahan, *Empty Vision*, pp. 130–77; Makransky, *Buddhahood Embodied*, pp. 329–34; Bokar Rinpoche, 1997, *Chenrezig – Lord of Love: Principles and Methods of Deity Meditation*, San Francisco, CA: ClearPoint; Khyentse Rinpoche, 1992, *Heart Treasure of the Enlightened Ones*, Boston: Shambhala, pp. 57–144.

27 Heim, *Depth of the Riches*, pp. 202–4.

creator makes God's grace (through Christ) the salvific power that redeems and saves humans from sin. But although the Buddhas guide, bless, inspire and quicken receptive persons in innumerable ways, they are not understood by Buddhists to be omnipotent, which means that persons must realize emptiness in the fullest way through some specific procedure of investigation or pointing out passed down in living tradition by a qualified guru, lama or Zen master that is not finally fulfilled simply by Buddha's (or God's) grace.[28] It is for this reason that I shy away from any theological pluralism that assumes Christians and Buddhists attain the very same religious fulfilments and ends in spite of specific differences in practice, especially with reference to Buddhist transmissions of remarkably effective ways to bring receptive persons to stable recognition of the empty nature of all experience, the very essence of freedom in Buddhist terms.

Christians, on the other hand, by upholding a theocentric vision that includes creation of human beings in the image of God, a God of justice and final judgement, might critique Buddhist traditions for their historic difficulty in distinguishing the dignity of human beings from other sentient beings sufficiently to justify truly effective social concern for human justice, poverty and the marginalized in human societies. And Christian ecclesiological understanding of spiritual community as God's very body, communally active in the world as God's own loving response to human need, contrasts sharply with much Buddhist rhetoric, retained from early Buddhism, of spiritual path as individual endeavour. That kind of Buddhist rhetoric translates much less directly than the Christian into spiritual praxis as effective communal social service (rather than spiritual practice just as individual virtue). Light from Christian communion and ecclesiology can send Buddhists back to resources in their own traditions with fresh eyes (as mentioned in note 3), perhaps helping them respond to such issues. The capacity not only to appreciate and learn from the other tradition but also to argue for a different vision and praxis is precious – part of what each

---

28 As in the texts mentioned in n. 23.

tradition can offer to and receive from the other, each for its own fuller self-understanding in our time.

In sum, Heim's model of diverse religious realizations, when reinterpreted in a Mahāyāna way, provides a framework to understand why a Mahāyāna Buddhist would be inspired by patterns of Christian communion and learn from Christianity with regard to the very reality that he understands himself to engage in Buddhist practice. He may thereby indeed recognize Christ as a remarkable *rūpakāya* manifestation of Buddhahood itself, a powerful means through which followers of Christ have indeed communed with and learned to embody liberating qualities of *dharmakāya* (though differences between the two traditions do seem to make a real difference in the ways such qualities are realized, integrated, and embodied). In addition, from within this framework, a Buddhist would be motivated to improve his understanding of liberation, ultimate reality and praxis in part through discussion and argument with Christian theologians and saintly practitioners, discussions that take note both of analogues and differences between Buddhist and Christian understandings of the natures and roles of love, wisdom, devotion, communion and emptiness.

12. Response to John Makransky

PERRY SCHMIDT-LEUKEL

First of all, let me state how delighted I am to find so many points of agreement with John Makransky in areas that are crucial when trying to make sense of the life, experience, message and impact of such outstanding figures as Gautama Buddha and Jesus Christ. Writing out of the heart of the Buddhist tradition Makransky clearly affirms the Buddhist belief in an ultimate, unconditioned and transcendent reality, characterized as 'the empty, radiant, all-pervasive, undivided ground of being (referred to as *dharmadhātu* and *dharmakāya*), the empty, lucid, intrinsic goodness of all experience (referred to as "Buddha nature"), possessed of limitless capacity for manifestation of divine qualities, forms, symbols and liberating powers.'[1] Unfortunately, such a view can no longer be taken for granted among Buddhists at a time when Buddhism is so often fused and confused with Western atheist materialism and frequently reduced to a sort of naturalist psychology or lifestyle – forgetting that classical India already had had its own genuine materialists, the Cārvākas, with whose doctrines, however, the Buddha was not at all satisfied, precisely because the Cārvākas did not believe in an afterlife, ultimate liberation and an ultimate, unconditioned reality without which (according to *Udāna* 8:3 and *Itivuttaka* 43) any real liberation would be impossible.

Moreover, speaking from his experience as a practising

---

1 J. Makransky, 'Buddha and Christ as Mediators of the Transcendent', Chapter 11 in this volume, p. 193.

Buddhist as well as from his sympathetic acquaintance with Christianity (the latter gained in part from his work in a Christian environment and participation in Christian practice), Makransky unequivocally acknowledges Jesus as an authentic mediator of liberating contact with the Ultimate, in Buddhist terminology: 'Christ as *rūpakāya*'.[2]

But, says Makransky, there is so much difference regarding Christian and Buddhist narratives and doctrines. First of all, is Jesus not understood by Christians primarily as a saviour who redeemed us through the atoning sacrifice of his life on the cross, while Buddha is regarded by Buddhists as an enlightened teacher who guides us towards salvation through the truth that he teaches and embodies? Makransky is surely right in that this is how many Christians would see it. But numerous Christian theologians nowadays reject the medieval idea that Jesus' death *constitutes* our salvation. The theological construct that God would require the bloody sacrifice of Jesus so as to be able to forgive our sins is as bizarre as it is repulsive. Our salvation is rooted in nothing else but in the grace of God – in God's universal salvific will – which is not constituted but *represented* through Jesus' life and death.[3] Jesus remained faithful to his embodiment of God's unconditioned love even in a situation of utmost hatred and enmity. His self-sacrifice is the climax of his self-lessness or self-emptying (*kenosis*) which made him fully transparent for God. Jesus teaches God's love through his life and through his death and it is through this sort of teaching that God reveals him-/her-/itself and is redeemingly mediated into our lives.

But still there is – as Makransky rightly emphasizes – the

---

2 Makransky, 'Buddha and Christ', Chapter 11 in this volume, p. 194.

3 For the helpful distinction between a constitutive and representational understanding of Jesus' role as saviour see S. Ogden, 1992, *Is There Only One True Religion or Are There Many?*, Dallas: Southern Methodist University Press, pp. 84–98. For a thorough theological critique of a constitutive understanding of Jesus' role see K. Rahner, 1975, 'Der eine Jesus Christus und die Universalität des Heils', in K. Rahner, *Schriften zur Theologie*, vol. 12, Zürich-Einsiedeln-Köln: Benziger, pp. 251–82; J. Hick, 1993, *The Metaphor of God Incarnate*, London: SCM Press, pp. 112–27.

huge difference between the theistic framework focusing on an interpersonal relationship between God and human, and human and human, on the one hand, and the *śūnyatic* framework, focusing on non-attachment and non-self on the other hand. To be sure, both result in an attitude of unconditional love and compassion, but on the Christian side we are dealing with a 'love within relatedness . . . involving distinctions between poles of relatedness that are irreducible, not non-dual',[4] whereas on the Buddhist side we find a 'compassion that has transcended even the distinction of "self" and "other".'[5] How are we to make sense of such differences without denying the liberative force and transcendent truth of the one or the other? This is the question confronting Makransky and indeed any Christian with some genuine insight into Buddhism.

In his solution Makransky draws on the inclusivist model of Mark Heim. What Makransky likes about Heim's approach is that it seems to allow for genuine diversity among the religious doctrines and practices – and consequently among their respective religious ends – without falling back into an exclusivistic denial of any salvific truth of the religious other and without 'downplaying' the power of their differences as, according to Heim and Makransky, the pluralist model does. But one must not be deceived. The price paid for such a 'recognition of difference' is that divergence becomes equal to inferiority. The other religious tradition is seen as wrong precisely in so far as – and precisely there where – it differs from one's own! Accordingly, the otherness of the other religious ends implies their inferiority: They do not represent the same high level of ultimate fulfilment as is purportedly available through one's own religious path. The result is a mutual inclusivism, with each side claiming the final superiority of its own religious path. However, mutual inclusivism cannot be a solution to the question posed by religious diversity. On the contrary, it is an exact description of the problem. All religions claim – traditionally – that they are

---

4 Makransky, 'Buddha and Christ', Chapter 11 in this volume, p. 196.
5 Makransky, 'Buddha and Christ', Chapter 11 in this volume, p. 196.

superior to all others, if not uniquely true. But if these claims all have the same referent then it is logically impossible that all of them are right. Analogously we might observe that in a given group of people it is impossible that *each* is older than the others. Let's say, however, that all of them are the same age – and then we might notice differences: Perhaps each has 'specialized', as it were, in a certain area of life, accumulating more or richer experience in this area than have the others; or each will have developed and progressed in a particular virtue for dealing with a given life experience, while none of them possesses all of these experiences or virtues at once.

For Heim the non-Christian religions are true and salvific in so far as they have some understanding of the divine reality. But since the true nature of the Ultimate is nothing else but the Christian Trinity, all other religions inevitably lack, in varying degrees, the full insight into the divine. (Parenthetically, we might ask Heim which of all the various versions of the Trinity promulgated throughout the history of theological discourse he has in mind as being the real one.) The other religions do, says Heim, recognize some true features of the Trinity – either divine emptiness (Buddhism), as the basis of mutual trinitarian interpenetration, or divine unity (Advaita Vedānta), or divine otherness in relation to the world (Islam), etc.[6] – but none of them has the full understanding of God's trinitarian nature as it was revealed in and through Jesus Christ. (Again, we might ask whether Jesus Christ himself had such a full understanding of the trinititarian nature of God.) Hence, according to Heim's reading, the religious ends pursued by the various religions represent but different forms of diminished contact with divine fullness. Their ends are not really ultimate ends, and Heim seriously hopes that in some sort of post-mortal progress the non-Christians might move up from their penultimate eschatological goals to the fully

6 See Mark Heim, 2001, 'The Depth of the Riches: Trinity and Religious Ends', in *Modern Theology* 17, pp. 21–55, particularly pp. 36–43; Mark Heim, 2001, *The Depth of the Riches: A Trinitarian Theology of Religious Ends*, Cambridge, MA: Eerdmans, pp. 209–39, 255.

and truly ultimate goal of Christianity.[7] Should they choose, however, to remain in their deficient 'ends', then these ends can no longer be seen as really salvific; rather, they represent some kind of eternal lostness.[8] It is more than obvious that the diversity of religious ends that Heim's approach can accommodate is nothing but the diversity of various *stages* on the way to the one and only true eschatological end represented by Christianity. The basis for Heim's grading of religious ends and of the respective paths of salvation is his assumption that the true nature of the Ultimate can be expressed in human terms and has found its best expression within Christianity.

Now Makransky adopts a similar approach for a Buddhist interpretation of religious diversity with Mahāyāna Buddhism on top of the scale. However, he does not follow Heim's model by making the rival, nevertheless analogous claim that Buddhism would offer the best, fullest and most accurate description of the Ultimate. This is a road which could hardly be taken by a Mahāyānist. Instead Makransky argues that the superiority of Buddhism consists in being better, more fully and more accurately aware of the emptiness of all our conceptual constructs. It thereby achieves superiority by avoiding any absolutization of our limited insights – and thus can be said to be absolute by virtue of its being non-absolute.

I must say I like that sort of dialectic – and it is not unknown to Christians. Quite a number of them do in fact hold that it is not Christianity that is absolute but God alone, and that any Christian claim to absoluteness, if rightly understood, can only mean the unconditioned assent to the absolute claim coming from God. But does it not remain the case that all of us – Buddhists, Christians, Hindus, Muslims, Jews, etc. – who fully subscribe to the insight that absolute truth pertains only to the Ultimate and that the Ultimate necessarily transcends conceptual grasping, have yet to draw the full consequences from this for our various

---

7 See Heim, *Depth of the Riches*, pp. 268, 278f.
8 See Heim, *Depth of the Riches*, pp. 288f.

religious discourses and in particular for our understanding of their diversity?

I suggest that neither the similarities nor the differences between Buddhism and Christianity can be neatly segregated. There are no well-demarcated areas of identical assertions on the one side and clear-cut differences on the other. The differences are through-and-through pervasive and leave no area untouched. Buddhism and Christianity represent different ways of realizing (in both of its meanings: as understanding and as enacting) human existence, the world and the ultimate. But on a functional – or better, a soteriological – level there are at the same time significant and recognizable similarities: Both traditions bring about – to quote John Hick – a transformation from self-centredness to a new centredness in ultimate Reality,[9] a transformation that manifests itself decisively in a liberation for love (*agape*) and compassion (*karuṇā*).[10] Nevertheless, the respective ideals of saintliness – representing in condensed form the goals of the respective paths – are as different as these paths are.[11] But is this necessarily a difference in degree on the common scale of 'better and worse', 'fuller and lesser', 'ultimate and penultimate', etc.? I do not at all deny that there are some real differences of that sort in the realm of religion. But what I dispute is the claim that *all* religious differences are inevitably of that sort. There can be forms of existence in relation to the Ultimate that are different but nevertheless equally valid as different expressions of salvation/liberation. This can be so in view of the fact that this relation always concerns the existence of finite human beings, whereas the only all-encompassing reality is not found in any religious doctrine or narrative but is the infinite ultimate reality itself, always exceeding that which can be caught in our conceptual webs. Diversity and (salvific) equality can be compatible because the infiniteness – in Buddhist terms, 'formlessness' – of

9 See J. Hick, 1989, *An Interpretation of Religion: Human Responses to the Transcendent*, Houndmills: Macmillan, pp. 299–342.

10 See Hick, *An Interpretation of Religion*, p. 164.

11 See Hick, *An Interpretation of Religion*, pp. 300–06.

the Ultimate leaves room for such a diversity of finite and equally valid engagements with it/her/him. The unity of the religions lies not in any doctrinal feature but in their ultimate point of reference. And since this is so, their diversity is thoroughly real but ultimately compatible and even complementary.

13. Response to Perry Schmidt-Leukel

JOHN MAKRANSKY

In my response to Perry Schmidt-Leukel's article, I will focus on three interrelated theses for which he argues: (1) It is reasonable for Christians to view the Buddha and for Buddhists to view Christ as authentic mediators of transcendent reality as each tradition understands transcendent reality; (2) 'God' and '*dharmakāya*' point to the same transcendent reality because (3) God and *dharmakāya* are functionally equivalent.

Regarding the first thesis, I think Schmidt-Leukel has done an excellent job drawing on Buddhist sources to show that Buddhists have indeed understood Gautama Buddha not merely as an exemplary human being but as the face of the unconditioned, which a Christian could reasonably understand as a mediation of God. He has also drawn on several contemporary Buddhist writers (including myself) to argue for the parallel position that Buddhists can view Christ as a genuine mediation of *dharmakāya* (Buddhahood) in its skilful means. My own chapter in this volume lends further support for the Buddhist side of this thesis. There I argued that Christ can be viewed at least by Mahāyāna Buddhists as a genuine mediation of *dharmakāya*. I also argued that the ultimate reality that Mahāyāna Buddhists engage as *dharmakāya* is what Christians engage as God differently understood. This supports Schmidt-Leukel's thesis (2) above. Thus far, our chapters are complementary and mutually supportive.

Thesis (3), however, is problematic for me – God and *dharmakāya* as functionally equivalent. The problem concerns ambiguities in Schmidt-Leukel's use of 'functional equivalence'. On page 170 he says that the terms 'God' and '*dharmakāya*' can be seen as 'functional equivalents', meaning that within different contexts, each term points to an 'unconditioned, transcendent reality which is the ultimate source of salvation or liberation.' He then asks whether this entails that 'God' and '*dharmakāya*' point to the same ultimate reality, and notes that this can only be established from the point of view of each tradition according to its own criteria. In exploring a Christian point of view on that question, he argues that any functional equivalent to God is genuine 'if it does not entail idolatry . . . and . . . is intrinsically linked to the evocation of selfless love'. Since *dharmakāya* complies with those criteria, he argues, Christians should regard it as a functional equivalent to God. But it appears that the meaning of functional equivalence has shifted in the course of this discussion. At first, functional equivalence means just that the two terms 'God' and '*dharmakāya*' function similarly in referring to posited transcendent realities. Later, it seems to mean that those transcendent realities, as they are conceived and engaged by Christians and Buddhists, function equally in their salvific potency, to impart qualities such as freedom from idolatry and evocation of love. When he equates the fruits of the Buddha's influence with those of Christ (freedom from idolatry and love), he appears to assume that the qualities of ultimate reality realized in the two traditions are just the same.

Thus, a further ambiguity arises over the precise scope of Schmidt-Leukel's use of the term 'equivalent'. Does it just mean that 'God' and '*dharmakāya*' refer to the same ultimate reality? Or does it also mean that God and *dharmakāya* (as ultimate realities conceived and engaged by persons) can be shown to function as fully equivalent in their saving potency? On pages 170–1, he asks: 'Can Buddhists identify the Christian God as a genuine equivalent to the *dharmakāya* and hence see Jesus as an authentic incarnation?' He goes on to argue that Buddhists can do so based on the Buddhist doctrine of skilful means – since the Christian God's incarnation in Jesus can be seen as a skilful means of *dharmakāya* for 'leading [persons] to enlightenment'.

Does this imply (as it seems) that Jesus leads persons to the complete enlightenment of a Buddha?

In my article 'Buddhist Perspectives on Truth in Other Religions',[1] I argued that Christian communion practice, centred upon Christ as mediation of God, could be viewed as skilful means of *dharmakāya*. Christian communion can evoke qualities that a Buddhist can recognize as supportive of the path to enlightenment, such as the willingness to surrender self-concern for an inclusive love beyond self-grasping. But I could not make the stronger claim that Christ and Christian communion lead persons fully to the enlightenment of a Buddha. That would require a rigorous analysis of the qualities that constitute a Buddha's enlightenment and whether each would be fulfilled through Christian practice.

In my chapter in this volume, I argued that 'God' and '*dharmakāya*' refer to the same reality, because my practice as a Mahāyāna Buddhist helped me recognize some of the liberating potency of Christian communion, as if the communion practice in each tradition genuinely expresses part of the structure of ultimate reality in its capacity to commune. This seems further confirmed by the ways that Christian communion unexpectedly sheds light for me upon Buddhist practices and understandings otherwise far removed from a Christian world-view (as in note 3 of my chapter). But to accept that 'God' refers to the same ultimate reality as '*dharmakāya*' (as both Schmidt-Leukel and I do) does not entail that the normative practices of traditions associated with God on one hand and *dharmakāya* on the other are equivalent in all ways that matter for salvation or liberation. From a Buddhist point of view, what functions to liberate persons is not just ultimate reality per se or one's concepts of it, but the specific practices associated with those concepts and their specific fruits.

In other words, Schmidt-Leukel seems implicitly to assert that those who engage in spiritual practices centred on the mediation

---

1 J. Makransky, 2003, 'Buddhist Perspectives on Truth in Other Religions: Past and Present', in *Theological Studies*, 64 no. 2, pp. 334–61.

of Christ and those who practise the Buddha Dharma can realize the same qualities of ultimate reality to the same depth or
fullness. But, I argue, the results of spiritual practice depend not
only on the nature of ultimate reality but also upon the ways that
specific practices render persons receptive to different aspects
and qualities of that ultimate reality.

As a Christian, Schmidt-Leukel posited functional equivalence
between God and *dharmakāya* in their power to free persons
from idolatry and to evoke selfless love. The Buddhist analogue
for idolatry would be 'mis-knowing' (Sanskrit: *avidyā*), defined
in Mahāyāna schools as the deluded consciousness that reifies
and grasps to a substantial sense of self and world, giving rise to
grasping, fear and consequent suffering. The goals of Mahāyāna
practice are to completely uproot that pattern of mis-knowing
by attaining a non-conceptual, non-dual realization of the empty
nature of all phenomena, and with love and compassion for all
who are still caught in such mis-knowing, to unleash vast activity so they may similarly awaken to the unconditioned freedom
found in the empty nature of all to which they grasp. Thus, the
Buddhist analogues of idolatry and selfless love are not just the
same as the Christian understandings, nor are the normative
practices.

In the two traditions, that from which persons are to be
freed (sin as broken relationship with God versus grasping to
substantiality within duality) and the main principle that frees
them (God's grace versus non-conceptual, non-dual realization
of emptiness) are differently defined. Therefore the practices to
bring about such freedom are differently targeted.

The practices of each tradition, since they are targeted so
differently, may function differently enough to make a real difference in salvific qualities realized and the type or degree of
liberation attained.

What I posit as a Buddhist, based on some similarity in Mahāyāna and Christian structures of communion and similarities in
some of the qualities of goodness that are realized through it
(love, compassion, relative freedom from ego-centred concern),
is that Buddhists and Christians are engaging the same ultimate

reality differently understood, through practices and beliefs, some of which are similar and others of which are different. This, it would appear, would affect which qualities of ultimate reality are realized in human life, to what degree, to what depth, and in what kind of integration with other qualities. Thus there would be difference within the similarities, differences which matter and from which each can learn from the other.

When I posit that the 'skilful means' of Buddhahood is operative in Christian life, as I did in prior writing, I meant that genuine enlightened activity is at work in more than one tradition – but that does not guarantee complete functional equivalence with regard to the attainment of enlightenment or salvation. Indeed different Buddhist schools over history have viewed each other's teachings as skilful means that are not fully equivalent for complete liberation – often one school viewing others as preparation for fuller accomplishment of awakening. Rather than declaring each school functionally equivalent for liberation and enlightenment, Buddhist scholars have continued to argue with each other over doctrine and practice, and in that way continue to learn from each other. Similarly, Buddhist and Christian traditions can avoid prematurely asserting the full functional equivalence of their traditions regarding salvation or enlightenment, even as they come into a new recognition of each other as genuine mediations of the same ultimate reality. That recognition can newly empower each tradition to learn from the other about the ultimate reality of its own devotion and the diverse ways that persons are authentically opened to it. But by avoiding a premature assertion of full functional equivalence between traditions, each can also learn from the other through friendly argument over what prevents persons from reaching their fullest openness to the goodness of ultimate reality and what can be done about it.

PART IV

THE QUEST FOR PEACE

14. Buddhism, Christianity and their Potential for Peace:

A Christian Perspective

KENNETH FERNANDO

The Ethnic Conflict in Sri Lanka

I come from a war-torn country in which we of different faiths have tried hard to come together in our quest for peace. I have myself been personally involved in some of these efforts and I can speak as a battered fighter for peace; battered but not defeated. I have served as a priest of the Church of Ceylon (Anglican) since 1960. I realized very early that the ethnic conflict in my country should be a major concern of my ministry.

Sri Lanka became an independent country within the British Commonwealth of Nations in 1948. My country had been under foreign rule continuously for 450 years. First the Portuguese had ruled Sri Lanka for 150 years beginning in 1505 followed by the Dutch and then the British for similar periods. When Sri Lanka became independent after that long period of subjection, we had to work out our ethnic relationships and the principles of state policy all over again. Indeed we opted for a parliamentary system of democratic government but very largely it turned out to be majority rule. The Tamils who constitute about 12 per cent of the population, very particularly, were of the view that their rights had not been recognized in the Constitution. The Tamils of Indian origin brought to the country to work on the plantations by the British have also felt that their rights have not been considered adequately. The Muslims who make up about 7 per cent are scattered in many parts of the country and have been engaged in a constant struggle for adequate recognition. Just now religious minorities, especially the Christians, have had to struggle for the preservation of their religious freedom. But the major struggle has been between the Tamils of the north and east and the predominantly Sinhala government in the south.

Early in the struggle the Tamils fought for language rights, criteria for admission to the universities that would be fair by them, non-discrimination in state employment opportunities and a colonization policy that would leave the east of the country with an unchanged demographic composition. The government of Sri Lanka failed to heed these grievances with sufficient sensitivity and sufficiently early. It persisted for too long with a policy that made Sinhala the only official language of the country. It implemented a policy of admission to the universities on a district quota basis that gave fairer opportunities to candidates from less developed parts of the country but seemed to discriminate against Tamils. And it established Sinhala colonies in the Eastern Province to mix up the various ethnic communities rather than set up ethnic ghettoes. At the time of independence in 1948 the percentage of Tamil persons in the professions and in government service was not in proportion to the Tamil population in the country. The government set out to restore the balance by limiting the recruitment of Tamil persons into government service. All this led to a non-violent struggle at first, marked by outbreaks of severe violence from time to time.

Since 1983 we have had a severe civil conflict between the Tamil people under the leadership of the Liberation Tigers of Tamil Eelam (LTTE) and the government, resulting in very great loss of life and property in all parts of the country. At about this time the demand changed from justice in relation to the various grievances to a demand for a separate state named Eelam. I would maintain that it has not been a conflict between the Sinhala and Tamil people because in all parts of the country, except the north, the two communities still live in harmony and there is no persecution by either of the two communities. The conflict is between the militant Liberation Tigers of Tamil Eelam and the government forces of Sri Lanka. However, the whole country has suffered much, our economy is severely affected and although there is a brittle ceasefire in place, various attempts to negotiate a settlement by successive governments since 1977 have proved futile hitherto.

Autobiographical

Very early in my ministry in Sri Lanka I realized that Christians had an important part to play in initiating and taking forward a peace process. Apart from some trade unions, we are among the few civil society organizations that count both Tamil and Sinhala people among our members. Consequently we had an opportunity and a duty to contribute what we could to a process of reconciliation. However, since the total Christian community in Sri Lanka is no more than 7 per cent of the population, there was very little we could do by ourselves. It was essential that we forge links and work with other religious communities, notably the Buddhists and the Buddhist Clergy. The Buddhist public wield much influence in our country led by about 20,000 monks.

I became the Director of the Ecumenical Institute for Study and Dialogue in Colombo in 1983. This Institute emphasizes Buddhist-Christian dialogue. As Director of this Institute I had the opportunity to study Buddhism in one of our Universities and also to forge personal links with some of our leading Buddhist monks and scholars. The year 1983 also happened to be the darkest year in the history of our conflict, marked by severe violence against Tamil civilians unleashed by Sinhala groups in Colombo and elsewhere in retaliation for the killing of thirteen Sinhala soldiers.

In December 1992 I was elected Bishop of the Diocese of Colombo. This Diocese extends right round the perimeter of the island and includes the north and east, where the Tamils predominate. The central parts of the island constitute another diocese. Tamil members of our diocese flouted a government ban on travel to the south and undertook the dangerous journey from the north and the east to be present at my consecration in Colombo in December 1992. My first pastoral visit was to Jaffna in the north in January 1993 despite the ban on travel.

Mr Prabhakaran, the leader of the LTTE, sent a message to me inviting me to come and talk to him. I accepted the invitation and met him for a two-hour dialogue. I was accompanied by the Roman Catholic Bishop of Jaffna, the Bishop of the Jaffna Diocese of the Church of South India and several other Christian clergy and lay people including the Archdeacon of Jaffna of our own diocese. We were very cordially received by the Tigers and they assured us that they would be content with a constitutional arrangement that would safeguard their rights. As he bade me goodbye he said, 'Come again, Bishop. Come with your friends. Come with the Buddhist monks.' This rather surprised me. He was aware that I had good contacts with the Buddhist clergy.

On my return to Colombo I reported all this to the government of Sri Lanka and to the press. I informed the Buddhist clergy leaders both formally and informally about my dialogue with the LTTE and tried unsuccessfully to go with them again to meet the Tigers. I continued to visit Jaffna every year, as it was my duty as the bishop of the people there. On every such visit Tiger leaders called on me, though I did not have the opportunity to meet Prabhakaran again.

In 1994 we had a change of government and with the election of a new president there was a change of government policy on the ethnic question. One of the first acts of the President, then Prime Minister, was to pay me a courtesy call and ask me to help with the peace process. From 1994 onwards and also sporadically earlier we have been engaged in a series of peace efforts and the President sent a number of delegations to have talks with the Tigers.

In 1995 a group of some seventeen police officers who had been captured by the Tigers started a fast seeking their release or their trial. The President sent me with another prominent civil rights activist to see what we could do to resolve the problem. At our request all the prisoners were released to me and because they were in a weak physical condition at my request the International Committee of the Red Cross brought them to Colombo.

In April 1995 the President requested me to go with two civil rights activists and the Secretary of the Presidential Secretariat to talk to the Tigers in the fourth round of talks initiated by her. In my view this round of talks went very well, we were able to clear up all issues to the satisfaction of all, and we parted on a very cordial note. But within a week hostilities broke out again with the sinking of some ships belonging to the navy in the Trincomalee Harbour. I have never understood the reasons for this. Subsequently a very severe war has raged and many lives have been lost in conflict and much property destroyed in Colombo and at the airport.

To my great surprise a group of leading Buddhist monks came to my office in 1998 and asked me whether I would accompany them to meet the Tigers. I readily agreed and within a week a group of twenty leading monks, a Roman Catholic bishop and another priest of that church went to the area occupied by the Tigers and had a most useful discussion with an LTTE delegation. There were mutual apologies and expressions of regret. It was the wish of the monks that as a last act we should meet in the vestibule of the holy shrine in Madhu and formally pledge to continue to work for peace until our efforts met with success.

In this long story I feel that Buddhist and Christian leaders have done what they could to promote peace in our country. We have created an atmosphere for peace negotiations. By choice we have not got into the area of discussing constitutional arrangements, which would be outside our sphere of competence.

Negotiations still continue amidst very great difficulties. The passage of time has meant that we keep running into new and unforeseen difficulties. But although the religious leadership for the most part remains committed to the peace process there has been a reaction and other voices hostile to the current peace process, including the voices of some Buddhist monks, can now be heard loud and clear. I myself retired from the Bishopric of Colombo in 2001 and now live in the countryside south of Colombo. But soon after I came here I had the unpleasant experience of having a hand bomb thrown in to my garden at midnight with a warning that I should not participate in the peace process any more. Although my car and house were somewhat damaged and debris came into our bedroom, my wife and I were unscathed.

Religious Loyalties in our World of Conflict

Despite the fact that sensitive and thoughtful people throughout the world give great priority to peace it is still true that we live in a world full of strife. It is very sad but true that in many of the conflicts now raging in various parts of the world, religion is one of the major causes. While religions can be a major resource for peace they have in fact become a major source of conflict. I do believe with Hans Küng that better inter-faith relations hold the key to better international and better inter-ethnic relations.

> No peace among the nations, without peace among the religions.
> No peace among the religions, without dialogue between the religions.
> No dialogue between the religions, without investigation of the foundations of the religions.[1]

I am well aware that religion is not a major issue in most societies of our secularized world and that in today's world people hang on to their religious loyalties only by a slender thread. But when religious loyalties and ethnic or national loyalties get intertwined then many people speak and behave as though religion is a very great issue in their lives. This is because for so many people religion is a factor that defines their identities. So in the world today we see in the midst of increasing secularization a most peculiar politico-religious revival. We see this phenomenon in many Islamic countries. Most notably in the United States and

---

1 Hans Küng, 1992, *Judaism: The Religious Situation of our Time*, London: SCM Press, p. xxii.

so many other countries under its influence, politics and religion and economic policies have been inextricably intertwined in the name of Christian fundamentalism.

Jacques Ellul has some very valuable insights into the way in which religion can be used to mould the attitudes of people in so many other spheres of thought as well:

> We are here in the presence of an organized myth that tries to take hold of the entire person. Through the myth it creates, propaganda imposes a complete range on intuitive knowledge, susceptible of only one interpretation, unique and one sided, and precluding any divergence. This myth becomes so powerful, that it invades every area of consciousness . . . controls the whole of the individual, who becomes immune to any other influence.[2]

Wherever this happens, there is bound to be a reaction and most serious threats to peace, both within nations and internationally. In India the resurgence of Hinduism is tied up with the demand for *Hindutva* ('Hindu-ness'): a political programme based on an idea of Hindu identity with polemical overtones against non-Hindu religions. In my own country, Sri Lanka, in response to Christian fundamentalism, there is a strong anti-Christian Buddhist nationalist movement that has led to some people demanding a Sinhala Buddhist state. For the first time in the history of Buddhism nine Buddhist monks sit as members of parliament. In so many countries the rise of Islamic fundamentalism has led Muslims to redefine their own identities in terms of religion. Fundamentalism is a feature today of all religions and since it seeks to control not only religious loyalties but also political and socio-economic and cultural loyalties it constitutes a grave threat to the peace of all people and nations. The whole

---

2 Jacques Ellul, *Propaganda: The Formation of Men's Attitudes*, quoted in Flo Conway and Jim Siegelman, 1982, *Holy Terror: The Fundamentalist War on America's Freedoms in Politics, Religion and Our Private Lives*, New York: Delta Books, Dell Publishing, p. 334.

question of fundamentalism as an international phenomenon is very relevant to our subject, but I do not intend to go into it at greater length in this chapter.

Inter-religious Relations: A New Paradigm?

Fundamentalism notwithstanding, it still remains true that the cause of world peace cannot be promoted without the active co-operation of the various religions that claim the loyalty of people. While fundamentalism is a perverse expression of religious loyalty, religious loyalties can also take many other more eirenic and accommodative forms. At its best, true religion encourages us to be appreciative and open to all religions. This is not a modern thought at all. I cannot do better than refer to the great King Aśoka of India who in the third century BCE, after his conversion to Buddhism, changed his lifestyle and policies and tried to make his whole empire follow Buddhist principles, so that it would be Dharma Rajjya, a kingdom of Dharma. With this aim in view he issued a number of edicts, some of them carved in stone, which survive to this day. Here is an extract from his Rock Edict no. 12:

> It is better to honour other religions for this reason. By so doing one's own religion benefits, and so do other religions, while doing otherwise, harms one's own religion and the religion of others. Whoever praises his own religion, due to excessive devotion, and condemns others with the thought 'Let me glorify my own religion', only harms his own religion. Therefore contact between religions is good. One should listen to and respect the doctrine professed by others. King Piyadasi (Aśoka) desires that all should be well-learned in the good doctrines of other religion . . . and the fruit of this is that one's own religion grows . . .[3]

3 *The Edicts of King Asoka*, an English rendering by Ven. S. Dhammika, The Wheel Publication 386/387 (1993), Kandy: Buddhist Publication Society, www.urbandharma.org/udharma/asoka.html.

Every true religion must define its teaching and mission in a way that does not threaten others but in fact promotes an environment that is conducive to peace. Indeed it must go further and promote dialogue among the various religions not merely at an academic level but by working together for common causes like peace-making, the preservation of human rights and the eradication of poverty. But this aspiration is not likely to be fulfilled unless and until we learn to relate with other religions in a friendly and respectful way. During the past half century or so we have debated the relative merits of exclusivism (as advocated by, for example, K. Barth, H. Kraemer, L. Newbigin), inclusivism (for example, H. Küng, J.N. Farquhar, R. Panikkar) and pluralism in different forms (for example, J. Hick, S. Samartha, W. Ariarajah). It is my contention that all these are attempts to build up a grand theory that covers all religions from a Christian perspective and is therefore triumphalistic. It is still a form of Christian imperial-ism which inhibits and is an obstacle to building up true inter-faith relations. In our multi-faith world we have to resent all tendencies to be judgemental and become the dominant partner. If we really need a model in which all religions can have a place we must work out such a model in dialogue with people of other faiths. Above all let us be pragmatic. Since all of us have to live together with people of different faiths in all our countries, let us learn to live together and learn from one another, enriching our respective faiths and growing in our understanding of one another and of the faiths of others. This is the basis on which the different religions in our world today can and must interact. This means indeed that we must all give up grand notions of conquering the whole world for our own religion, which is a prescription for conflict.

This effort to bring the whole world into the ambit of our own religion is generally based on the presumption that we alone have the key to salvation. This arises from the belief that there is no salvation outside my own religion. Salvation should not be looked upon as a gift available within any particular religion, which we can appropriate for ourselves. It should rather be looked upon as an experience into which we can enter. If one can claim that in one's own religion one has found freedom and release from one's fears and anxieties and also found meaning and purpose both personally and socially for one's life, then indeed such a person can claim to have found salvation within that religion. It is a personal experience. I do believe in evangelism. But it must be evangelism carried out eirenically, patiently, respectfully and in personal terms, following the example of Jesus Christ himself and the Buddha.

There is no way in which conflicts with a religious component whether in Sri Lanka or anywhere else can be finally resolved unless the religious leaders of all the various religions act in co-operation. There are indeed many teachings common to all religions that contribute to peace. I would like to emphasize some Buddhist teachings that make for peace.

The Buddhist Potential for Peace

Chief among the Buddhist teachings conducive to peace would be the *brahma vihāra* which provide a basis for the social expression of Buddhism. The *brahma vihāra* – or 'Four Sublime States' – are: *mettā*, universal unlimited 'love' and 'goodwill' extended to all living beings without recognizing any boundaries at all; *karuṇā*, 'compassion' for all those who suffer any kind of affliction or discrimination; *muditā*, the 'joy' we experience when we share the success, welfare and happiness of others; and *upekkhā*, the 'equanimity' we must cultivate in all the changes and experiences of life. These *vihāra* lend themselves to imaginative interpretation and may well provide a basis for establishing peace.

Of crucial importance also is the Buddha's attitude towards the issue of caste. It is true that we in South Asia still live amidst caste and ethnic differences. But this happens despite the very clear teaching of the Buddha. In ancient India there was a belief that the four different castes were derived from the head, body, hands and feet of the great Brahman. The Buddha rejected this myth and clearly taught us that our status in life is determined not by our birth but by our deeds. 'One born of a Brahmin's womb is not a Brahmin. When he has no defilements and is captive to nothing, I call him Brahmin.'[4] The whole of humanity is descended from a single source and we are therefore all brothers and sisters. Unlike in the case of birds, fishes and animals, 'in humans various attributes are not evident at birth'.[5]

The Buddha himself is described in the Pāli *Tipiṭaka* as a peace maker:

> Thus does he live (the Buddha), as a builder together of those who are divided, an encourager of those who are friends, a peacemaker, a lover of peace, a speaker of words that make for peace.[6]

This is illustrated by a story related in the Buddhist scriptures that the Buddha came across two tribes, the Koliyas and the Sākiyas, that were in conflict over the waters of the River Rohini. The Buddha asked what value the water had and pointed out that it was not worthwhile to quarrel over water.[7] In this story the Buddha teaches us that material things, the things of this world, whether it be water, or land or oil are not worth fighting about, since man is called to a higher destiny, to live a noble life free of material greed and acquisitive habits. Surely it is the greed, materialism and competitiveness of our society that are the root causes of conflict in our world. The Buddha totally rejects the resort to violence as a method of resolving conflicts. As the *Dhammapada* teaches us in a well-known stanza (verse 5):

> Hatred is never appeased by hatred in this world;
> It is appeased by love.
> This is an Eternal Law.

---

4 *Vāseṭṭha Sutta, Majjhima Nikāya* (ii 119) 98.
5 *Vāseṭṭha Sutta, Majjhima Nikāya* (ii 118) 98.
6 *Brahmajāla Sutta, Dīgha Nikāya* I (i 6).
7 See *Jātaka* 536. Also related in various commentaries, e.g., *Dhammapada Aṭṭhakathā* III, 254–6.

This is the teaching that gave rise to Mahatma Gandhi's belief in the power of non-violence. Its power has been proved in practice by people like Martin Luther King, Jr and Nelson Mandela.

Our Historical Track Records

Buddhists can claim with much justification that the history of Buddhism is largely free from religiously motivated violence. It seems that Buddhism has never been propagated by violent means. What of Sri Lanka? I can affirm that thoughtful Buddhists in my country have agonized over this issue and it is with the greatest reluctance that some of them have consented to the use of violence in the defence of the unity and the integrity of Sri Lanka. But none has sought to defend such a course of action on religious grounds, and there is no attempt to formulate a theory of a just war in Buddhism. I am aware of some efforts made by scholars both in Sri Lanka and abroad to find justification for war on historical grounds and quote various incidents from the *Mahāvaṃsa*. But the *Mahāvaṃsa* is a historical chronicle compiled many centuries after the Buddha's life and can in no way be placed on a par with the canonical literature.

By contrast Christianity has a most regrettable track record. We need to remind ourselves constantly of the religious wars fought in Europe over the centuries and perhaps being fought even now. The European colonial enterprise was political and economic and in order to further those ends the colonizing powers treated our indigenous cultures and our religions with cruelty and violence. Folk memory and the ruins of temples and shrines of other faiths found scattered in Asia bear ample testimony to these facts even if documents are hard to come by. We need to be reminded of the heartless manner in which the Native Americans were treated in the United States and Canada and the way in which aborigines were decimated, and in some places like Tasmania actually annihilated. Perhaps the most shameful war in which Christians have been engaged is the war against the Muslims in the Holy land, the Balkans and Spain – a war that is not yet over.

But this dark cloud has a silver lining. We who belong to the Third World must be grateful to the colonizers for modern education including access to foreign languages. They have also left behind a small coterie of liberal-minded persons of all faiths who in the Third World stand up for such values as human rights and the peaceful resolution of conflict as understood generally by the modern international community. This coterie has a great responsibility to lead their nations from narrow nationalist loyalties to an appreciation of the values and ideals of the whole international community. We can also take heart from the fact that several significant Christian leaders very clearly refused to give their approval to the war in Iraq, adopting Christian stances at long last, after so many centuries of giving their blessing to crusades and other wars they considered holy.

I would have preferred not to refer to this sad history of Christian mission in the Third World, but I felt constrained to do so because this history is not something of the past that we have got over. I am deeply concerned that extremist Christian fundamentalists are still making deep inroads into our countries, setting at nought our cultures and our religions and making efforts pell-mell to win converts to Christian fundamentalism. Unfortunately, many of our religious and political leaders in the Third World see this endeavour as being motivated by some new-found Christian enthusiasm and fail to see the well-hidden political and economic motives of this enormous worldwide campaign.

The Christian Potential for Peace

What we can do in the face of this sad history, in which Christians have been involved in persecution and war, is to be penitent and seek the pardon of those whom we have harmed, in a truly Christian spirit. Despite our track record and past history, a few of us in the Third World still profess the Christian faith because of the potential for peace and human community contained in the teaching and life of Jesus Christ. Hence I turn now to my own somewhat individualistic understanding of contemporary Christianity. I do not apologize for the use of the word 'individualistic', because in my view the traditional understanding of Western European Christianity needs much rethinking, especially in the Third World, if it is to be relevant and intelligible, and a resource for conflict resolution in our world today.

Creator and Parent God

I consider the teaching of Jesus, that the transcendental Reality whom we call God must be conceived as our parent, Father, is a very radical and, in the time of Jesus, innovative understanding of Reality and the Eternal. It certainly would appear to be so from an Eastern and Buddhist perspective.

The creator and parent of us all requires first of all that we all regard creation as an ongoing process. It is God's way to do things gradually and, as St Gregory of Nyssa reminds us, God created *semina* (seeds).[8] We are stewards of creation but we have not always been mindful of that trust. It is absolutely essential that we treat our world and its resources with much respect and a sense of responsibility if we are to establish world peace. Our great desire to exploit oil is one of the main causes of international tension and war in our world today. Soon we shall be fighting over water and a cleaner atmosphere. We simply do not have the right to exploit and pollute the earth because it is not ours but God's.

Our belief in God as parent means that the whole community of humankind are brothers and sisters, those near us and those who are far away, and those yet unborn. If we remember that responsibility, there simply cannot be strife among people of different colour, people of different faiths, ethnicity or class and caste. This teaching is a very special resource for peace and we have not believed or lived by it in the past.

This parent God is also the lord of history. In my part of the world, people find it very difficult to think of God being actually involved in human historical processes. But the Old Testament

---

8 St Gregory of Nyssa, *Apologia in Hexaemeron* in *Patrologia Graeca* 44: 61–124, *passim*.

is very clear that God is the parent of Abraham and Isaac and that God led his people from slavery in Egypt across the Red Sea and into the Promised Land. These are historical and political processes. I insist that God has been active also in the history of India, China, Sri Lanka, Africa, etc. God has spoken to our forefathers and revealed the divine nature throughout history. But the most important thing is that God is active in the political processes of our own day and generation. It is very difficult to accept that, when we think of all the terrible events that take place in our world today. But it is true that God seeks to establish God's Kingdom in our world today and God is active in seeking reconciliation and the liberation of all humankind from all that enslaves us, like racial prejudice, economic exploitation and grinding poverty. Christians must discern God's activity in the world today and co-operate with God. This means indeed that the true place for Christians to live out their faith is out in the world. But I must also add the warning that this belief in God at work in the world can and often does lead to a most serious perversion. 'I am God's person, my political party is God's own instrument and my country is the country that God has chosen to save the world.' Such self-aggrandizing identification with God is very common in our world today and so we have nations identifying what they believe to be the source, or axis of evil and setting out to destroy it.

Christianity not only teaches us to take history with the utmost seriousness, it also requires that we should be totally involved in the things of this world, as Jesus was. 'The Word (Dharma) became flesh.' This important and radical teaching means that we Christians simply cannot withdraw from worldly concerns. This is where we are right now and the things of this world, like peacemaking, eradicating poverty and establishing the rights of all, are rightly our concern.

The Teaching of Jesus

The birth of Jesus was anticipated by Isaiah long before he was born and hailed as the 'Prince of Peace'.[9] His last farewell to the disciples included the words 'My peace I leave with you my peace give I unto you'.[10] Taking his cue from Jewish teaching, Jesus reaffirmed the goal of shalom. The concept of shalom is well defined in several parts of the Old Testament as each person sitting under his own fig tree and his own vine and drinking from his own well.[11] It is a picture definition of peace. Picture definitions are more expressive than legalistic ones and they stand the test of time better. Isaiah 66.17–25 describes very well what happens to people in war and what happens when peace is restored. Shalom is very much more than the absence of war; it is ensuring the freedom and right to self-determination of all nations; respecting the human rights of every person, and the abolition of all forms of racial and social oppression and discrimination; and the protection of the environment. In so many war-torn countries including my own, we have been trying to establish peace by making constitutional arrangements. But the task of peacemaking goes far beyond that, as Isaiah makes clear.

Jesus built upon the Old Testament understanding of peace and produced a radically new concept that he called the Kingdom of God. This was, in my view, the one topic on which all the teaching of Jesus was based – how to establish God's reign (Kingdom) and to work for the extension of that reign. God reigns wherever God's will is done. I am very glad that the Second Vatican Council,[12] almost all churches and so many theologians are agreed that this emphasis on the Kingdom of God is central to the teaching of Jesus. I say it is the only thing he taught about. The Kingdom is the subject of all his parables, his signs in St John's Gospel, and all his teaching. He was identified so much with the Kingdom he preached that, even when he was on the cross, he was recognized as the Kingdom man by the penitent

---

9 Isa. 9.6.
10 John 14.27.
11 2 Kings 18.31; Isa. 36.16; Micah 4.4.
12 *Lumen Gentium* 1, section 5.

thief: 'Remember me when you come in your Kingdom.' The chief task of every Christian, then, is to recognize the will of God and do it both in our personal lives and in the life of the nation. When his will is done, his Kingdom comes.

I would like to emphasize two hallmarks of the Kingdom. One is love as understood by Jesus: limitless love that transcends all barriers. Jesus taught that Samaritans are capable of loving Jews (the Good Samaritan). How difficult it is in situations of conflict to say that there are Arabs who love Jews, or Iraqis who love Americans or vice versa. It would be very difficult in my country to say that there are Sinhalese and Tamils who love one another across our ethnic divide. But this is a very essential Christian teaching, and it is this kind of thinking that makes for peace. We deal with people not categories.

Very closely allied to this teaching is the most revolutionary teaching of Jesus about forgiveness. There can be no peace without acknowledging the wrongs we have done to others, apology, forgiving one another, reconciliation among ourselves, restoration of equality and the establishment of fellowship (*koinonia*). St Paul has some unforgettable words about Jesus the reconciler: 'He is our peace, who hath made both one, and hath broken down the middle wall of partition between us.'[13] Indeed I am thinking of South Africa, where the miracle has happened before our very eyes. I am sometimes challenged to give an example where peaceful methods of reconciliation and conflict resolution have succeeded and I have no hesitation in quoting the example of South Africa. This is something that a few years ago we considered impossible. Jonathan Sacks has written, 'Forgiveness . . . represents a decision not to do what instinct and passion urge us to do. It answers hate with a refusal to hate, animosity with generosity.'[14] Love can literally liquidate your enemy by allowing your love to destroy every trace of hatred in their hearts.

---

13 Eph. 2.14, KJV.
14 Jonathan Sacks, 2003, *The Dignity of Difference: How to Avoid the Clash of Civilizations,* rev. edn, London: Continuum, p. 179.

The Death and Resurrection of Jesus

Christians know that the death and resurrection of Jesus take the central place in their faith. In my own view these events have been interpreted in the scriptures in a number of ways to suit the various contexts in which the scriptures were compiled – sacrifice, substitution, example, victory, etc. I submit that any understanding of the death and resurrection of Jesus that is relevant and meaningful to our age must fulfil the following conditions:

1. It must keep these two events, death and resurrection, together. If Jesus on the cross is understood solely as the sacrificial lamb, what happened at the resurrection?
2. Military metaphors like victory are not helpful in non-military, non-triumphalistic societies.
3. In an age which values the rule of law we cannot understand how one person can pay for the sins of another. Pay whom?
4. There are many examples of persons who have lived and given up their lives for a cause but no one, having done so, literally regained life.

If the Kingdom of God is the sole teaching of Jesus we must understand and interpret the death and resurrection of Jesus in Kingdom terms. We need a 'basileic' (Kingdom-related) understanding of the atonement if it is to be meaningful and relevant in our conflict-ridden world of confusion. Jesus died for the Kingdom because no one can work for it without being ready to die for it: 'If any man will come after me, let him deny himself, and take up his cross daily, and follow me.'[15] Jesus said 'Blessed are the peacemakers, for they shall be called the children of God'[16] because he knew the cost of peacemaking. It means being ready to be condemned by both sides and being ready to suffer and die for peace. There is no Kingdom building or peacemaking on the cheap.

---

15 Luke 9.23, KJV.   16 Matt. 5.9, KJV.

It is not possible to participate in an activity so difficult and dangerous as peacemaking unless one is convinced that one is on the side that will win ultimately. Peace will come in every situation. The Kingdom cannot fail. Jesus Christ is risen from the dead. This message of hope is one of the important contributions Christians must bring to any peace process. We never give up because we know that we will win. Christian hope is the assurance that God is at work, that he reigns. It is not blind optimism. It is a sure and certain hope based on the truth of the resurrection.

The Holy Spirit

Christians believe that God's Holy Spirit is at work in the world, bringing order out of chaos, and promoting beauty, goodness and truth in our world. The Spirit of God is as gentle as a breeze, quiet as a still small voice, mighty and unpredictable as the wind, invisible as the air, life-giving as breath, enlightening and enabling as a flame.

This God is still among us, despite all human passion and vileness to one another. The Spirit of God will continue to be the still small voice that speaks to every human conscience.

Conclusion

All religions throughout human history have been and indeed still are sources of conflict. But they can also be resources for peace.[17] But this will require that the religions we believe in should not confine us to our respective camps but set our human spirits free – free to explore all that is good, beautiful and true in human experience; free to seek partners and colleagues wherever they may be found; free to reach out towards true human community and peace and all that makes for what is best and worthwhile

---

17 On this see also Perry Schmidt-Leukel (ed.), 2004, *War and Peace in World Religions*, London: SCM Press.

in human life. Let me conclude with the words of Rabindranath
Tagore:

> Where the mind is without fear and the head is held high;
> Where knowledge is free;
> Where the world has not been broken up into fragments by
> narrow domestic walls;
> Where words come out from the depths of truth;
> Where tireless striving stretches its arms towards perfection;
> Where the clear stream of reason has not lost its way into the
> dreary desert sand of dead habit;
> Where the mind is led forward by thee into ever widening
> thought and action –
> Into that heaven of freedom, my Father, let my country
> awake.[18]

---

18 Gitanjali 35, www.allspirit.co.uk/gitanjali.html.

15. Buddhism, Christianity and their Potential for Peace:

A Buddhist Perspective

HOZAN ALAN SENAUKE

> The accomplishing work of great peace has no sign;
> The family way of the peasants is most pristine –
> Only concerned with village songs and festival drinking.
>
> Zen Master Tiantong[1]

Not Turning Away

Buddhists and Christians share a difficult spiritual practice. Our teachers have shown us how to turn towards human suffering . . . and not to look away. This is an ongoing challenge to us. In Luke 4.18 Jesus preaches in Nazareth from the Book of Isaiah:

> The Spirit of the Lord is upon me because he has anointed me to preach good news to the poor. He has sent me to proclaim release to the captives and recovering of sight to the blind, to set at liberty those who are oppressed . . .

In our time, the Vietnamese Zen monk Thich Nhat Hanh writes:

> It is important for us to stay in touch with the suffering of the world. We need to nourish that awareness through many

---

1 Thomas Cleary, 1990, *Book of Serenity*, Hudson, NY: Lindisfarne Press, p. 21.

means – sounds, images, direct contacts, visits, and so on – in order to keep compassion alive in us . . . (but) We need to stay in touch with suffering only to the extent that we will not forget, so that compassion will flow within us and be a source for the energy of our actions.[2]

Returning in the heady days of the late 1960s from a decade in Asia, the poet Gary Snyder published an essay entitled *Buddhism and the Coming Revolution* that even today seems radical and completely to the point – in later revisions the piece was more moderately re-titled *Buddhism and the Possibilities of a Planetary Culture*. Snyder set terms for an inter-faith practice of peace that we are still trying to accomplish. He wrote:

The mercy of the West has been social revolution; the mercy of the East has been individual insight into the basic self/void. We need both. They are both contained in the traditional three aspects of the Dharma path: wisdom (*prajna*), meditation (*dhyana*), and morality (*sila*). Wisdom is intuitive knowledge of the mind of love and clarity that lies beneath one's ego-driven anxieties and aggressions. Meditation is going into the mind to see this for yourself – over and over again, until it becomes the mind you live in. Morality is bringing it back out in the way you live, through personal example and responsible action, ultimately toward the true community (*sangha*) of 'all beings'.[3]

The challenge of peacemaking is to turn towards our own suffering, then to go back into the world with just the right tools to change people's minds. But as an old Buddha said, 'The mind of a sentient being is difficult to change.' To change minds and to find our way in this world we need the harmonizing actions

2 Thich Nhat Hanh, 1993, *For A Future To Be Possible,* Berkeley, CA: Parallax Press, p. 13.
3 Gary Snyder, 1999, *The Gary Snyder Reader*, Washington, DC: Counterpoint, pp. 42–3.

and teachings of bodhisattvas and the righteous voices of prophets. I was born into a Jewish family, given a patriarch and prophet's religious name – Abraham. So I embrace both of these archetypes – the prophet and the bodhisattva – and vow to bring forth peace.

Here in the West the voices of prophets and bodhisattvas can still be heard. Tragically, they go unheeded, and wars spread like a virus. When Gary Snyder published his essay the United States was mired in Vietnam. In 1968 we were losing more than 300 soldiers a week, while casualties among Vietnamese soldiers and civilians on both sides were geometrically higher. This in a war that even intelligence analysts at the time conceded was unwinnable and counter-productive. These were my own student days and I remember them well. I have a prominent lump on my skull as a reminder.

Violent irrationality still rules the political roost. In 2003 the United States entered another escalating and unwinnable conflict, this time in Iraq. While the USA represents a yearning for freedom for much of the world, it has tragically become a source of armed and structural violence at home and around the world. We live in a relentless climate of fear and reaction, while simultaneously serving as a beacon of democratic freedoms, freedoms that are badly tarnished, but enduring. A cursory look around the world, though, finds similar stalemates in Israel/Palestine, and in Kashmir, as well as ongoing civil wars and conflict in Burma, Haiti, Sri Lanka, the former Yugoslavia, Sudan and many other parts of the world.

In this troubled moment I write not as a scholar, theologian or political scientist, but as a Buddhist practitioner, an inter-faith activist and a religious pluralist. In brief this means to me: (1) that I believe people's true nature is one of enlightenment covered over by habits of greed, anger and delusion; (2) that human interconnectedness and compassion yearn for liberation despite religious and cultural differences; and (3) that spiritual truth can not be reduced to any one set of beliefs or experiences, rather it is widely available and various. On this point, the Catholic monastic Brother David Steindl-Rast writes, 'The territory is so vast that no one path can do justice to it . . . different traditions may say very different things; they are exploring the same territory but in very different areas.'[4]

Buddhist Tools and Stories

Buddhism, the path I know most closely, provides countless tools for peacemaking, a wide array of precepts, principles and practices. These precepts reduce to a single instruction: Do not live one's life at the expense of others' lives. This prescription resonates with Christ's words in the Sermon on the Mount: 'Do unto others as you would have them do unto you';[5] and with the Jewish teacher Hillel's words, almost contemporary with those of Jesus: 'That which is hateful to thyself, do not do to thy neighbour. This is the whole law, and the rest is its commentary.'[6]

Foremost among Buddhist principles is Śākyamuni's great teaching of dependent origination. Like life, the truth of dependent origination is unimaginably complex, and yet it simply means: 'When this exists, that comes to be; with the arising of this, that arises.'[7] Or, 'Because there is the base, there are jewel pedestals, fine clothing.'[8] Because there is war, I know there is also peace. But if I think of peace as something that can be described and cling to the idea that it is outside myself, conditions for war inevitably arise. There is, however, a peace beneath and beyond our ordinary notion of peace. This peace is not the act of avoiding wrong. Neither is it some pleasant idyll. True

---

4 Robert Aitken and David Steindl-Rast, 1994, *The Ground We Share: Everyday Practice, Buddhist and Christian*, Liguori, MI: Triumph Books, p. 7.

5 Matt. 7.12, KJV.

6 *Hillel Babylonian Talmud*: Tractate Shabbath Folio 31a, translated by H. Freedman, www.come-and-hear.com/shabbath/shabbath_31.html.

7 *Bahudhātuka Sutta, Majjhima Nikāya* 115. Quoted from B. Bodhi, B. and B. Nanamoli, 1995, *The Middle Length Discourses of the Buddha*, Boston: Wisdom, p. 927.

8 Thomas Cleary (ed. and trans.), 1980, *Timeless Spring: A Soto Zen Anthology*, New York: Weatherhill, p. 41.

peace has for me a gritty quality. It means that I recognize my own deluded impulses – dislike, anger, greediness, violence – and choose not to give them power over my actions towards myself and others. This is a difficult practice. I need a lot of help with it. In my own Zen school of Buddhism we practise together in community or *sangha*, and our practice of *zazen* or meditation is simultaneously the door to peace and its expression.

Buddhist meditation involves what His Holiness the Dalai Lama calls inner disarmament: 'you try to reduce negative emotions such as hatred, anger, jealousy, extremism, and greed, and promote compassion, human affection, tolerance . . .'[9] In meditation we become intimate with our disquiet or *duḥkha*. What the Buddha called *duḥkha* is variously translated as 'suffering', 'dissatisfaction' or 'lack' – the seemingly ceaseless flow of self-centred thoughts. The meditation hall is a kind of laboratory – an environment that is intentionally simple and quiet – in which we begin to deconstruct busy habits of mind that veer away from peace. But the meditation hall is also where we sit together, embodying the essentially social nature of human life.

The Buddha taught that what we call a 'self' is not a fixed entity or 'soul'. The Buddha refrained from saying whether in fact there was or was not a soul. He explained that what we conventionally see as self is a miraculous interdependence of forms, causes and conditions. Thich Nhat Hanh advises us to 'Look into the self and discover that it is made only of non-self elements.'[10] He calls this 'interbeing'. We can realize this non-separation of self and other as a direct and transformative experience. Martin Luther King expressed it this way: 'For some strange reason I can never be what I ought to be until you are what you ought to be, and you can never be what you ought to be until I am what I ought to be. This is the inter-related

---

9 Tenzin Gyatso, the fourteenth Dalai Lama, 1999, 'Dialogue on Religion and Peace', in David Chappell (ed.), *Buddhist Peacework: Creating Cultures of Peace*, Boston: Wisdom, pp. 189–97 (p. 190).

10 Thich Nhat Hanh, 1998, *The Heart of the Buddha's Teaching*, New York: Broadway, p. 126.

structure of all reality.'[11] We wake up in relation to others, who are integral to our own being. We work towards peace from inside out and from outside in, because there really is nothing 'outside' ourselves. In the words of an old Zen saying: there is no place in the world to spit. This is a stark way of saying that holiness is everywhere. And yet too often we just miss it. Stories, my own and others', reveal this truth in action.

Rainy Night at San Quentin

The state of California, where I live, still has capital punishment. There are about 650 men and 15 women on death row – the largest population of condemned prisoners in the world – many of them warehoused for fifteen or twenty years before they run through their appeals and face execution by lethal injection in a mock-clinical setting. Executions are infrequent – unlike in Texas and Florida – but on an execution night many people gather at the gates of San Quentin prison. One such evening a thousand people came to protest the execution of Jay Siripongs, a Thai national and a Buddhist, convicted of a 1983 murder in Los Angeles. Sheets of rain and cold wind beat down on all of us – death penalty opponents, a handful of death penalty supporters, reporters and state troopers. A large, diverse group sat in meditation up against the prison gates, gazing at San Quentin's high stone walls. My robes were soaked by the heavy rain and my meditation cushions sat in a deepening puddle. Ten feet away across a chain link fence, fifteen helmeted guards stood in a wet line, rain falling as hard on them as on us. I felt a flash of connection: here were Buddhist students – many in black robes – sitting in attention in the rain, protecting beings as best we knew how; and black-slickered police officers standing at attention in the rain, protecting beings as they knew how. Together we expressed our respective training. We were linked to the grim

---

11 Martin Luther King, Jr. Papers Project at Stanford University, 'King On War and Peace', <www.stanford.edu/group/King/about_king/warandpeace/wpquotes.htm>.

activities within the prison. We were connected to the victims' families, to the governor who let the execution go forward, and to the guards who had to carry out his order. Despite our different feelings and motivations, a single community of beings was fully absorbed in this one painful activity. I saw that we were all part of a larger functioning – a reality of mutual involvement. In that bleak moment a bodhisattva's challenge was to turn our functioning in the direction of life, not death.

As War Came Close

As the Iraq War approached in 2003 the Buddhist Peace Fellowship joined activists of other faiths in vigils against the United States' senseless and self-defeating violence. We organized meditations and sat in silence at countless peace demonstrations. We undertook civil disobedience to carry more widely our opposition to the killing on both sides. We spoke from many stages, trying to offer an alternative to the anger and self-righteousness of many activists. More than a hundred San Francisco Bay Area clergy gathered in front of the San Francisco Federal Building as the first bombs fell in Iraq. We offered a statement of spiritual solidarity and determined civil disobedience. It was a powerful moment. A circle of readers each took a paragraph, adding their voice to our protest, as we shared a letter to President Bush, Secretaries Powell and Rumsfeld, and our Congressional representatives, which said in part:

As clergy and people of faith we are aware of the great responsibilities you bear for the wellbeing of Americans, and your concern for the people of Iraq . . . Together, we can create a world free from fear, poverty, disease, and war. This will never arise from self-centeredness, greed, national pride, empire, and intolerance. We believe that the consequences of this pre-emptive war in Iraq will spin the whole world into a downward spiral of fear and untruth . . . Boastful predictions of easy victory and welcoming Iraqis turn out to be a pipedream. What did you really expect? So now the battle will be in earnest. Death and destruction will bury the sweet dream of peace and freedom.

Yet, it is never too late to awaken to the common spirit flowing in our veins. We know that this spirit is strong and unstoppable. It grows like grass coming up through cracks in the sidewalk. When we listen to this spirit, we oppose war and encourage diplomacy. We wholeheartedly welcome the return of our troops now and offer our enemies a generous peace and reconciliation. Such a course may seem naïve, but we know this to be ancient and universal wisdom.[12]

What I remember most clearly was how we had to work with the Federal Police in charge of building security. Though free speech is fundamental to American society, the government was actively rolling back civil rights, so we needed permits and permissions to gather in a public space. We also felt it was proper to alert the officers to our intention to commit civil disobedience. We tried to talk with these officers as neighbours, as we would talk with each other. It became clear that, despite their jobs, some of them supported our positions and intentions. Some officers were friendly and, of course, some were less so. Some were surprised to see ministers there from their own churches. When we broke the law they were bound to handcuff us and led us away to a holding area, but the respect we had showed them engendered respect in turn when they came to arrest us.

Stillness and Activism

Meditation is stillness right in the middle of a dynamic universe. In the Mahāyāna schools of Buddhism there is no separation between *nirvāṇa*, or the world of enlightenment, and *saṃsāra*, the world of suffering. Buddhism posits original enlightenment rather than original sin. Suffering, the flip side of enlightenment,

---

12 This section is quoted from Buddhist Peace Fellowship's 'Statement on the Beginning of the Iraq War', drafted by Alan Senauke in the spring of 2003.

differs from original sin in that it seems to be built into our human mechanism, and yet this is really a kind of mind/body illusion. Because our bodies are subject to all kinds of habits and attachments, we are unable to see our enlightened nature until attachment to desires, dislikes, and impermanence falls away. That falling away is the point of Buddhist practice. It is also the gift that the many buddhas share with us all the time. It is a kind of grace.

When Śākyamuni Buddha was enlightened at the foot of the Bodhi tree, he said, 'Now I see that I am enlightened together with all sentient beings.' Christ endured the cross for the sake of our misdeeds. Peter says to us of Christ's death, 'He himself bore our sins in his body on the tree . . . by his wounds you have been healed.'[13] For Christ and Buddha, for prophets and bodhisattvas, the practice of peace must be done with one's own body. Here is where Buddhists and Christians find common ground. And yet there are differences too.

August of 1995 was the fiftieth anniversary of Hiroshima and Nagasaki. To mark the date I attended an inter-faith vigil and civil disobedience at the Nevada Nuclear Test Site. The site itself occupies 1,400 square miles of mountain and desert, pockmarked by craters from more than 900 nuclear tests – 800 of them under-ground, and, before 1963, 100 in the open atmosphere. Their mushroom clouds could easily be seen in Las Vegas, only sixty miles away. Even today this madness of nuclear weapons has not ended. The US Department of Energy is working on a new generation of nuclear weapons.

The evening after our vigil, clergy, activists and Hibakusha – Japanese survivors from the Hiroshima and Nagasaki bombing – drove back to Las Vegas to bear witness to our experiences and feelings at the test site. The harrowing recollections of Hibakusha brought tears to our eyes, as did stories of US veterans forced to march on to 'nuclear battlefields' in the 1950s, and what we call 'downwinders' sickened by fallout on ranches near the test site.

---

13 1 Peter 2.24.

As we considered Hiroshima and Nagasaki, Christian and Jewish clergy asked how could this happen? How could churchgoing generals and politicians have planned to use such weapons? How could chaplains have blessed pilots and aeroplanes before their mission of mass death? For these clergy men and women, it seemed clear that the high ethical standards of religion should not allow this to have taken place. Standing on a moral high ground, looking back in time, some of us today seemed to separate ourselves from our brothers of 1945.

I asked myself: If I had been a president, a general, a soldier, or a priest, what would I have done in that summer of 1945? Right there, that evening in Las Vegas, I didn't know. That question continues to trouble my mind. I wish to think I would have been wise enough to suggest another course. I also believe those men who ordered and carried out this bombing were not evil. They may have believed they were saving lives on all sides by avoiding an all-out invasion of Japan. (That has long been the historical justification for the bombing.)

The startling fact that emerges from a Buddhist analysis of self is that I (and all of us) are capable of terrible things. It is simply a matter of causes and conditions. We choose among those conditions, and cultivate right view, right speech, and right action. This is inner training, which I hope and pray will help me choose life rather than destruction when the chips are down.

There is a 'proto-Buddhist' story from the Native American tradition.

An elder was teaching his grandchildren about life. He said to them, 'A terrible fight between two wolves is going on inside me. One wolf represents fear, anger, envy, greed, arrogance, self-pity, resentment, lies, and ego. The other wolf stands for joy, peace, serenity, humility, kindness, generosity, truth, compassion, and faith. This same fight is going on inside you, and inside every other person, too.'

The children thought about it and then one asked her grandfather, 'Which wolf will win?'

The old man replied, 'The one I feed.'[14]

Those Las Vegas questions have stayed with me. I was uncomfortable with an attitude proclaiming, 'Not me! I'd never drop those bombs.' And I was unable to rest with a soft-minded acceptance of 'things as they are' often passing for Buddhism. This is the personal and dynamic tension within what Gary Snyder referred to as the mercy of the West and the insight of the East. We actually need both . . . at once. We must work for justice, and for an end to suffering and war. We must be able to recognize that the world's marvellous and ever-changing perfection exists even within the most disturbing conditions of life.

Truth's Price

God speaks directly through the old prophets. They embody God's voice and authority, conveying his difficult truth. This is a great burden for any man or woman to bear. Thus the prophets paid dearly when they stood up for peace and 'speak truth to power'. The Hebrew prophets were scorned, exiled and murdered. Christ was crucified.

The old Buddhist texts have little to say about justice. There are no prophets in Buddhism, since the essence of 'God' is in us and never apart from us. But all of us have to bear the trials of worldly life, which are enough to make or break us. While Buddhist ancestors didn't usually suffer the bitter fate of biblical luminaries, there are many ancient and modern tales of monks and nuns who endured hardship and abuse as the price of their single-minded practice. Today, Buddhists in Tibet have many such stories to tell.

In the 1960s Thich Nhat Hanh was asked which side, North

---

14 I could not confirm the source of this story, perhaps apocryphal. I heard it in a Buddhist teacher's lecture several years ago, and found a number of similar versions online, none clearly attributed.

or South Vietnam, he supported in the ongoing war. He replied,
'I'm for the centre.' For his belief in non-violence he was exiled
from Vietnam, mistrusted by Communists in the North as an
American sell-out, mistrusted by the puppet government in the
South as a secret Communist. Thirty-five years later he has still
not been allowed back. Repressive political power correctly
understands that principles of peace and non-violence are radical
and dangerous to regimes based on violence and exploitation.

Martin Luther King, Jr shouldered a prophet's burden in the
same years that Thich Nhat Hanh was exiled from Vietnam.
King began his work by addressing injustice and oppression
against African-Americans in America's South. The more deeply
he engaged injustice, the wider his eyes were opened. In time
he dared to move beyond civil rights to speak out against the
war and against a system of US imperialism that generated war
abroad and racism and economic injustice at home. Reading
King's sermons going back to the Montgomery Bus Boycott in
1955 one can see the germ of this view very early on. As he broad-
ened his critique and his commitment to non-violence, King took
a firm stand against the war in Vietnam. This cost him support
among many Black leaders in the Civil Rights movement who
failed to see that their struggle and the anti-war struggle were
one. King's interconnected vision of human suffering rendered
him more vulnerable to assassination. That came all too soon.

Many religious people have paid a high price for speaking and
acting on their vision of peace. Some have paid with their lives.
The work of peace, with all its urgency, impossibility, frequent
failure and hardship, can lead us far from peace into a frighten-
ing spiritual wilderness. We see a world everywhere on fire, and
of course we want to douse all flames. We can't do it. Not even
God seems capable of extinguishing all the flames (although she
may simply be testing us!).

Buddhists have an eleven-headed image of the Kuan Yin, the
bodhisattva of compassion. Just to take in all the suffering, her
head split into so many faces. But for us the all-too-common
result is that we lose ourselves in busyness and burn-out. It
simply stands to reason that if we are not at peace, how can

we be in service to peace? In *Conjectures of a Guilty Bystander* Thomas Merton wrote:

> There is a perverse form of contemporary violence to which the idealist fighting for peace by non-violent methods most easily succumbs: activism and overwork. The rush and pressure of modern life are a form, perhaps the most common form, of its innate violence. To allow oneself to be carried away by a multitude of conflicting concerns, to surrender to too many demands, to commit oneself to too many projects, to want to help everyone in everything, is to succumb to violence. The frenzy of the activist neutralizes work for peace. It destroys the fruitfulness of work, because it kills the root of inner wisdom which makes work fruitful.[15]

As Buddhists or Christians, when we raise a prophetic voice for the sake of peace we should try to strike just the right tone to unlock people's hearts and our own. Even if enemies drive us into exile or raise hands against us, we should not be in exile from ourselves. Neither should we drive others away by the energies of our passions. We all need to be around for the long haul.

At Last, Justice

In 1886 Leo Tolstoy – who inspired Gandhi's non-violence – wrote these words:

> It is as if I were sitting on the neck of a man, and, having quite crushed him down, I compel him to carry me, and will not alight from off his shoulders, while I assure myself and others that I am very sorry for him, and wish to ease his condition by every means in my power except by getting off his back.[16]

---

15 Thomas Merton, 1966, *Conjectures of a Guilty Bystander*, New York: Doubleday, p. 86.

16 Leo Tolstoy, 1890, *What To Do? (What Must We Do Then?)*, London: Walter Scott, p. 68.

We who live in the United States – whether we are Christians, Buddhists, Jews, Muslims, Hindus or Pagans – have saddled ourselves upon the world's poor. Without intending to, half-asleep, we fasten our hands around their throats and squeeze the life from them. This is the heart of injustice. We are numbed by our privileges and by our own fears, a nightmare from which only love can awaken us. Martin Luther King, Jr said:

> Nonviolence is absolute commitment to the way of love. Love is not some emotional bash; it is not empty sentimentalism. It is the active outpouring of one's whole being into the being of another.[17]

In Buddhist terms this love is simply taking care of ourselves and others in peace, in justice, without differentiation. Non-violence is also a practice. It is a matter of instinct shaped by training.

To enact this practice I call upon Kuan Yin, the Bodhisattva of Compassion. Her name means 'the one who sees the cries of the world'. She is often depicted with a thousand hands. Each hand has an eye, and each hand holds a tool useful for liberating beings. An old Zen story asks 'What does the Bodhisattva of Great Compassion use her many hands and eyes for?' Zen Master Wu replies, 'It's like someone reaching back groping for a pillow in the middle of the night.'[18] In the middle of the night we don't stop to think how. Nor do we worry whether we deserve to be at ease. We just make ourselves comfortable.

The Buddha did not speak about justice as such. The idea of justice arose in the prophets' cultures. But when we act from deepest instinct, as the Buddha taught, we cannot fail to be just. When we can embody the practice and truth of peace – God's peace or Buddha's – we act readily and naturally to put others at ease. We do this at the risk of failure. We even risk our own safety.

---

17 Martin Luther King, Jr. Papers Project at Stanford University, 'Popular Requests', <www.stanford.edu/group/King/popular_requests/>.
18 T. Cleary and J.C. Cleary (trans.), 1977, *The Blue Cliff Record*, Boulder, CO: Shambhala, p. 571.

And yet we also know that as ordinary men and women we have faults and inconsistencies. Few of us are as awake as the great saints and bodhisattvas. If our realization falls short of St Francis or Layman Vimalakīrti, we need what Catholics would call 'discernment' as an equal partner to human instinct. To the extent that we are even partly deluded – and each of us is – we need to discern the wholesomeness of our actions deeply within ourselves and check it out with those we trust. As long as we carry even the smallest bit of self-centredness, making peace is, alas, not so easy as reaching back for a pillow in the night.

The great peacemakers are more than archetypes. They are real people who suffer doubt and pain. They walk and talk and practise faith with their bodies. Martin Luther King, Jr or Mother Teresa or the Cambodian monk Maha Ghosananda or the Berrigan brothers are bodhisattva models for us because of what they did in the world, because they kept faith in the face of violence, discouragement, and countless dark nights of the soul. Their work continues – as does the work of Buddha, Jesus and Gandhi – because when we meet such beings, whether or not we understand them or agree with them, we feel confirmed, embraced, and we respond in kind.

16. Response to Hozan Alan Senauke

KENNETH FERNANDO

We have very good reason to be grateful to Alan Senauke for his paper. Alan and I deal with the same subject, he as a Buddhist and I as a Christian, while being open to each other's religions.

But I perceive a more important difference between us. I am very political in my approach because I admit that I am a political person. I like to deal with social and political issues primarily on the basis of political and social analysis rather than on the basis of individual responses. While Alan agrees that we need both social revolution and individual insight and quotes Gary Snyder to support that view, I hope I can say without being unfair to him, that his emphasis is on the individual contribution to the peace process and on what individual insight has to contribute to peacemaking.

Basically he is right and we cannot contribute to peacemaking unless and until we take a deep look at ourselves and ensure that we are doing all we can for peace as individuals with integrity. However, I am of the view that peace-loving and peaceful individuals may not necessarily make up a peaceful country. The people of my country, both Sinhala and Tamil, are indeed peace-loving peoples. But we have no peace. In the same way those who engaged in the slave trade in the sixteenth to nineteenth centuries were not bad people. Many of them were good Christian people. But their trade was horrible and it degraded people. Examples can be multiplied. The people of the United States are a fine peace-loving community. But the policies of that country, supported by its people who are not fully aware of what they are doing, cause much suffering and conflict in the world. Moral and peace-loving people can constitute an immoral and strife-torn society or country. So in my view a wholly individualistic approach will not be adequate to meet the challenges of our time and people of religion like ourselves must not think that our religions constrain and constrict us to the sphere of the individual to solve problems of peace. Basically the problem of maintaining peace is a political and social issue and we must seek social and political solutions. So while Alan Senauke is of the view that the 'practice of peace must be done with one's own body' I would interject that it must be done with the body politic.

Our task as Buddhists and Christians is, I believe, to develop criteria by which to assess and evaluate the political, social and economic systems of our times and then to discover strategies to contend with them. This must be done not only by like-minded groups but also through relevant political action.

I often insist on the concept of the Kingdom of God, which I contend is primarily a social concept. Much harm has been done by those who translate Luke 17.21 as: 'The Kingdom of God is within you'. It should be translated: 'The Kingdom of God is among you.' The word 'you' is plural and therefore the latter translation, I suggest, is the correct one. Somehow people of religion seem to prefer interiorization of these concepts and hesitate to give them their full social significance. I believe that the social significance of our religious insights is primary and the individual significance follows. But I do agree that there should be no such dichotomy.

Alan Senauke's statement that the 'old Buddhist texts have little to say about justice' set me thinking. In the Theravāda texts I know, the *Cakkavatti Sīhanāda Sutta* (*Dīgha Nikāya* 26) says that the monks must advise the king obviously on issues of justice and fair play. The *Sigālovāda Sutta* (*Dīgha Nikāya* 31) deals at some length with just and fair social relationships, and the social and political implications of these Suttas must be worked out. The *Aggañña Sutta* (*Dīgha Nikāya* 27) has a story to describe how contention and evil came into our world because of the greed of people and so concepts of fair play and just dealing had to be developed. Furthermore the 550 *Jātaka* stories have much useful material where attempts are made to apply Buddhist values to the issues of life.

So while Alan Senauke and I are struggling to do all we can to make peace in our world and in our respective situations, we have to recognize that we are parts of great social and economic structures, which by their very nature threaten peace. Strife and war are systemic in our societies, which are built upon the foundation of competition. We have to change these structures, and individual action even when carried out in groups can be of little avail until we use tools of social and political analysis to expose what in fact is going on and struggle against political powers politically. Otherwise we shall be like Don Quixote fighting against windmills. Alan Senauke indeed concedes this point but there is a difference of emphasis between us.

However, peacemaking is such a difficult task as all peacemakers have learnt. For Alan Senauke it means a bump on his head. Others have wounds in their hearts. It is for this reason that inner strength is essential for all would-be peacemakers, and interiorization, 'zazen', meditation are absolutely essential in that aspect of peacemaking. To their cost Christians do not emphasize this sufficiently.

Finally I feel constrained to comment that our struggles for peace and justice have to be sustained by hope. How else can we carry on in the face of seeming defeat? I am sure that Zen Buddhism too provides sources for such hope. But where and of what nature are these? May I recommend this as a question for future research? I would be very interested in this.

17. Response to Kenneth Fernando

HOZAN ALAN SENAUKE

Bishop Fernando's paper begins with a brief overview of the Sri Lankan predicament. A majority Sinhalese Buddhist community is entangled in a violent ethnic conflict with the Sri Lankan Tamil community. This conflict has deep roots, often ascribed to national myths, some derived from the *Mahāvaṃsa* and *Cūlavaṃsa*. But it seems to me that the proximate source of the conflict is the inheritance of British colonialism, and its self-serving policies privileging one ethnic group (usually a minority) over another in its colonies, backing up those policies with force of arms. Kenneth Fernando alludes to this. The history of British imperialism and post-imperial conflict in Sri Lanka, Burma, India, Pakistan, Palestine and elsewhere continues to haunt us.

Meeting Kenneth Fernando, and listening to his stories, I was moved by the directness of his faith and courage. Many Buddhists in the West are engaged with society. We teach dharma in prison, we organize against a new American *imperium* and its wars, we feed and house the poor, and we stand against racism in our communities. But the risks taken by Kenneth Fernando, working as a Christian mediator in a civil war, are very high, and not at all abstract or theological. I bow to him in admiration and respect.

In this brief response to Kenneth Fernando's paper, I can touch on just one point. But his paper invites many long and essential discussions.

Writing about Buddhism's potential for peace, Kenneth Fernando cites the Buddha's successful mediation of a conflict between the Sakiyas and the Koliyas, as told in the introduction to *Jātaka* 536. A little later in talking about the Christian potential for peace, he writes:

> It is not possible to participate in an activity so difficult and dangerous as peacemaking unless one is convinced that one is on the side that will win ultimately. Peace will come in every situation . . . This message of hope is one of the important contributions Christians must bring to any peace process. We never give up because we know that we will win. Christian hope is the assurance that God is at work, that he reigns. It is not blind optimism. It is a sure and certain hope based on the truth of the resurrection.

When Kenneth presented his paper, my ears perked up at these words, very different from the teachings I have received as a Buddhist practitioner. I recalled the following story, also found in the *Jātaka* tales (465).[1]

Towards the end of his life, the Buddha witnessed the destruction of his Sakiya clan in a battle between them and the neighbouring Kosalans, led by prince Viḍūḍabha. Because of past deceptions and insults, Viḍūḍabha had an intense hatred for the Sakiyas. The Buddha, in his survey of the universe, saw the impending fall of his clan. He journeyed to a place near Kapilavatthu, at the border between the Sakiyas and Kosalans, and sat down beneath a dead tree that offered little comfort. The shady banyan trees of Kosala were nearby.

Viḍūḍabha arrived with his army, and came to pay respects to the Buddha. He invited the Buddha to refresh himself under the wide banyans of Kosala. The Buddha responded, 'The shade of my kindred keeps me cool.' The prince was touched by the Buddha's words and turned his army back to its own capital.

But Viḍūḍabha remained restless and impatient. He mounted

---

1 E.B. Cowell (ed.), 1969, *The Jataka or Stories of the Buddha's Former Births*, vol. 4, London: Luzac, p. 96.

a second campaign against the Sakiyas. Once more, the Buddha appeared to him before battle. Viḍūḍabha turned homeward again, but his burning hatred soon returned. He made a third attempt, with the same result. But on the fourth try the Buddha realized that war was imminent, and that the evil *karma* of the Sakiyas had led to their destruction. In battle that day the Sakiyas were wiped out.

Despite his best efforts, the Buddha failed to bring peace. Other commentaries and versions of this story go into horrific detail about the slaughter of the Sakiyas, and relate the very human fact that from this event forward, the Buddha was plagued by headaches. What interests me here is in response to Kenneth Fernando's Christian belief that, 'We never give up because we know that we will win.' Buddhist teachings of mutual causation in general, and *karma* in particular, delineate very different spiritual laws.

Although the Buddha was blessed with many supermundane powers, even he was not single-handedly able to suspend the working of cause and effect. *Karma* translates as 'action', but more precisely it means intentional thoughts, words and deeds. The traditional view is that our human life in the present and in the future is strongly conditioned by intertwined strands of *karma*. But this is not a mechanistic sense of fate. Though we are never able fully to see the web of *karma*, by wholesome actions we are able to transform our present and future life.

Karma is only one kind of causation. The Buddha outlined laws of nature, the *niyamas* (including *karma*), which explain the orderly ways of the natural world, to the extent that it was understood in his time. The *niyamas* have no moral force, but they speak to a kind of self-regulating universe. Events that may be seen as disaster to humans – like the recent Asian tsunami, earthquakes, cyclones – can be seen as the planet seeking to re-balance its natural energies.

There is a complexity to a Buddhist understanding of causation that is far beyond our ordinary understanding. In this sense, our notions of success and failure are necessarily incomplete. What seems like failure or victory at one point in time may ripen into success later. And vice versa. This brings to mind an old Taoist tale from the *Huainan-Zi*.[2]

Near the Great Wall lived an old farmer who had a fine horse. One day his horse ran away, and his neighbours came to commiserate. 'Bad luck', they said. 'Maybe so,' the farmer responded. The next morning the horse returned, in the company of three wild horses. 'How wonderful,' the neighbours said. 'Maybe so,' the farmer responded. His son went to ride one of the wild horses, was badly thrown, and broke his leg. The neighbours returned to offer their sympathy. 'Maybe so,' said the farmer. The next day, the emperor's recruiters came through town, conscripting all local young men into the army. Since the son's leg was broken, they didn't take him. The neighbours congratulated the farmer on this happy outcome. 'Maybe so,' said the farmer.

Buddhist teachers also encourage us to have 'no gaining idea', to practise good without attachment to an outcome. They propose a kind of radical hopelessness, rooted in boundless connection rather than despair. The Buddhist social thinker David Loy writes, '. . . we do not live a certain way for the recompense of our meritorious actions will bring us, either in this lifetime or in a future one. Rather, to become a different kind of person is to experience the world in a different way.'[3]

From a Buddhist perspective, if one has attachment to a particular outcome, that attachment is usually linked to a self-centred concept or motivation. But if there is effectively no discoverable self to centre on, then we are liable to fall into delusion. The very outcomes we hope for are self-centred instead of all-centred. We forget the very fact of our connection to all beings.

And yet . . . in my heart, I feel that the distinction I am drawing between my view and Kenneth Fernando's view is merely a theological difference. We hold our faith quite differently, and could compare and contrast from now until the cows come home. But I

---

2 *Huainan-Zi*. 'He lost his horse, but gained good luck', www.ancient-china.info/chinese-idioms2.htm.

3 David Loy, 2003, *The Great Awakening: A Buddhist Social Theory*, Boston: Wisdom, p. 8.

feel that our common spiritual root is selfless love. The teachings of Christ and Buddha go beyond words and ideas to the heart of things. In *Dhammapada* 5, the Buddha says, 'Never by hatred is hatred conquered, but by readiness to love alone. This is eternal law.'[4] In Matthew 22 Jesus says, 'You shall love your neighbour as yourself.' Either way is the path of peace, if only we give of ourselves completely.

---

4 *Dhammapada* 5, transl. Munindo, www.ratanagiri.org.uk/Book/book5/index.htm.

Subject and Name Index